THE COMPANION GUIDE

to Outer London

£7—

⅓

THE COMPANION GUIDES

GENERAL EDITOR: VINCENT CRONIN

*It is the aim of these guides to provide a Companion,
in the person of the author, who knows intimately
the places and people of whom he writes, and is able to
communicate this knowledge and affection to his readers.
It is hoped that the text and pictures will aid them
in their preparations and in their travels, and will
help them remember on their return.*

LONDON · THE SHAKESPEARE COUNTRY · EAST ANGLIA
THE COAST OF SOUTH WEST ENGLAND
DEVON AND CORNWALL · NORTHUMBRIA · NORTH WALES
SOUTH WALES
THE WEST HIGHLANDS OF SCOTLAND
THE SOUTH OF FRANCE · SOUTH WEST FRANCE · NORMANDY
BURGUNDY · THE ILE DE FRANCE · THE LOIRE
ROME · VENICE · FLORENCE
MADRID AND CENTRAL SPAIN
TURKEY · JUGOSLAVIA · MAINLAND GREECE · THE GREEK ISLANDS
THE NORTH ISLAND OF NEW ZEALAND · SOUTH AFRICA

Certain of these guides are also available in limpback

In preparation
NEW YORK

THE COMPANION GUIDE TO

Outer London

SIMON JENKINS

COLLINS
St James's Place, London
1981

William Collins Sons and Co Ltd
London · Glasgow · Sydney · Auckland
Toronto · Johannesburg

Jenkins, Simon
  A companion guide to outer London.
  1. London metropolitan area – Guide-books
  1. Title
  914.21′704858   DA679
  ISBN 0–00–216186–9

First printed in Great Britain 1981
Maps by Les Robinson
© Simon Jenkins 1981

Photoset in Times Roman
Made and Printed in Great Britain by
William Collins Sons & Co. Ltd., Glasgow

Contents

১৯

ERRATA

CAPTIONS

See caption for *Cutty Sark* on page 32

See caption for the Gothick Gallery at Strawberry Hill on page 97

See caption for Kenwood House Library on page 192

List of Illustrations

২১

List of Maps

Introduction

MORE than any other city in the world London is the sum of its parts. In the sixteenth and seventeenth centuries the pressure of numbers within the medieval walls drove its monarchs and nobles to seek the open spaces and clear air of the northern and southern heights and of the land upstream along the Thames. The Georgian era saw them followed by a new bourgeoisie able to afford weekend retreats within a few hours' drive of the City. But it was the coming of the steam engine which led what George Cruikshank satirized as the march of bricks and mortar across the landscape of the London basin, as clerks, tradesmen and even manual workers streamed out of the polluted capital like refugees from some terminal holocaust.

This migration, sometimes a ripple, sometimes a tidal wave, caused casualties among the towns and the villages in its path. The historic centres of Uxbridge, Enfield and Kingston, for instance, are now all but submerged. Yet for the most part London's suburbanization was graced (at least until the last war) by domestic and civic architecture of high quality and human scale. Courtiers, speculators, bankers and their various dependents arrived, made their contribution and passed on. The buildings they left behind them managed to reflect their identities but without doing violence to their surroundings. Their London was an organic growth.

This is the theme I have tried to trace in describing a metropolis which is still, for most visitors, a disjointed series of places, known and half-known. Its variety is extraordinary. Hampstead, Richmond and Blackheath are survivals of suburban communities from the pre-motor car era. Villages such as Ham, Dulwich, Highgate and Pinner claim antecedents as authentic as any rural equivalent. And in among them are the giants. Two of these, Hampton Court and Greenwich, are among the great monuments of Europe. The mansions of Ham, Syon, Osterley and Chiswick are the finest of

11

their period in England. The galleries at Kenwood and Dulwich are second only in this country to the National Gallery and the Tate. Kew yields precedence to none. I believe all can stand the same test of quality as that applied by David Piper in his companion volume to this one on inner London.

The buildings of outer London thus need no patronizing and I have deliberately not dealt with those parts of the metropolis which lack outstanding monuments or whose attractions are mainly of local or specialist appeal. The method adopted has been to base each chapter on a major house, gallery or historic centre and make forays out from it into the surrounding territory. Inevitably this method leaves some gaps. There is less about south and east London because they contain fewer of the spectacular features so plentiful to the north and west. Of the pre-railway suburbs I have chosen Islington rather than Clapham or North Kensington, because it compresses the diverse characteristics of such places into the smallest area. Of the inter-war suburbs, Pinner is preferred to Gidea Park or Petts Wood because I regard it as the best of its genre. I pick out the old more often than the new because buildings acquire associations and personality with age. There is in old buildings the voice of history speaking, a voice that is more garbled the more recent the structure.

The process of writing this book has been enthralling. No town or city anywhere reveals itself so reluctantly as London. Veil after veil can be lifted – one from the train, one from a passing car, another on foot. But always the place is holding something back for next time. There are disappointments. The majority of London's churches are now locked and many are virtually inaccessible except during services. Locking a church is allowing the vandal to win. Surely schools or scout troops or someone could stand guard over these microcosms of local history? Even more dismaying is the dreadful quality of public architecture in London since the war. The period 1955–75 appears to have been the worst. It coincided with the abandonment of brick in favour of concrete, notably on public housing estates, and the imprisonment of tenants in towers and slabs, where they still bewail the loss of the traditional terraced houses which they rightly believe were their birthright. Too many areas of London now lack what is essential in any city: places of human congregation which lift the heart and make the lonely feel at home. However much tastes change, I cannot believe future generations will admire these buildings as distinctive memorials to our post-war culture.

Yet in years of wandering round London's suburbs, I have found the delights have greatly outweighed the disappointments: the astonishing richness of London's Victorian heritage, still largely unrecorded; the exhilarating architectural parade of the Thames bank above Chiswick; the infinite inventiveness with which the London builder down the ages – be he architect or speculator, jerrybuilder or navvy – has gone about the task of putting a roof over peoples' heads. There is the miraculous ingenuity of the London gardener, who can transform the meanest patch of sooty earth into a horticultural wonderland. And there is the sainted army of those who *fight*, historians, photographers, conservationists, guides, pioneers – raising their flags over districts and styles which later generations will, we must hope, hold more precious than we appear to do. Even today it is largely through them that we are able, despite our economic troubles, to preserve and maintain in outer London one of the architectural treasure-houses of Europe.

I know that even in the most obscure byways I am treading in the footsteps of others. London bibliographies are notoriously indigestible and, for individual parts of the capital, impossibly long. From a list of hundreds I would just like to refer to those who kept me entertained as well as informed on my travels. Of those long dead, Edward Walford haunts every corner of the metropolis with his *London Old and New* (1883), as does his engaging precursor, James Thorne, whose *Environs of London* (1876) excoriates the builder with all the venom of a modern conservationist and delights at finding wheatfields still in Acton.

Of more recent works, Michael Robbins' *Middlesex* (1953) is a masterful introduction to that late-lamented county, Philip Howard's *London's River* (1975) is the best companion on a trip up the Thames and the indefatigable Arthur Mee leaves no historical stone unturned in his *London North of the Thames* (1972). Alan Jackson's *Semi-detached London* (1973) is the seminal work on the twentieth-century suburb. Pevsner's various guides are indispensable, though much in need of revision. And Ian Nairn's quirky *Nairn's London* (1966) is an effervescent combination of booze and brilliance. Two guides to post-war architecture, by Nairn for London Transport and by Charles McKean for the Royal Institute of British Architects, stand alone in a neglected field.

On the important subject of refreshment, foreign visitors should learn English licensing hours by heart. Sadly the traditional English teashop has all but vanished from London, as has its tepid successor, the coffee bar. But no local institution is now thriving so vigorously as the London pub. After a disastrous period of chemical beer and corporate design in the 1960s, the pub has flowered once more as a real centre of community life. Their proprietors have realized the value of restoration rather than demolition. And in restoring them many have discovered a storehouse of local tradition. Managers have learned to serve fresh food, real beer and, at long last, coffee. As a general rule, pub food is more reliable than cafeteria food. But any food outside pub opening hours is hard to come by, and a cup of tea or coffee on its own is a near impossibility. The most regular exceptions are Indian and Chinese establishments – in many areas the only oases of traditional hospitality.

Finally a word on transport. I have assumed that most chapters will be walked on foot, though forays usually call for a vehicle of some sort. The desperate unreliability of many London bus routes is a particular handicap. But the top of a traditional double-decker – that swaying queen of the road, the 'RT', or her more sedate daughter, the Routemaster – has always been the best way of seeing London. Gardens can be peered into, architectural features noted, destinations spotted, while ordinary mortals down below are still fuming through the traffic. Cars, tubes and bicycles may be swifter and more convenient; but there is no better overture to outer London than the journey there by bus.

CHAPTER ONE

Greenwich I

GREENWICH has always been the gateway to London. From its heights Roman legionaries marching down Watling Street would catch their first glimpse of Londinium. Tudor monarchs would send their galleons off to sea from its river front. Here Charles II was welcomed back from exile. And to tens of thousands of sailors throughout history, Greenwich Reach, with its palaces climbing up the hillside behind a forest of masts, signalled journey's end and home.

Maritime Greenwich has long been submerged by noble architecture and genteel suburbs. But down on its pierhead, where all visits to Greenwich must start, it is still possible to recapture some of that seafaring spirit. The **Cutty Sark** (open 11.00 to 6.00, Sundays, 2.30 to 6.00) was one of the last and certainly the finest of the tea clippers. Built on the Clyde in 1869 she embodied the pride of the tea merchants and their obsession with speed. The first ship to bring the new season's tea crop back from China made its owner's fortune. And *Cutty Sark* was designed to do just that. Her line demonstrates what were then revolutionary hydrodynamic features. Narrow stem with curved 'clipper' bow, gradually widening to enable her vast hold to slide through the water with ease; copper bottom to resist the drag of marine growths; raked masts and high rounded stern. Fully-rigged she could carry thirty thousand square feet of canvas, requiring some thirty boys to scramble aloft. Despite a life of searing ropes, freezing waves and rotten food, hundreds of boys would every year 'run away to sea' for the excitement of it.

The Suez Canal opened soon after *Cutty Sark* entered service, giving the new steamers substantial advantages on the tea run. The clippers were then switched to the Australian wool route, still closed to steamers because of inadequate coaling. And it was on this run, under her famous master, Captain Woodget, and in competition

15

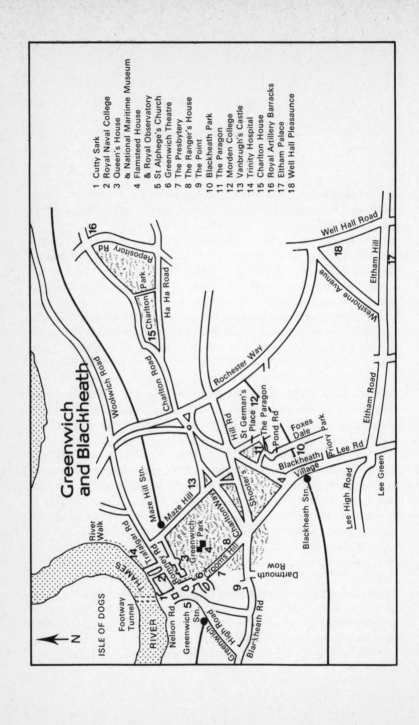

Greenwich
and Blackheath

1 Cutty Sark
2 Royal Naval College
3 Queen's House
& National Maritime Museum
4 Flamsteed House
& Royal Observatory
5 St Alphege's Church
6 Greenwich Theatre
7 The Presbytery
8 The Ranger's House
9 The Point
10 Blackheath Park
11 The Paragon
12 Morden College
13 Vanbrugh's Castle
14 Trinity Hospital
15 Charlton House
16 Royal Artillery Barracks
17 Eltham Palace
18 Well Hall Pleasaunce

with her rival *Thermopylae*, that *Cutty Sark* captured the nautical imagination. She sailed, in some form or other, until 1922, when she was bought by a devoted enthusiast named Captain Dowman, who fought a long battle for her preservation. She finally arrived at Greenwich in 1954 and the enthusiasm surrounding this arrival was immense. I remember as a schoolboy signing on as a 'junior shipmate' and learning by heart every spar and rope of her rigging. I would dream of the day when some tidal wave would wash her from her concrete bunker and send her creaming out to sea, topgallants slapping in the wind.

Cutty Sark took her name from a poem by Robert Burns, a free version of the words *courte chemise*, the garment worn *deshabillée* by the lady on her prow. Figureheads such as these were a combination of owners' emblems, mascot and sailors' good luck charm. Below decks is an exhibition of thirty-eight of them, collected by a businessman, Sidney Cumbers (also known as Long John Silver), whose fascination with the sea led him to amass the largest collection of figureheads in the world. Visitors can also see the holds, the cramped crews' quarters and the relatively spacious poop deck where the officers could warm themselves round a real coal fire.

As you step 'ashore' it is worth trying to imagine ships crowding the river front, with masts, sails and riggings filling the sky. For all the hardship and danger the 'tall ships' inflicted on those who lived by them, they possessed greater beauty than any other form of transport before or since. To John Masefield, 'They mark our passage as a race of men; earth will not see such ships as these again.'

Across from *Cutty Sark*'s concrete harbour lies another monument to seamanship, Sir Francis Chichester's **Gipsy Moth IV**. In this tiny craft, Sir Francis was, in 1967, the first man to circumnavigate the globe single-handed. The Queen knighted him, here at Greenwich, with the same sword Elizabeth I had used to knight Sir Francis Drake after his circumnavigation in 1581. Like *Cutty Sark*, *Gipsy Moth IV* was built for speed. Chichester had hoped to equal *Cutty Sark*'s average time to Australia of a hundred days – failing only by seven days. It is possible to squeeze on board and experience Chichester's cramped quarters, including the cooking galley and desk on which he worked over his charts, swung on gimbles to counteract the roll of the sea. Look up from it towards the cockpit and imagine a forty-foot sea bearing down on the stern off Cape Horn. *Cutty Sark* is cosy by comparison.

From ships, to shore. Greenwich enthusiasts will now plunge into the tunnel near the landing stage and walk under the river to the Isle of Dogs opposite. The tunnel is an eerie experience but the view back over the river is stupendous, especially on a misty day when the surrounding buildings recede and Greenwich becomes an enchanted palace shimmering over the water. A similar view can be had more simply by following the 'European Heritage' path along the shore and stopping at the main axis of the **Royal Naval College** buildings by the landing steps. Either way, the view is not to be missed. This is one of the architectural set pieces of Europe, a magnificent procession of palace, court and colonnade, an ordered setting more suggestive of continental absolutism in town planning than of casual British understatement. But of that, more anon.

First, some history. Under the smooth lawn which stretches in front of the College lie the remains (briefly excavated in 1971) of a succession of buildings on this site dating back to Saxon times. The first of which we have any architectural record was Duke Humphrey's riverside palace of Bella Court. Humphrey, founder of the Duke Humphrey library at the Bodleian in Oxford, fell out of favour during the Wars of the Roses. Henry VI and his wife, Margaret of Anjou, whom Humphrey had, as Protector, entertained here on their honeymoon, now seized it and renamed it their palace of Pleasance. Henry VII rebuilt the palace completely as Placentia, by all accounts a beautiful place in redbrick and stone dressings, with a banqueting hall and tiltyard, and crowned with the pinnacles and gilded vanes of Tudor fashion. His son, Henry VIII, made it his principal palace – until he wrested Hampton Court from Wolsey. Here at Greenwich his second wife, Anne Boleyn, gave birth to the future Elizabeth I, and from here she set out to the Tower and her execution. Perhaps for this reason Queen Elizabeth was less attached to the place than her father. But she held court at Placentia in the summer months, conferring with her admirals, visiting the royal shipyards at Deptford and Woolwich and receiving ambassadors up the steps from the river. It was here that one of those delightful scenes which enliven the history of the British crown reputedly took place. As the Queen was entering the palace gate, presumably from the muddy Woolwich Road on the far side of the building, an ambitious young adventurer named Walter Raleigh stepped forward and threw his cloak across a 'plashy place'.

The Stuart monarchs established their court at Whitehall and St

James's, and Placentia went into decline. But in 1616, James I commissioned a summer resort for his queen, Anne of Denmark, in the old palace grounds straddling the Woolwich Road. This 'curious devise' consisted of two parallel blocks connected by a bridge across the road. Its architect was Inigo Jones, then known chiefly as a designer of courst masques and stage sets. At Greenwich, Jones was eager to interpret in more permanent form the styles and motifs he had observed on his recent travels in Italy. The architecture of his time was still that of Hatfield and Hardwick Hall. Sir Adam Newton's Charlton House, just over the hill, had recently been completed in considerable splendour to a traditional Jacobean E-plan, with turrets, bay windows and stone mullions. Half a century later, Sir Christopher Wren would still be adhering to similar features in his Observatory on Greenwich Hill. Indeed, so advanced was Jones' building that it is widely assumed he saw it more as a stage set than a real home – a diversion for a queen and a storehouse for her works of art.

The Queen's House was the stylistic outcome of Jones' study of the works of Andrea Palladio. Palladio's villas were themselves a turning away from the excesses of the Baroque, back to the order and proportion of classical antiquity. Jones was thus bringing to English architecture a transfusion more drastic than any before or since – with the possible exception of the Bauhaus 'modernism' of the 1930s. In architecture, Jones wrote, 'Ye outward ornaments ought to be sollid, proporsionable according to the rulles, masculine and unaffected.' Indeed, only in the curving staircase in front of the house does Jones allow himself a brief flourish of baroque motion, and even here it is curtly turned back behind the terrace, looking from a distance like two tears running down from the façade. The house was first occupied by Charles I's queen, Henrietta Maria, who completed it in 1635 and filled it with many of the works of art collected by her husband. It is her name which appears high on the façade.

The Commonwealth saw the old palace in its final decline and following the Restoration Charles II began its demolition and re-building. The first block, the **King Charles Building** on the immediate right, was designed by Inigo Jones' son-in-law and pupil, John Webb, in his master's careful Palladian style. The ornate window surrounds and the pediment carvings, however, suggest the pomp of a royal palace not the 'devise' of a lady's retreat. The vertical emphasis of Webb's design and his grouping of the volumes on his façades demonstrate the early stirrings of an English Baroque which Wren, Vanbrugh and Hawksmoor later developed with such bravura.

Charles' palace was to have three sides facing the river. But money ran out, and after the completion of the west range the massive edifice was left empty, towering over the adjacent slums of Greenwich. Not until 1692 did William and Mary turn their attention to the place and decide to convert the original scheme into a naval hospital. Sir Christopher Wren was commissioned to plan the remainder of the buildings accordingly. He at first proposed to continue Webb's three-sided plan, but Queen Mary was attached to the new view from the Queen's House, and Wren had to think again.

What we now see is the composition for which Wren was ultimately responsible. Webb's King Charles Building is matched by an identical façade opposite. But the third side is broken by a processional way guarded by Wren's colonnades, pediments and domes: all in a sort of mock obeisance to the altar of their progenitor, Inigo Jones, whose Queen's House is made to seem almost domestic in the distance. This remarkable essay in architectural compromise is completed by Wren's Observatory. It was built on the site of Humphrey's old castle to the command of Charles II as an aid to navigation and, in Wren's words, 'for the Observer's habitation and a little for Pompe'. It is one of the most charming small buildings in London. From this angle, it neatly deflects the perspective of Wren's composition (yes, the same Wren) and laughs at the continental nonsense going on down below. It is this final lapse from symmetry which sets Greenwich apart from the baroque masterpieces of France and Italy and makes it so endearing.

The Royal Naval Hospital lasted nearly two centuries in these buildings, but was never popular with its inmates. Perhaps, as Dr Johnson concluded, it was all 'too magnificent for a place of charity'. But its bad reputation may also have had something to do with the authoritarian way it was run – the old men persistently complained of the cold, the bad food and the corrupt administration. Finally in 1869, its medical functions were moved into the Dreadnought buildings, which continue to function as a seamen's hospital. The pensioners left and in 1873 the Royal Naval College moved in from Portsmouth. Though with diminished student numbers it remains in use today and is open to the public only for a few hours each afternoon (2.30 to 5.30 and not on Thursdays).

To enter it, we retrace our steps alongside *Cutty Sark* and pass two great stone globes, one terrestrial, the other celestial, but sadly too decayed to be decipherable. To the right can be seen the west façade of the **King William Building**, by Wren's successor as surveyor at Greenwich, Sir John Vanbrugh. It is a bold composition in red brick, its massive frontispiece and corner pavilions linked by diminutive two-storey bays with windows and doors heavily over-decorated as if to compensate. Turning into the main court and trespassing through the colonnades, we see that the other (east) façade of this building is even odder, with giant arches, pilasters, pediments and curiously shaped windows scattered across the entrance. It is as if Vanbrugh, frustrated at the comparative orderliness of Wren's legacy, had let rip with every item in the baroque pattern book. With characteristic restraint, Sir Nikolaus Pevsner calls it merely 'wilful'.

At right angles to Vanbrugh's building is Greenwich's pride and joy, the **Great Hall** and its painted ceiling. The hall was designed by Vanbrugh's associate, Nicholas Hawksmoor – the last of the baroque triumvirate who succeeded the Palladians Jones and Webb at Greenwich. It is a stunning sequence of vestibule, hall and upper hall, divided not by walls and doors but by pillars and steps. Above the vestibule soars Wren's cupola, flooded with light even on the darkest day. The main hall is equally light, despite the pervasive brown and gold paint in which columns and murals are decorated to imitate fluting and perspective. Here Nelson's body lay in state after the Battle of Trafalgar in 1805. Thousands besieged Greenwich to pay homage to the fallen hero in one of the most remarkable outbursts of national emotion England has ever seen.

The **ceiling** and the mural in the upper half were painted by Sir James Thornhill. They took him nineteen years (from 1707) and are one of the great achievements of baroque art in England. Thornhill was the first native artist to compete with Verrio and Laguerre for commissions to decorate the noble houses of late-seventeenth-century England – and the first to be knighted for his work. His output was enormous, but this ceiling is unquestionably his masterpiece. William and Mary, surrounded by the four virtues, hand the cup of liberty to Europe. Tyranny, in the form of Louis XIV of France, is seen trampled beneath William's feet. Architecture (a voluptuous maiden) points to the plans for the hospital, while

John Wall, a ninety-seven-year-old pensioner at the time, watches her and warms his hands at a fire. What a slice of English history he must have seen! The central oval is supported by *trompe l'oeil* arches, themselves surmounting two vast galleon sterns, one a Spanish man-of-war, the other the *Blenheim* loaded with the spoils of war. The whole gigantic work is difficult to take in from any one point of view, and mirrors are provided to prevent the cricking of necks.

In the upper hall, the two monochrome **murals** on the left and right walls show respectively George I and William III arriving in England, somewhat improbably in Roman dress. On the ceiling is Queen Anne and her husband, George of Denmark, surrounded by a celestial retinue of gods and angels. But the main work, again by Thornhill, fills the facing wall: George I and his family as a group of rather self-satisfied Hanoverians waited on by Providence, Time, Peace and Plenty. In the background rises the dome of St Paul's in honour of Wren, and down in the right foreground is a self-portrait of the artist, his hand outstretched to present his patrons to the public. Legend has it that his quizzical expression and left palm open behind his back are a reference to the constant delays in payment which he experienced during the commission. He was paid £3 a foot for the ceilings and £1 a foot for the walls.

On the other side of the courtyard is the **chapel**, part of the Queen Mary Building erected behind Wren's colonnade by the least distinguished of the Hospital's architects, Thomas Ripley, in 1735. His chapel was destroyed by fire in 1779 and rebuilt by James Stuart in 1789. Nicknamed 'Athenian' for his enthusiasm for the Greek revival, Stuart brought to Greenwich the simple lines and delicate decoration best known in the work of Robert Adam. The chapel is a Handel oratorio compared to the military marches of the Baroque outside. The ceiling roundels and gallery door arches draw the eye upwards and outwards in a *trompe l'oeil* of plaster rather than paint. And the intricate scrolls and brackets in soft Wedgwood colours seem a far cry from the sea. Only the extraordinary coat of arms on the gallery balustrade reminds us where we are: a sailor and a lion rampant, but turning into fish halfway down! On the pulpit are scenes from the life of St Paul and the painting over the alter depicts St Paul's shipwreck on Malta – which can hardly have comforted any departing seamen. It is by the

American artist, Benjamin West, one of the few Americans to migrate to Europe in the eighteenth century.

We now cross Romney Road to the Queen's House and Maritime Museum before climbing the hill to the Observatory, dodging lethal skateboarders as we go. Romney Road – the old Woolwich Road – is a torrent of traffic suddenly released from the whirlpool of central Greenwich. There have been plans to divert it, close it, bury it even, but still it thunders on. This is the road which used to pass directly under the Queen's House, where its course is still visible. It was diverted when colonnades were built in 1807 to link the two halves of what was then the Royal Naval Asylum, a school for young seamen. The length of the colonnades and the decorum of the two wings excellently offset Inigo Jones' building, an achievement for which the architect, Daniel Alexander, received the congratulations of his professional colleagues.

The house is part of the **National Maritime Museum**, established here in 1934. The collection was built round the Nelson relics which had been kept since his death in the painted hall of the Hospital. It is now the largest maritime museum and art gallery in the world – and is not to be undertaken lightly.

Broadly speaking, the west wing (on the left facing inland) contains the nineteenth-century and modern exhibits; the Queen's House contains the earliest pictures and models, including a series of seventeenth-century portraits contemporary with the house; and the west wing is devoted to the eighteenth century, but contains also the Nelson collection and, in the new Neptune Hall, exhibits illustrating the history of seafaring from prehistoric times to the present day. It is best to work out in advance what one wants to see – there is no comprehensive guidebook and the museum's 'twenty-five things to see' is useful but brief. (The museum is open 10.00 to 6.00, Sundays 2.30 to 6.00, closed at 5.00 in winter.)

The Queen's House is the best starting point. What seemed so chaste from outside now flowers into a luxuriant palace. The main hall, the **Cube Room**, was a breathtaking innovation to a people still accustomed to Elizabethan panelled halls. The deeply coffered ceiling was originally painted by Gentileschi, but his work was later removed by Queen Anne's favourite, the Duchess of Marlborough, to her house in St James. Among other celebrated painters invited to adorn the interior were Rubens, Giulio Romano and Jordaens, on whom Charles I laid the special instruction to make 'ye faces of ye women as beautiful as may bee, ye figures gracious and svelte'. It was in this house, in February 1642, that Charles and Henrietta Maria spent their last night together before she fled to France. Perhaps it was this memory that kept her devoted to the house when she returned to it after the Restoration. The floor was designed by the sculptor, Nicholas Stone, to reflect the coffering of the ceiling. Its abstract pattern, when seen from above, swirls outwards in motifs of startling modernity – it could be a work of 'op art' by Bridget Riley.

The Queen's House paintings depict the early years of British sea power: the Tudor wars against Spain and the seventeenth-century wars against Holland. Downstairs, the early sea pictures begin the collection with the 'Battle of Lepanto' (the last sea engagement to be fought under oars) and a delightful Portuguese 'sea piece', presenting war at sea as an almost balletic activity. There are also portraits of admirals such as Drake and Hawkins, looking stiff and uncomfortable in a court painter's studio. But it is the Van de Veldes which deserve pride of place. The two Dutchmen, father and son, were invited to London from the Netherlands to record the exploits of British ships in the reigns of Charles II and James II. When in Holland, they had been given a boat at government expense to record the Dutch fleet at sea and this experience they were now able to place at the service of 'the other side'. The father did the drawings, while his son (working, it is believed, in a studio in the Queen's House itself) 'put the said draughts into colours'. The result is a thrilling combination of historical accuracy, decorative detail and the huge drifts of sea and skyscape so beloved of Dutch painters. The 'Battle of Texel', hanging in the Cube Room, is perhaps the finest: the billowing sails seem to scoop the action up from the waves and engulf all nature in the struggle.

Off a corner of the Cube Room rises the **Tulip Staircase**, the first spiral staircase in Britain. It derives its name from the tulip motif in the iron baluster, though this is rather intended to represent the *fleur de lys* emblem from Henrietta Maria's homeland of France. To gaze up the spiral, through what Jones termed the 'vacuum in ye middell', induces the same giddying effect as Stone's mosaic out in the hall. What amazing geometers those Jacobeans must have been!

On the **first floor** State Rooms double as galleries. The Queen's drawing room has monograms of Charles I and his wife set into the ceiling and two pictures by Van Dyck, including the famous portrait of Henrietta Maria in profile. This room also contains 'Peter Pett and the Sovereign of the Seas', painted by Lely (or at least the portrait probably was). Launched in 1637, the *Sovereign* was in its day the biggest and most costly ship ever built. It was in Pepys' words, 'a glorious vessel being for defence and ornament the richest that ever spread cloth before the winds'. Pett, master shipwright at Woolwich, was the son of its designer, Phineas Pett, and he sits here taking a quiet pride in his family's creation. The *Sovereign* was finally destroyed by fire in 1696 after a career lasting sixty years.

What had originally been an H-shaped building was later turned by John Webb into a complete square by the insertion of two additional wings, east and west of the original bridge. Walking in a clockwise direction, we come to the first Cabinet Room, containing portraits of Cromwell's admirals, Deane and Blake. Then comes the East Bridge Room and another Cabinet Room, leading in turn into the King's Bedchamber. All are filled with stirring pictures of seventeenth-century naval scenes by the Van de Veldes and others, culminating in a magnificent portrait by Ferdinand Bol of the 'enemy' commander, the Dutch admiral De Ruyter. It was he who sailed up the Medway in 1667 and wrought havoc on the British fleet, causing poor Samuel Pepys no end of trouble.

From this point, we can look out through the columns of the loggia at a view which has changed little over three centuries – grass and trees sweeping upwards to the sky, and not a vehicle in sight. The rooms on the west side of the house contain more Van de Veldes, including the dramatic painting of 'An English Squadron Beating Windward' – carrying, I should have said, rather too much sail for the state of the weather. Here too is Kneller's portrait of Pepys, full of conceit and humour, and with just a hint of debauchery about the eyes. The Queen's bedroom is Jones' masterpiece of interior decoration. Its ceiling displays the motifs with which he had crammed his notebooks in Italy, though the effect was impaired by Thornhill, who later inserted some frolicking cherubs into the central panel.

We return to the gallery of the Cube Room which contains a portrait of Inigo Jones himself by Hogarth (after Van Dyck): sensitive and thoughtful in comparison with the hauteur of the Stuart portraits we have just seen. On the other side of the balcony, however, is a bizarre Jonesian signature. The cartouche above the Bridge Room door looks from a distance like mere decoration. It is, however, an actor's mask complete with grotesque eyes and a nose. Only sixteen years had passed since Shakespeare wrote 'All the world's a stage'. The mannerist in Jones has the last word.

Downstairs and across the roadway is a series of galleries devoted to yet more Dutch sea paintings as well as a collection of pictures illustrating the history of Greenwich itself. Here we can see portrayed the ancient palace of Placentia and the Queen's House as it was when first constructed, with its road still passing beneath it. Here too is the famous Canaletto, of Greenwich from the Isle of Dogs. His Italian sense of classical propriety compels him to reduce the Queen's House to diminutive scale, while the equally un-baroque Observatory vanishes almost completely. Indeed Canaletto's marvellous transparency of colour manages to carry the whole scene off to the Venetian lagoon – with Thames watermen as gondoliers in the foreground.

A detailed guide to the rest of the museum would occupy the remainder of this book, so this is no more than a series of signposts. The best route begins with the **West Wing** and the three galleries covering the eighteenth century and the wars against the French. Here are works by Hogarth, Kneller, Reynolds, and a series of dockyard pictures by Nicholas Pocock. **Gallery 6** contains the Cook–Hodges collection, depicting Cook's voyages of discovery along the east and west coasts of Canada down to the Antarctic and through the South Pacific. He was the first European to visit Australia and New Zealand and to map the South Sea islands, where he met his end at the hands of Hawaiian natives in 1779. The gallery contains works by the artists who travelled with him, notably Hodges and Webber, as well as a splendid study of Cook painted by Nathaniel Dance in 1776. Here also is the reconstruction of Cook's murder by Zoffany, based on lurid accounts given him by surviving members of the expedition. Great care was nonetheless taken to portray the 'savages' as 'noble'.

The galleries now take us through the Seven Years' War and reach their climax in the heroics of Nelson's campaigns against the French. The eighteenth-century portraits remain determinedly un-nautical in flavour – even the fearsome Admiral Hood looks more like a hunting squire than a sea captain, and the Romneys might all be of country gentlemen. But the sea battles are truly blood-thirsty affairs, the skies enveloped in smoke, sails ragged with gunshot and seas filled with contorted bodies of drowning men. Nowhere is this better illustrated than in the many paintings produced by the battle of Trafalgar. Here in the **Nelson Galleries** is everything the Nelson enthusiast could ask for: the hero's uniform and medals on the day he died, his chair and letters from his mistress, Lady Hamilton. There are portraits galore, including the two well-known studies of Nelson's fatal wounding on the deck of the *Victory* and the death scene below-decks afterwards. But over all towers Turner's picture of *HMS Victory* at Trafalgar. It is surely the finest representation ever made of battle at sea. The clash of the two floating fortresses and the agony suffered by the human participants are transformed by Turner into a stupendous drama. The sky itself is ablaze with the fire of battle. Here is none of Van de Velde's serenity. It is a picture which roars like a lion.

From Nelson we can retrace our steps to the Navigation Room, filled with globes, astrolabes, sextants and quadrants. Or we can go on down to the new **Neptune Gallery**, designed round the steam tug, *Reliant*, proudly described by the museum as 'the world's largest ship in a bottle'. Built in 1907 and in use until 1968, she was taken apart and reassembled here piece by piece. Inside we can see a series of cabins reconstructed from early ocean liners (what we miss by travelling by plane). Adjacent to the hall lies the **Barge House** containing the museum's pride and joy, the state barge built for Frederick, Prince of Wales in 1732 by William Kent. The carvings, including the six lions on the bow, were done by Grinling Gibbons' successor as master carver to the crown, James Richards. After Frederick's death in 1751 it became the principal state barge, last used by Prince Albert in 1849. Queen Mary's shallop, on display next door, was its 'reserve'. The gallery also includes two navy ordnance barges, used to convey navy commissioners between London and the various Thames-side dockyards.

We end the tour in the **East Wing**, devoted to ships of the nineteenth and twentieth centuries, to the decline of sail and the rise of steam. Two sections deal with the mass migration of Europeans across the Atlantic to America and Canada – and the often horrific conditions they experienced *en route* and on arrival. In the basement is a recreation of the voyage of Sir John Franklin in search of the north-west passage through the Arctic in 1845.

Upstairs we pick up again the story of the British navy since the age of Nelson. The last of the huge 'wooden walls' is represented by a painting of Queen Victoria arriving to visit the Emperor Napoleon III at Cherbourg. Here too is a model of the *Queen*, last of the big ships of the line to be powered by sail. She fought in the Crimea, but was later converted to steam-engine and screw propulsion. Further galleries tell the story of the royal and merchant navy in the two world wars – though they are poor cousins of the displays in the Imperial War Museum. There is, however, an eerie tableau of a convoy at sea, with sounds and lights describing its attack by U-boats.

After the heroics of the maritime museum, the grass of **Greenwich Park** comes as a relief. Although it cannot boast the rolling acres of Richmond or Hampstead, Greenwich's short, sharp climb and magnificent view have always made it a popular excursion. There is a deerpark on the south side, and flower gardens, sports grounds and some dramatic woods and dells along the escarpment. To the west of the Observatory buildings, mounds said to represent early Saxon settlements have been found, while to the east are the foundations of an extensive Roman villa.

The park was first enclosed by Duke Humphrey in 1433, and is thus the oldest of London's royal parks. The present two-mile wall encircling it was built by James I in 1619 and still has much of its original brickwork. Charles II invited the French garden designer, Le Nôtre, to prepare plans for Greenwich in the style of gardens which he and his mother, Henrietta Maria, had admired during their exile in France. In 1955 an original plan for the garden was discovered in Paris, and experts have wondered whether Le Nôtre (who is not known to have visited England) was aware that Greenwich Park lay along a steep hill. His formal vistas and ordered rows of trees reflect the classicism of Jones' architecture, but show scant respect for the contours of the hillside. Either way, the plan as executed involved a broad tree-lined avenue, leading to a series of tiered steps up the hill, and continued as a narrower avenue to the Blackheath gate in the distance. Today the steps have gone, but the rudiments of Le Nôtre's layout can still be detected beneath the encroaching parkland.

Wildness of another kind has always been attracted to the park. It was first opened to 'friends of patients' in 1705 and soon became a major place of recreation. A fair was established, bringing its inevitable entourage of prostitutes, footpads and swindlers. Dance halls and taverns sprang up, where 'soldiers caught nursemaids and children caught colds'. It was described by Dickens as a 'three-day fever which cools the blood for six months'. By 1825 a petition was complaining bitterly at the 'numbers of the profligate part of the lower orders', and by 1857 the fair had been suppressed. But Londoners still indulge in the ancient sport of 'tumbling' down what were once Le Nôtre's steps, while some two million visitors a year troop up to admire the view. They share the prospect with a huge statue of the conqueror of Quebec, General Wolfe, shrouded in a conspiratorial black cloak.

The whimsical façade of Wren's **Flamsteed House** and **Observatory** has been described from the riverside. We now see that it conceals an open courtyard and a six-sided structure curiously set on a conventional seventeenth-century house. Until 1948 this was the residence of the Astronomer Royal, an office whose origins lay in the claim (by a French friend of one of Charles II's mistresses) that a ship's longitudinal position could be determined by relating the position of the moon to that of the stars. Charles decreed that an observatory be built for the first Astronomer Royal, the Reverend John Flamsteed, with Wren, himself a keen astronomer, as architect. It was from these high windows that the initial measurements were made which eventually established the Greenwich meridian and the time zones based on it. In 1884 Greenwich Mean Time was finally accepted and zero degrees longitude described as the 'meridian passing through the centre of the transit instrument at Greenwich'. The instrument is housed in the Meridian Building on the south side of the courtyard, the skylights in the walls and roof showing where successive meridians were plotted. A line across the courtyard marks the meridian itself, usually covered by jostling crowds of tourists eager to be photographed with a foot in each hemisphere.

The Observatory buildings are now a comprehensive museum of the early history of astronomy and time-keeping, with lucid explanations pinned to the walls for the scientifically minded (opening times as for the Maritime Museum). In the upper room of Flamsteed House are ancient telescopes as well as the Tompian Clocks, with thirteen-foot pendulums, with which Flamsteed checked 'mean time' against the more erratic solar time. Downstairs are the simple quarters in which the astronomers lived. Charles' original patronage was by no means lavish, and Flamsteed had to survive on what he termed bitterly his 'incompetent allowance' of £100 a year, with which he also had to pay a 'surly, silly' assistant. From this eyrie, he engaged in almost continual warfare with his distinguished contemporary, Sir Isaac Newton, including some spectacular name-calling sessions at the Royal Society ('Robber! Thief! Puppy!').

We now pass through a series of galleries named after past Astronomers Royal. The Edmund Halley Gallery is devoted to armillary spheres and astrolabes: strange and often beautiful instruments for finding the position of the sun, moon and stars. In the Nevil Maskelyne Gallery are the museum's sundials, with the bigger ones fastened to the wall outside. The Nathaniel Bliss Gallery contains, among other time-keeping instruments, the nocturnals (for night-time observation) and a beautiful set of hourglasses. Downstairs, the Spencer Jones Gallery is devoted to mechanical and electrical methods of time-keeping, including the development of marine chronometers.

Across the garden is a reconstruction of Flamsteed's first observatory. Inside is a facsimile of his quadrant and of the huge sextant through which he had to peer lying flat on his back. There follows a series of rooms devoted to the instruments used to measure the meridian, culminating in Airy's Transit Circle. Here visitors can look directly along zero degrees longitude – one of tourist London's less thrilling experiences.

On the wall outside the observatory can be seen Shepherd's electric twenty-four-hour clock, always set to Greenwich Mean Time. Erected in 1851, its makers fervently hoped that twenty-four-hour clocks would soon become the rage. But even today, with quartz clocks and twenty-four-hour timetables, the twelve-hour dial is still universal: perhaps because most of us can still tell day from night. Beneath the clock are standard measurements of distance – good British feet and yards, that is. And up above Flamsteed House, we can watch the red ball rise and drop every day at 1.00 p.m. precisely. It was intended as a signal by which ships on the river could set their chronometers before setting sail.

Behind the Observatory buildings are three structures each built to house later instruments. The largest, the terracotta South Building, once housed the Observatory's two large reflecting and refracting telescopes. In 1948 London smog and emissions from the two power stations, visible left and right on the river, finally drove the observatory out to the clearer air of Hurstmonceux in Sussex. The South Building has been converted into a planetarium where there are afternoon programmes for visitors and schoolchildren.

CHAPTER TWO

Greenwich II and Blackheath

2⁀

WE now turn from royal Greenwich to a place of a very different texture, the discreet suburb which developed slowly after the departure of royalty but which blossomed with the coming of the railway in the 1830s. We start once again at the *Cutty Sark* and follow a wide arc of some four miles before returning to the river.

From the pierhead we make our way into the small grid of streets nestling beneath the walls of the Royal Naval College. The old medieval core of Greenwich has vanished completely, as have the monastery, the palace and the tall ships which were its lifeblood. In the 1820s the central area was almost completely demolished (or is Turnpin Lane the relic of some ancient alley?). In its place, Joseph Kay, surveyor to the Hospital, laid out the handsome terraces and streets which fortunately survive to this day. The façades of Nelson Road and College Approach are strongly reminiscent of Nash's work in the West End at the same time. And in College Approach is the columned entrance to a covered market which is still in use today – as, we hope, is its carved motto: 'A false balance is abomination to the Lord, but a just weight is His delight.' Above the entrance is an old music hall, sadly out of commission. Once the 'high street' of Greenwich, this neighbourhood has been transformed into a succession of antique shops, boutiques and restaurants, their predominantly tourist customers undeterred by the aggressive confrontation between traffic and pedestrians.

Facing on to Greenwich High Road is the parish church of **St Alphege**. It marks the legendary spot on which Bishop Alphege was put to death by marauding Danes in 1012. The medieval church on this site, where the future Henry VIII was baptized and where Thomas Tallis was organist, must have seen every vicissitude of Greenwich's long history. Here Samuel Pepys went for a 'good sermon, a fine church and a great company of women' (a typically Pepysian escalation of epithets). More frequent visitors would have

Cutty Sark at rest with the church of St Alphege, Greenwich, through the rigging.

South-eastern splendour:
above The Queen's House and Royal Naval College, Greenwich, with the Isle of Dogs beyond;
below The Royal Artillery Barracks, Woolwich.

been the grief-stricken relatives of sailors lost at sea. When its old roof fell down one November night in 1710 the parishioners petitioned Parliament that no fewer than three thousand widows and children had recently been left destitute by storms and disasters at sea 'and are chargeable on the parish'. Parliament voted funds under Queen Anne's 'Fifty New Churches Act' to enable Nicholas Hawksmoor to design a new church for the town. It stands today with a 'Wren' tower by John James somewhat spoiling an otherwise strong Hawksmoor outline. But the east front has a characteristic bold arch inside the pediment, the plan is a simple cross and there are few of the swags and ornaments favoured by Hawksmoor's baroque contemporaries. St Alphege's impressive melancholy is heightened by the sparseness of the interior decoration: an incendiary bomb in the last war destroyed its Grinling Gibbons carvings.

Hawksmoor can at least give us courage to face the scene opposite. The area of Stockwell Street and Greenwich High Street was as recently as 1960 a friendly collection of old shops, together with the Victorian terminus building of one of Greenwich's railway lines into London. No ravage of storm or war has inflicted greater damage on the town than the council bulldozers which descended on this swathe of land, leaving it half car park, half derelict. (Another Victorian station, and an excellent one, survives farther up Greenwich High Road.)

A few determined strides, however, bring us to the **Greenwich Theatre** at the foot of one of the handsomest hills in London. Opposite the theatre stands what is left of the Spread Eagle coaching inn, its tall gateway still visible next to an old bookshop. The theatre itself was once Crowder's Music Hall and passed through a number of non-theatrical uses before being reopened with a company of sufficient quality to put it on the 'first night' circuit of the West End critics. Apart from the theatre itself, the building contains a restaurant and bar and is used for a variety of community purposes.

Croom's Hill began life as a track leading from Blackheath down to the river. With its surrounding land it developed as a typical royal palace *banlieu*, with houses built for attendance on the crown by a number of famous Tudor and Stuart families: Audleys, Courtenays, Comptons, Dudleys, Cecils and Howards. By the eighteenth century most of these had departed westwards with the court, and Croom's Hill settled down to the more modest role of providing

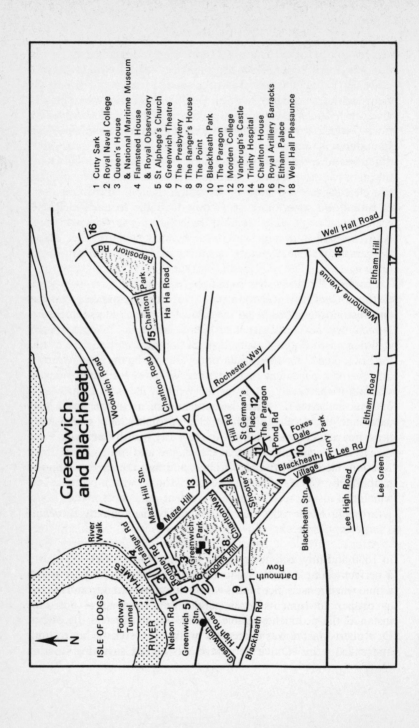

Greenwich and Blackheath

1 Cutty Sark
2 Royal Naval College
3 Queen's House
  & National Maritime Museum
4 Flamsteed House
  & Royal Observatory
5 St Alphege's Church
6 Greenwich Theatre
7 The Presbytery
8 The Ranger's House
9 The Point
10 Blackheath Park
11 The Paragon
12 Morden College
13 Vanbrugh's Castle
14 Trinity Hospital
15 Charlton House
16 Royal Artillery Barracks
17 Eltham Palace
18 Well Hall Pleasaunce

genteel houses for the Hanoverian and Victorian middle class. Few London streets better illustrate their taste. The hill changes its tune every few yards, but the harmony is always constant. The series of Georgian terraced cottages on the left was described when built as 'five fair tenements' yielding £6 a year to help poor children of the town – which apparently they still do. On the right are more substantial town houses, built in the eighteenth century and each subtly different: a carved door bracket here, a bay window there. Off to the right runs Gloucester Circus, of which only the south side was completed as planned. Note the rhythm of the four-four-four pattern of round and square arched windows and the reducing height of each storey: Inigo Jones' sense of Palladian proportion writ small. And compare it with the utterly uninspired modern block across the central garden. Architecture students should spend their detentions here.

Croom's Hill continues round the edge of the park with more textbook Georgian. The doorcase of No. 30, for instance, is classical and restrained, dating from the middle of the eighteenth century. No. 32 beyond is at least thirty years earlier, its foliated bracket well demonstrating the exuberance of domestic architecture during the brief reign of the English Baroque. Farther up the hill and jutting out over the pavement (heaven preserve it from a road widening scheme) is the gazebo built for Sir William Hooker, Lord Mayor of London, in 1672. With the contempt of a courtier for a City merchant, Pepys tells us that 'A plain, ordinary, silly man I think he is, but rich'. Hooker was one of the many wealthy men who came to live in Greenwich to escape the plague and the polluted air of London. He bought the old Grange, and had the gazebo designed probably by Wren's colleague, Robert Hooke, with a pretty ceiling which can just be seen from the pavement outside. Hooker's house is farther up on the right, much altered and lying unobtrusively behind a large copper beech.

After the terrace of 'Sayes Court' comes the old **Presbytery**. Built in 1630 and now belonging to the Catholic church next door, it is a perfect example (both inside and out) of English architecture at a time when renaissance motifs were being introduced from Holland as proper adornments for a gentleman's residence – note, for instance, the pedimented gable and first-floor pilasters. Its owner, Dr Robert Mason, was immensely proud of its stylistic innovations and called it his 'Dutch hermitage'. Its closest surviving London

35

parallel is the 'Dutch House', later George III's palace, at Kew.

Next door, the Catholic Church of our Lady Star of the Sea dates from 1851. Its most prominent feature is the fine spire which punctuates the western view out of the park. Croom's Hill now becomes a succession of villas built (illegally) by Stuart developers on the 'waste' land owned by the Crown between the park wall and the roadway itself. One of these, Park Hall, was believed to have been the home of Sir James Thornhill while he worked on his painting at the Royal Hospital. On the right, set back from the road and facing away to Blackheath, is the old Manor House, a William and Mary mansion built in 1695 for another City merchant, Sir Robert Robinson.

Opposite stands another 'waste' villa, the White House, once occupied by a couple named Lawson, whose daughter Elizabeth was courted passionately by the young James Wolfe. Wolfe's parents had moved from Westerham in Kent to live at Macartney House next door. For four years, whenever he returned from campaigning, Wolfe visited Elizabeth to ask for her hand. She persistently refused him and finally he gave up hope. She died unwed in 1759. Later that same year, Wolfe himself was killed during the conquest of Quebec. The whole of England celebrated his victory. But Greenwich kept its peace in deference to his heart-broken mother on Croom's Hill.

An avenue, once of huge chestnuts, leads us to what was the grandest of the 'waste' villas, the **Ranger's House** (formerly Chesterfield House). Built in the late seventeenth century it was acquired by the Earl of Chesterfield as a retreat in 1748. He added a bow-fronted gallery to the south side – later balanced by another to the north – creating a mansion of considerable proportions. Chesterfield was a leading statesman of the Whig ascendancy and the much-derided patron of Dr Johnson during the agonizing preparation of the latter's dictionary: Johnson defined 'patron' in his dictionary as a 'wretch who supports with insolence and is paid with flattery'. He was, however, an avid collector and writer, perhaps best known for the homilies with which he educated (or plagued) his son, whom he wished quite simply to be 'as near perfection as possible'. The son was no more appreciative than Johnson and broke his father's heart by marrying beneath him and in secret. Chesterfield, however, found consolation at Blackheath: 'My acre of ground here affords me more pleasure than kingdoms do kings.'

In 1814 the house was taken over as the official residence of the Ranger of Greenwich Park (a Crown sinecure) and sold in 1902 to the London County Council. In 1975 it was finally converted to display the unsold remainder of the collection of the Earls of Suffolk (open 10.00 to 5.00, closed at 4.00 in winter), in particular a series of full-length Jacobean portraits attributed to William Larkin. Despite the formality of the faces and poses – the seven paintings of the 'Berkshire Marriage' contain two virtually identical pairs – the portraits are bursting with the wealth and self-confidence of James I's court. Roy Strong, who 'discovered' Larkin in the course of his research into Tudor portraiture, calls them 'the most important series of portraits to survive unbroken from this period'.

The most magnificent is that of Richard Sackville, 3rd Earl of Dorset, on the occasion of the wedding of the king's daughter in February 1613. We are told that 'Lord Dorset dazzled the eyes of all who saw the splendour of his dress.' Nothing produced by the wildest imaginations of modern fashion could equal his astonishing ruffs and garters or his intricately embroidered stockings. The eighteenth-century pictures in the collection look funereal by comparison. But the moving portrait of a 'Howard Boy' of 1627 should not be missed. He stands in a dress holding a bow and arrow, his face filled with adult wisdom.

From the Ranger's House we walk past the site of the last of the 'waste' villas. Montague House was occupied by the Prince Regent's wife, Caroline of Brunswick, after her rejection by her husband for, among other reasons, her refusal to take baths or change her underwear. Here, it is alleged, were committed the 'indiscretions' which gave rise to the rumour that she was mother of an illegitimate child. A committee was appointed to conduct a 'delicate investigation', and though it censured her somewhat loose conduct it acquitted her of the charges laid. She went into self-imposed exile, returning only to claim her throne as Queen at George IV's coronation. Despite widespread public sympathy for her cause her husband refused to include her in the ceremony, and she died soon afterwards. Perhaps to obliterate the memory of his treatment of her, George promptly had Montague House demolished. Ironically in view of her personal habits, nothing survives of Caroline's ownership but a stone bath standing in the grounds.

We are now on **Blackheath** proper. This sweep of grass once ran for four miles to Woolwich and was the natural point of assembly at the south-eastern approaches to London. Wat Tyler led his Peasants' Revolt here in 1381, and in 1497 Henry VII massacred an army of rebels who had marched up from Cornwall. It was here too that Henry VIII staged his magnificent welcome for his fourth wife, Anne of Cleves. He had rashly become betrothed to her on the strength of a portrait by Holbein (in the Victoria and Albert). The sight of the poor woman in the flesh so appalled him that within six months he had divorced her for 'non-consummation', describing her as 'that fat mare of Flanders'. Holbein's reputation nonetheless appears to have survived this trauma.

Even on the finest day, Blackheath contrives to look desolate. Its convex contour has denuded it of trees and the surrounding buildings seem to be in perpetual retreat, slinking off down the hillsides to hide. Nonetheless, the circumference of Blackheath presents a perfect complement to Croom's Hill as a gallery of Georgian development. Proceeding anticlockwise from the top of the hill, we reach the summit of Blackheath Hill at **The Point.** Here the main Dover Road offers us a spectacular view of central London. Beneath our feet are caves and passages which have long been the object of speculation but which are nothing more exciting than disused lime quarries. Beyond runs the Dartmouth Estate, developed in the eighteenth century and containing many original houses in Dartmouth Row (especially Nos. 21-3). A brisk walk brings us via the gloomy mansions of Granville Park and Grope's Buildings into the delightfully named Tranquil Vale – now usually howling with traffic. Despite the intrusion of some discreet modern housing, this area of London retains very much the appearance of a century and a half ago. The Church of All Saints juts up from the heath at the entrance to Blackheath Village in a mid-nineteenth-century Gothic style aptly described by Ian Nairn as 'sit up and beg'. Locals once had less flattering words for the steeple, calling it the 'Devil's toothpick'.

A detour from the heath at this point takes us down through Blackheath Village, now a fashionable neighbourhood high street, and along Lee Road as far as Priory Park. **Blackheath Park Estate** to the left is south-east London's answer to the villas of Richmond or Highbury. The land was originally part of the extensive manor of Wricklemarsh, with a house built by Sir Gregory Page in 1723 for the then (and still) astronomical price of £90,000. The architect was John James and the grounds were landscaped from the heath down to Lee Green. After Page's death in 1783, the estate was bought by a Mr John Cator, who promptly demolished the building, sold the rubble and laid out the park as building lots. A route from Priory Park up to Blackheath Park, Foxes Dale and Pond Road takes us past a series of leafy Victorian villas in a multitude of suburban styles. Of more recent interest are the small estates laid out for the Span development company by the architect Eric Lyons from 1957 onwards, some of the first speculative housing designed after the war in a modern, rather than neo-Georgian, style. Its crisp 'spick-and-span' outline has mellowed with age and vegetation is beginning to blend the buildings into their surroundings. Will we ever regard it as favourably as its Victorian forebears? No. 10 Blackheath Park, by 'office of Patrick Gwynne' (McKean), is an exotic black slate insert of 1969. The Church of St Michael, in Blackheath Park, was built for the estate in 1830 at a time when Italianate houses were invariably offset by a Gothic Church. It has the narrowest spire I have ever seen.

Pond Road leads us back to Blackheath. Here, at what was the summit of the Wricklemarsh estate, Cator laid out one of his first developments, the **Paragon**, built in the 1780s and reputedly making use of columns from the old house itself. It is a beautiful set piece: seven houses four storeys high linked by a stucco colonnade, forming a crescent facing the heath. We might almost be in Bath. To the left of the Paragon the ground falls away towards the Kidbrook, a tributary of the Ravensbourne running into the Thames between Greenwich and Deptford. The stream flows through a series of attractive hollows, above one of which stands **Morden College**, designed by Sir Christopher Wren. It was begun in 1695 by a former owner of the Wricklemarsh estate, Sir John Morden. He was a merchant in the Turkey trade who founded a settlement 'for poor, honest, sober and discreet merchants who shall have lost their estates by accident and perils on the seas' – alms-houses for the respectable poor. Wren's buildings, forming a courtyard with a chapel and carvings attributed to Grinling Gibbons, have an appropriately discreet opulence. Morden and his wife are commemorated by statues in niches above the main entrance. Although trade with Turkey is not what it was, or is not so risky, the charity is still in existence and the college is still filled with pensioners. Individual visitors are welcomed and shown round.

Our route now runs past St German's Place to the villas of

Shooter's Hill Road and then down Maze Hill, which parallels
Croom's Hill to the east of the park. Here stands **Sir John
Vanbrugh's house** – unmistakable on the corner of Vanbrugh Park
(but not open to the public). This 'castle' was designed by the
architect himself in 1717 and is notable as the first residence in
the eighteenth-century picturesque or 'folly' style. Its machicolations
and turrets give it a Scots baronial air; but it was designed to be
reminiscent of the Bastille – Vanbrugh was proud to have been
imprisoned there as a spy in 1692. It is best seen rising majestically
through the trees from the top of Greenwich Park. Vanbrugh built
a number of smaller villas on the estate behind his house, the last
of which was demolished in the 1950s.

From the bottom of Maze Hill, Park Vista turns towards the
Maritime Museum. It is worth braving Trafalgar Road ahead, however, to reach the river beside the power station. Here the **River
Walk** leads downstream for some two miles to the Blackwall Tunnel
at the head of what were once called Bugsby Marshes. It is one of
the longest stretches of continuous river walk in London and an
exhilarating sequence of warehouses, docks and bracing views
across to the Isle of Dogs. At Execution Dock (moved downstream
from Wapping) mutineers and pirates were hanged and their bodies
left putrefying in cages on the foreshore for three tides to wash over
them, a grim deterrent for departing sailors.

Turning instead upstream at the power station, we come across
another of those Greenwich surprises: **Trinity Hospital**, with its
quadrangle and tidy garden and a raised seat overlooking the river.
The charity was founded in 1613 by Henry Howard, Earl of
Northampton, though the present façade is early nineteenth-century.
The hospital is still a charity and has some twenty pensioners. Its
whitewashed courtyard, cowering beneath the cliff-like wall of the
power station, has an almost Sevillian intimacy. In the chapel is
some sixteenth-century stained glass and a statue of the founder
kneeling devoutly in prayer. Permission is required to enter.

The path back to *Cutty Sark* runs past two historic pubs, the
Yacht, with a terrace overlooking the river, and the more famous
Trafalgar. The latter was one of a pair of 'whitebait' inns (the other
was the Ship, destroyed in the war) to which customers would be
rowed down river from as far as Westminster. Dickens described
its menu in *Our Mutual Friend* (a splendid Thames-side novel) as:
'What a dinner – specimens of all the fishes that swim in the sea

surely had swum their way to it.' After years of neglect the Trafalgar was rescued in 1965 and reopened as a pub, restaurant and 'banqueting suite'. The restoration is handsome and whitebait can once again be had – at a price. Seen from the upstairs window, Greenwich Reach moves silently back and forth, ruffled only by the occasional pleasure launch or sculling oarsman. Pepys, writing during the Great Plague, remarked of Greenwich: 'Lord, what a sad time it is to see no boats upon the river.' We could say the same today.

East of Blackheath, just when London seems to be sloping off into Kent for good, we find a series of isolated but important monuments. **Charlton House** (reached along Charlton Road) is, since the loss of Holland House in the last war, the only major Jacobean house left in London. It was begun in 1607 and has an entrance of such exotic Renaissance detail that many have attributed it, at least in part, to Inigo Jones, who lived nearby. The view west over Greenwich and London was stupendous – 'For city, river, ships, meadows, hills, woods and all other amenities one of the most noble in the world,' said Evelyn. So finely polished was the black marble on one of the many fireplaces that a seventeenth-century owner reputedly caught sight of a robbery on Blackheath reflected in it through the window. Later owners were the Maryon-Wilson family who ruled, or misruled, their Hampstead manorial domains from here. The present owners are Greenwich Council who use it as a community centre. Opposite is St Luke's Church, prettily situated on the side of the hill overlooking the Thames.

Beyond Charlton, Maryon-Wilson Park leads us into Ha-Ha Road and the Woolwich domain of the **Royal Artillery**. We reach first an extraordinary landscape of grassy mounds and hollows where the Victorians stored their ammunition for safety and practised gun drill in rugged battlefield conditions. A large collection of guns and cannon are littered about the park as if expecting aggression from every quarter. In a good fog, this could still be the field of Waterloo. To the south is James Wyatt's Royal Military Academy for artillery and engineering officers, now housing the **Royal Artillery Museum** (open weekdays 10.00 to 12.30, 2.00 to 4.00). The curious Rotunda in Repository Road, designed in the form of a tent by John Nash, is an outpost presenting the history of the gun. To the north are the **Royal Artillery Barracks**, an enfilade of buildings a quarter of a mile long constructed at the end of the eighteenth century. It is London's only structure which, as Pevsner says, can be compared with the façades of St Petersburg – yet how many Londoners know it?

Down in Woolwich lie the noble but dejected remains of Sir John Vanbrugh's Royal Arsenal. The building is closed to the public and there are no firm plans for its re-use. Its vast entrance gate looms over Woolwich town centre, begging for salvation.

The answer is not to be found a mile to the east where the G.L.C.'s new town of **Thamesmead** is emerging in all its municipal horror from the Plumstead and Erith marshes. There is a place here where the architects have tried to recreate the harbour of Port Grimaud on the Côte d'Azur, with piazzas, lakes and sailing boats. Rubbish fills every corner; the concrete is stained and ugly and small boys wander about indolently smashing bottles and vandalizing cars. It is worth a visit to see how wrong-headed paternalist British architecture in the 1960s could be.

At the eastern extremity of the marshes, however, is high drama: **Crossness Pumping Station** on the Southern Outfall Sewer, the sister building of Abbey Mills on the north bank. Built by Sir Joseph Bazalgette in 1865 (that *annus mirabilis* of Victorian architecture) and still containing its four giant James Watt beam engines, it is a monument which ranks with the Palm House at Kew and Scott and Barlow's St Pancras Station. It is normally inaccessible but I did once penetrate its defences and found myself in a cathedral of foliated columns, gantries, and spiral staircases decorated with the most exuberant ironwork. The rust comes away in handfuls. Will no one save it?

South-east of Blackheath lie the remains of the medieval palace of **Eltham**. Here amid the prosperous suburbs of SE9 stands a three-storey timbered building dating from the sixteenth century and a small version of Westminster Hall, built by Edward IV. Inside is a magnificent hammerbeam roof (open 11.00 to 7.00, closed at 4.00 in winter) with each member carefully carved and decorated appropriate to its royal owners. The gardens, laid out by Sir Stephen Courtauld in the 1930s, are filled with fragments of the old palace. Bridge, brickwork and stone pop up among the trees and flowers to form what the Tudors would have called a 'pleasaunce'. For good measure a real pleasance lies to the north in the grounds of the Tudor **Well Hall**, once home of Sir Thomas More's daughter

Meg. Though the house has gone, its moat and grounds survive as does the extensive brick barn, now an art gallery and restaurant. Hugh May's **Eltham Lodge** of 1663 lies east of the old palace, an immaculate Restoration mansion but with none of Ham's intriguing eccentricities. It now houses the Royal Blackheath Golf Club, the first golf club in England when its original course was laid out on the heath by James I; the club moved here in 1923.

Four miles due west of Eltham and nestling in the angle of the A2 and the old River Cray is one of the most endearing survivors of all London's historic buildings. **Hall Place**, now in the custodianship of Bexley Council (open 10.00 to 5.00, Sundays 2.00 to 6.00 except in winter), is a rural Tudor house with seventeenth-century additions behind it and an old-fashioned garden running down to the river. In the grounds is a delightful set of heraldic beasts carved in topiary.

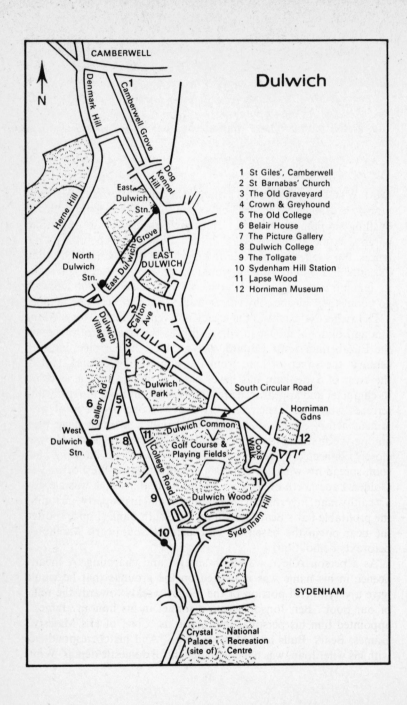

Dulwich

1 St Giles', Camberwell
2 St Barnabas' Church
3 The Old Graveyard
4 Crown & Greyhound
5 The Old College
6 Belair House
7 The Picture Gallery
8 Dulwich College
9 The Tollgate
10 Sydenham Hill Station
11 Lapse Wood
12 Horniman Museum

CAMBERWELL

N

Denmark Hill

Camberwell Grove

Dog Kennel Hill

Herne Hill

East Dulwich Stn.

East Dulwich Grove

North Dulwich Stn.

EAST DULWICH

Dulwich Village

Calton Ave

Gallery Rd

Dulwich Park

South Circular Road

Horniman Gdns

West Dulwich Stn.

Dulwich Common

Coxs Walk

College Road

Golf Course & Playing Fields

Dulwich Wood

Sydenham Hill

SYDENHAM

Crystal Palace (site of)

National Recreation Centre

CHAPTER THREE

Dulwich

৯১

DULWICH always seemed forbidden territory. Even that queen of buses, the stately No. 68, which swung us as children through the bustling shopping streets of Camberwell on its way to our grand parents' home at Norwood, was not allowed to penetrate its defences. No sooner had it mounted the slopes of Denmark Hill than its confidence would wane. It would cough apologetically and make its ignominious way round by Herne Hill. Residents of Dulwich go about their business by car or train – but certainly not by bus.

Dulwich's exclusivity is the legacy of a remarkable history. Alone among London's suburban villages it was the creation of one man, the Elizabethan actor **Edward Alleyn**. Since the early seventeenth century, the sweep of land from the summit of Denmark Hill to the crest of Sydenham has never changed hands, and as a result its character and appearance are wholly different from the sprawling terraces which now encircle it. Alleyn was one of the most prominent actors of the Shakespearian period, and must have been among the first portrayers of Hamlet, Macbeth and Lear. He was closely connected with the running of the Globe on Bankside, but soon spread his wings to establish his own theatre, the Fortune, in Golden Lane north of the city. By his early thirties he was already a wealthy man, investing in entertainment and in property, including the profitable Paris Bear Garden on the South Bank (I once spotted the bear pit in the basement of a derelict Southwark warehouse before its demolition).

As a person Alleyn was both shrewd and charming. A theatre licence in his name was requested on the grounds that he would 'give a very liberal portion of the money weekly towards the relief of our poor'. Ben Jonson wrote a sonnet in his honour. James I appointed him his personal impresario as 'Chief of His Majesty's Games, Bears, Bulls and Mastive Dogs'. And his correspondence with his wife, Joan, was filled with delightful domestic details. While she showered him with affectionate concern on his many journeys, he responded with terms of equal endearment: 'Mouse, you send me no news of anything. You should send of your domestical matters, such things as happens att home ... And, Jug, I pray you, let my orayng tawny stockins of wolen by dyed a very good blak, against I come home, to wear in the winter.'

In 1597, at the age of just thirty-one, Alleyn retired from the stage to devote himself entirely to business. In 1605 he began buying land in and round the old Manor of Dulwich, well situated in attractive country but convenient for his South Bank activities. Here, eight years later, he commenced the building of the college to which he devoted the rest of his life. Rumour had it that one of his motives was to do penance for a rumbustious theatrical career which ended terrifyingly with the appearance on his stage of a ghostly 'thirteenth spirit' in a cast which called for only twelve. The Puritan historian Fuller commented, 'Some, I confess count [the college] built on a foundered foundation, seeing in a spiritual sense none is good and lawful money save what is honestly and industriously earned.' Yet it was not uncommon for wealthy Elizabethans to invest their life's savings in charitable ventures in and round the capital, as Harrow and Highgate found to their benefit. And Alleyn was certainly among the wealthiest. The charities at Dulwich cost him what was for those days the huge sum of £100,000.

Alleyn's **College of God's Gift** consisted of a chapel, almshouses, and a school room for the benefit of the poor of the four parishes with which he had been connected – Bishopsgate, Finsbury, Southwark and Camberwell. The constitution and activities of the charity were laid down with meticulous care, Alleyn subsequently revising them to ensure their continuance after his death. Thus the eighty boys in the educational part of the college were to receive 'a cup of beere' for their breakfast and 'beere without stint' for dinner. Beef and mutton for their meals were to be 'sweet and good' and their coats were to be of 'good cloth, of sad cullor, the boddys lined with canvass'. Governors were to be drawn from the four benefiting parishes. The complexity of these statutes gave rise to constant litigation, and a series of legislative reforms in the nineteenth century were deemed necessary to put an end to eighteenth-century maladministration. This enabled the charity to adapt to Victorian educational expansion and the gradual suburbanization of south London by separating the educational charities from the revenue-raising Estates Governors, whose task was solely to administer the property. This administration has not always been popular. A writer in the 1880s could remark that 'It is an astonishment to those who know his wishes to observe the disregard of Alleyn's courteous provisions.' And even a modern historian, William Darby, feels it necessary to plead with his local readers that the governors 'do not, contrary to suspicion, have horns and a tail'.

Base camp for any assault on Dulwich must be **Camberwell**. In the early nineteenth century this was the 'city tradesman's *beau idéal* of a suburban retreat', but by the 1870s it was experiencing the most dramatic suburbanization of any parish in London. In 1887 *Building News* wrote that, 'The speculative builders and kin societies called building societies are depriving the glade or the meadow of its pastoral sward and the thicket and grove of their folial richness.' By 1900 Camberwell boasted more clerks per head of its population than any other part of London – including the Pooters' Holloway.

Some sense of that folial richness survives in **Camberwell Grove**. This street makes its graceful way up Denmark Hill above one of the best early-Victorian churches in London, St Giles Camberwell, built in 1844 by Sir Gilbert Scott on a church site thought to date back to Saxon times. The Grove is a remarkable recluse, concealing its terraces and crescents behind a thick screen of chestnuts and planes. It is probably the longest, and certainly the most decorous, Georgian residential street in any London suburb.

We reach the summit of the Grove at Dog Kennel Hill and can look across the valley of the lost river Effra to Sydenham Hill beyond. This view once held travellers entranced as they emerged from the London smoke. In 1827 William Hone recorded that, 'Below me, yet wearing its sober livery of brown, lies the wood, the shadowy haunt of the gipsy tribe ... a rich variety of upland and dale, studded with snow-white dwellings.' Yet by 1900 the prospect had changed completely. To Walter Besant it was a 'deadly monotony of row upon row of identical houses', and many modern visitors might feel the same. In 1936, even Joseph Paxton's Crystal Palace vanished from its horizon, burned down in one of London's most spectacular fires.

Nonetheless, **East Dulwich** is the most complete example extant of the craft of the late-Victorian speculative builder. The houses are not identical – unlike their Georgian predecessors. Streets twist and turn in desperate contortions to avoid monotony and capture some corner of what was, by the mid-1880s, a saturated market for suburban housing. This was the lowest of lower-middle-class development, houses at an annual rental of £20–£30. The area round Melbourne and East Dulwich Groves is the result: a fretwork of roof ridge-tiles, carved bargeboard eaves and gabled porches heavy with cheap decoration. Bay windows are coated with what H. J. Dyos, in his history of Camberwell, called 'architectural millinery'. There are sham balconies and balustrades, pilasters with fruit and foliage for capitals, and a constant inventiveness in the colour and textures of the brickwork: red, yellow, black, any brick that might be different. Punctuating these terraces are the 'amenities' the developers were careful to provide. Churches, chapels, working men's clubs, public houses, schools and the magnificent Dulwich Hospital, complete with 'Hatfield' entrance façade, rise up like galleons on a sea of slate. (Connoisseurs may care to look at some extraordinary examples of Speculators' Gothic a mile to the east at Therapia and Marmora Roads.)

East Dulwich is a poor district, lately colonized by immigrants spilling over from Brixton and New Cross. As we squeeze the visual character out of central London, friendly terraced neighbourhoods such as these will come to seem no less attractive than Chelsea or Islington. For the present, however, the boundary between East Dulwich and the ordered sanctuary of the Estates Governors is plain to see. At Carlton Avenue, the air becomes rarer, the voices in the street more refined and the ghost of Edward Alleyn hovers over the ivy and magnolia. Alleyn's Dulwich begins with the **Church of St Barnabas**, opened as Dulwich's first proper parish church in 1894, the tower being added in 1908. It is a London rarity, a late-Victorian church in Perpendicular Gothic and executed in sandstone with a north-country robustness.

Such robustness is short-lived. Those who regard the English suburb as an exercise in illusion need look no farther than **Dulwich Village**. Visitors in the eighteenth century were exhorted to 'lose the world amid the sylvan wilds of Dulwich yet by barbarous hands unspoiled', and its residents ever since have been on a perpetual offensive against urban encroachment. They call themselves a 'hamlet' and their high street 'the village'. They have a common, an ancient graveyard, a parish noticeboard, old-world shops, finger-post road signs and chestnut trees in abundance. There

Edward Alleyn (1566-1626), Shakespearian actor, impresario and founder of Dulwich College. His manorial estates remain almost intact, as one of London's most distinctive and jealously guarded suburbs. (From a portrait in Dulwich Picture Gallery.)

Sydenham Hill Station: 'Lose the world amid the sylvan wilds of Dulwich, yet by barbarous hands unspoiled.'

Above The Observatory at Flamsteed House, designed by Wren for Charles II.

Below South London craftsmanship: *left* Corinthian pilasters and entablature on John Webb's King Charles Building (1664), Greenwich.
Right Victorian bargeboards and pargetting on the gable of The Crown and Greyhound, Dulwich.

are no factories within Dulwich's borders and it harbours, most precious of status symbols, London's last operating tollgate. Yet all this is merged so carefully into the urban fabric as to seem without affectation. So be warned not to use the word 'suburb' within the hearing of any military looking gentleman you may see tending his roses beneath a Georgian wall.

The old **graveyard** at the junction of Carlton Avenue and Dulwich Village was given to the people of Dulwich by Alleyn himself in 1616. Its most remarkable inhabitant is 'Old Bridget', last authentic Queen of the Gipsies, who died in 1768 and whose clan would have encamped each year on neighbouring Gipsy Hill. The heights of South London were home to thousands of these people until the end of the nineteenth century (they still come to Epsom Downs on Derby Day). Another local gipsy, Margaret Finch, who died in the eighteenth century aged 109, had sat cross-legged telling fortunes for so long that she had to be buried in a deep wooden box, still in that position.

The village greets us in style next to the graveyard with a large Georgian house and a guard of honour of chestnuts and beeches. The adjacent group, Nos. 61–7, are not Georgian at all but reproduction Georgian, in keeping with the Governors' post-war 'house style'. The **Crown and Greyhound** pub is an amalgamation of two former pubs on opposite sides of the road. Here Ruskin would bring his worker-pupils to tea after a visit to the Dulwich Gallery. And here the Dulwich Club, a local dining club, would meet to hear speakers such as Dickens and Thackeray. Perhaps as a result of one such visit, Dickens decided to retire his ebullient Mr Pickwick to Dulwich, where he could enjoy 'with a large garden, one of the pleasantest spots near London'. When the old pub was demolished this retirement was celebrated by naming the new road on the site Pickwick Road. The modern Greyhound is an excellent example of 'gin and tonic' pub architecture, with marble columns and mahogany woodwork, topped with oriel windows rising to a heavy bargeboard gable.

The village illusion is sustained by Ye Olde Village Tuck Shoppe opposite. A number of stores still have their canopied colonnades, as at Highgate. And on the left, the Estates Governors are even up to a tease: which Georgian townhouse is a real one? Nos. 93 and 95 are devised to look early eighteenth-century but were built in 1934. But Nos. 97–105 are solid examples of mid-Georgian merchants' houses, shaded by a row of huge chestnuts which form an avenue leading to the white buildings of Alleyn's college in the distance.

The **Old College** sits round three sides of a quadrangle in roughly its original Jacobean form: almshouses on either side with the chapel and administrative buildings in the middle. In contrast to the care Alleyn took over the constitution of his college, he let his builders get away with murder: in 1638 the steeple collapsed; in 1664 one wing and part of the other fell down; and in 1703 the 'College porch with ye Treasury Chamber, etc., tumbled down to ye ground'. These and later disasters mean that the college as we now see it is almost entirely a nineteenth-century structure, both left and right wings in stuccoed mock-Tudor, the central cloister and tower in stone. The chapel is not open to the public except for services, but contains a graceful marble font designed by James Gibbs in 1729, as well as elaborate Victorian choir stalls and a 1911 altarpiece showing Dulwich boys in the costume of Alleyn's time. Old prints show the college scruffy and bustling in a properly collegiate manner. For some reason, today it has the atmosphere of a clinic.

To the right of the Old College at the corner of Gallery Road stands the **Old Grammar School**. The building is a testament to the pricked consciences of the early Victorian Governors. As fee-paying scholars took up more of their 'charity', they were criticized for neglecting the local poor – again, as happened at Harrow and Highgate. This picturesque school room was the result, designed in 1842 by Sir Charles Barry, architect to the Governors. A boisterous local playgroup was appropriately in residence when I was last there.

A detour up the surprisingly rural Gallery Road (complete with hedgerows) brings us to **Belair House**, one of the last of the grand mansions which graced the valley below Sydenham. The house was built in 1785 (though not, as claimed, by Robert Adam) and was in private hands until 1938, after which it passed to the local council. Neat cricket pitches now cover the lawn, and the steps down which the daughters of Victorian merchants would have run with croquet mallets now lead to municipal changing rooms. But the old stables are still standing, trees sway romantically in the wind overhead, and Belair in the autumn twilight can just shake off its twentieth-century tawdriness and take us back to a time of house parties, carriages in the drive and the tinkle of sophisticated chatter.

Opposite Belair and immediately south of the Old College is the **Picture Gallery and Mausoleum**, opened in 1817 and the first public art gallery in London. The collection was created round a nucleus of Alleyn's own pictures, chiefly of Tudor royalty, augmented by the William Cartwright bequest of theatrical pictures given to the college in 1687. The bulk of the Dulwich collection, however, and the gallery which houses it, arrived by a different and most curious route.

In the 1770s a young Frenchman teaching in London, Noel Desenfans, fell in love with one of his pupils, Margaret Morris, and duly married her. Margaret inherited a large enough fortune to encourage her new husband to set up as an art dealer, abetted by his friend, Francis Bourgeois. Desenfans expanded his business and was eventually commissioned by the King of Poland to amass pictures for the formation of the Polish National Gallery. But no sooner had the collection been made, and paid for out of Margaret's fortune, than the king was overthrown and reduced to the status of a St Petersburg pensioner. Desenfans was left with the pictures unpaid for and nowhere to put them. He first offered them to the British Treasury as the basis for a National Gallery, but the offer was refused. (It took a further twenty-five years for such a gallery to be established in Trafalgar Square.) So Desenfans eventually bequeathed them to his friend, Bourgeois.

Bourgeois had been much impressed by Dulwich's custodianship of the Alleyn and Cartwright collections. So he in his turn left the collection to Margaret (who had, of course, paid for it) with a reversion to Dulwich on her death. It was she who supervised the building of the gallery and stipulated that a mausoleum be built adjacent to it for the three creators of the collection. She personally paid for the gallery buildings and insisted that they be kept open to the public. They were to be inspected each year by the Royal Academy to ensure the paintings were well looked after – given the reputation of the Governors, clearly a necessary precaution. Money, and a dinner service, were given for the Academy's entertainment.

The architect chosen to design the Gallery and Mausoleum was Sir John Soane, who completed it in 1817. Most of what we see today was rebuilt after a direct hit from a bomb in the last war. The entrance façade is new, a Soanian pastiche, but the rear, west side and the adjacent mausoleum are original. The group is not easy to comprehend at first glance, but its flavour can best be appreciated in the mausoleum, one of the oddest yet most peaceful of structures. It takes the form of a circular antechamber of Doric columns leading into a taller room containing the three coffins of Bourgeois, Desenfans and his wife. The whole space is lit from above with a deep orange glow from stained glass windows. To Soane's most fervent disciple, Sir John Summerson, the simple intersecting lines and spaces of Dulwich Mausoleum achieve 'a level of emotional eloquence and technical perfection rare in English or indeed in European architecture'. To my less tutored eye Soane's variations on a classical theme are intellectually intriguing rather than emotionally uplifting. But it is this very restraint which makes it so exhilarating to find inside such caged lions as Rembrandt, Rubens and Van Dyck.

The gallery has suffered a series of mishaps since its reopening after the war. These included the theft in 1966 (and subsequent recovery) of eight of its most important paintings and the sale by the Governors of its famous Domenichino. Under new direction it has embarked on a major rehanging – making a detailed guide to the rooms impossible (open weekdays except Mondays 10.00 to 5.00, Sundays 2.00 to 5.00, closed at 4.00 in winter). Works by the northern European masters predominate in the collection, especially the Dutch and Flemish schools, but Desenfans taste was remarkably Catholic.

Dulwich's most precious treasures are undoubtedly the three works by Rembrandt, at present hanging at the southern end of the gallery. The first, 'A Girl at a Window', ruddy complexioned, hair tousled and hand playing with her necklace, is surely Rembrandt's most vivid presentation of youthful coquettishness. Next to it is a portrait of maturity, the head of Jacob de Gheyn III, calm and direct. And third is the artist's son, Titus, a vulnerable face, invested not just with a father's hopes but with his cares as well – so intense it might almost be of the painter himself. Both Titus and his mother Saskia died relatively young, leaving Rembrandt in old age the isolated figure of his great Kenwood self-portrait.

Examples of the more flamboyant Flemish school include some characteristic works by Rubens, including 'Hagar in the Wilderness' and a painting of Venus squirting milk into the mouth of Cupid – to predictable schoolboy titters. There is also a delightful portrait of Catherine Manners, much put-upon wife of the first Duke of

Buckingham, favourite of James I. Chief among Rubens' pupils in Antwerp was the young Van Dyck. (The latter's skill at copying his master's style once enabled him to save a fellow apprentice who had damaged a Rubens canvas in a rumpus.) In the 1620s Van Dyck went to Italy to broaden his education and to obtain the lucrative portraiture commissions available there at that time. It was in the course of a visit to Palermo in 1624 that he produced the painting of Emmanuel Philibert, Governor of Sicily, which hangs at Dulwich. In 1632, Van Dyck was persuaded by Charles I to settle in England, where he worked for six years and was awarded a knighthood, the first artist to be so honoured. His studio turned out a phenomenal number of portraits of the English nobility – Van Dyck himself often contributing only the head – in the decade before the Civil War. Hindsight lends them all a sense of tragedy.

One such portrait is believed to be of William Russell, 5th Earl of Bedford, and son of the creator of Covent Garden. It was William who married the impoverished Anne Carr of Chiswick House, much to his parents' disgust (*see* Chapter 7). He began the Civil War as a Parliamentary officer, but changed sides to support the king – and then changed back again. He finally decided to retire from politics to engage in the steadier pursuit of draining the fenlands of East Anglia. (The sitter, however, could be not Bedford but the Earl of Bristol, says the new catalogue!)

Thomas Gainsborough is represented by a painting of Mrs Moody and her children and by the famous portrait of the Linley sisters. These girls were daughters of the eighteenth-century composer, Thomas Linley of Bath, and were much admired for their singing voices. Elizabeth, the elder, was so plagued by suitors that in desperation she decided to flee to a French convent. The playwright Sheridan offered to escort her on the trip – and caused a great scandal by marrying her in private near Calais. The two girls look poised and knowing, and more than a match for their brother, Samuel, whose portrait hangs nearby. Reynolds' famous portrait of the actress, Mrs Siddons, as the Tragic Muse, is accompanied by a delightful self-portrait of the same artist, wearing a pair of spectacles. The Dulwich Murillos include his 'Flower Girl' and two pictures of peasant children at play, as powerful a portrayal of the Spanish character as any painting by Goya. The French collection is strong in Poussins and Claudes. 'Jacob with Laban and his Daughters' is the sort of landscape which so excited the Palladians on their grand tours and which Kent and Burlington sought to recreate in the grounds of Chiswick.

Among the Italian pictures, the Florentine Renaissance is represented by Piero di Cosimo's 'Young Man'. There is a strong Guido Reni of 'St John the Baptist' and works by Veronese and Agostino and Annibale Carracci. A series of Tiepolos appear to have floated down from the ceiling of some Venetian saloon; and there is a Canaletto, painted when he was in England, of old Walton Bridge. He makes even this quaint structure look as glorious as the Bridge of Sighs; and his Surrey gentlemen seem hot-foot from the Rialto.

However, it is the Dutch and Flemish landscapes and domestic interiors which are most characteristic of the Dulwich collection. Those local beneficiaries of the Desenfans' bounty must have responded instinctively to the Cuyps, Hobbemas, Pynackers, van Ruysdaels and Boths, full of the rural naturalism they so prized in their immediate neighbourhood. The morning sun catches the sails of Ruysdael's windmills and the flanks of Cuyp's cattle as it must have caught the trees and cottages of old Peckham and Denmark Hill. The fanciful slopes with which the Dutch masters scattered their canvases might almost be Sydenham.

As we depart, the kindly faces of Edward Alleyn himself and his 'sweet harte and mouse,' Joan, gaze down benevolently over the foyer. Dulwich Gallery is one of the treasures of London. It deserves to be more widely known and patronized.

Opposite the gallery is **Dulwich Park**, seventy acres given by the Governors to the London County Council in 1888. In return for their generosity they demanded that the L.C.C. pay for the erection of a statue of Alleyn by the entrance. Lord Rosebery, accepting the park on behalf of the Council, replied that he would 'not dare promise execution of such an unpardonable act of extravagance as the requested statue, though he might provide 'some very cheap stone which would not materially affect the rates'. No monument was ever erected, but the L.C.C. scored the winning goal by naming the park gates after Rosebery himself. Though heavily municipalized with herbaceous borders, boating pond, huts and benches, Dulwich is one of the most attractive of London's smaller parks.

College Road now acquires the character of a hallowed precinct. Villas are set back from the road behind white-post fences, schoolboys carry satchels over their shoulders and each house emphasizes its individuality with a name – Pickwick Cottage, Bell House, Papplewick, Howlettes Meade. This is the territory through which Browning walked to write: 'The lark's on the wing, the snail's on the thorn,/God's in his Heaven, all's right with the world.' We can see why. Note especially Bell House, a handsome building of about 1770, with twin pediments and rusticated door surround, the style repeated on the stable block to the left. Perhaps the work of an imaginative suburban builder, allowed to roam free through his pattern book? The house is a Junior section of Dulwich College.

We now reach the road named 'Dulwich Common' which does a Jekyll-and-Hyde act with London's South Circular. Since Mr Hyde is usually dominant it is to be treated with respect. Regency villas and town houses with splendid gardens line it to left and right, their period flavour fighting a losing battle with the traffic. But not even the South Circular can overpower the adjacent buildings of **Dulwich College**, moved uphill from the Old College buildings in 1870.

The Governors were able to provide £100,000 for the new school out of profits made by permitting railway companies wayleave south through the estate. The result was undoubtedly the most florid Victorian school building in London. (New local free schools were also built at this time: Alleyn's for boys and John Allen's for girls.) The architect was Charles Barry Jnr, son of the designer of the old grammar school down the road, and the style chosen was 'northern Italian Renaissance', much in fashion in the late 1860s. The plan consists of three blocks linked by colonnades, with the big hall and administration in the centre block and the junior and upper schools on either side.

I used to visit Dulwich as a boy to play rugby against the school on cold winter afternoons. These awesome buildings loomed over the playing field, personifying the menace of the opposition. I dreaded them then but they have grown on me since. The façades are enriched with some of the most intricate coloured brick, stone and terracotta work to be found anywhere in London, surmounted by turrets, pinnacles and a filigree of balustrading. The school is not open to the public, but behind the central window is a massive hall with a hammerbeam roof to rival St Stephen's Westminster. In the master's common room is a fireplace incorporating what are improbably claimed to be painted panels from the original Golden Hind.

Directly opposite the college gate is a carefully maintained village mill pond. Overlooking it, the weatherboarded **Pond Cottages** might have stepped straight out of a rural crafts museum. They have been here ever since this was a country lane and the centre cottage is a claimant to the title of smallest house in London (there are many others, including one in Dulwich village itself).

We now reach the **Tollgate**. If we have a vehicle, we must dig into our pockets for 3p, or 'For beast, per score and so on in proportion, 10d, for sheep, lambs or hogs per score, $2\frac{1}{2}$d.' Would they really accept pre-decimal coinage were anyone to collect the necessary livestock and try them? This is not a particularly ancient or historic tollgate. It was established by a local tenant in 1789 to pay for the maintenance of a track through some fields he had rented from the Governors. The college kept it in operation even after the 1864 Act abolishing such tolls on public roads. It is still defended on the grounds that it might deter drivers from taking this short cut to Sydenham – and besides, 'It's quaint.' Although it can hardly pay its keeper's wages and is left open at night, it is a unique survival of London's economic history.

Dulwich now changes character. The upper end of College Road crosses what was once the woodland belt round the hills of Sydenham and Norwood. Of this wood, which used to shelter some of the finest houses in suburban London, only a fragment is left in a wild state. Playing fields lap round its slopes and the woods themselves are interlaced with roads, crescents and drives where the Estates Governors have capitalized on rising property values since the war. There is nothing here of special interest, but a good leafy walk for about a mile to the Horniman Museum.

Sydenham Hill Station, on the right of College Road, is lost in its fairy-tale dell and is one of my favourites. Here weary commuters alight at the original platform of the London, Chatham and Dover Railway Company and are led up steps and along iron catwalks before emerging through the woods on to the road. Behind them down the tracks, the thundering anvils of the metropolis can scarcely be heard above the singing of the birds in the trees. Not even Metroland encapsulates the spirit of suburban escape so effectively. Across the road, Great Brownings (yes, the poet) is London's answer to the all-American suburban estate. It is modern and cottagey, with individuality sprayed on from the architect's catalogue – shades of East Dulwich – in the pattern of the bricks, the tone of the hung tiles, even the colour of the garage doors. Here are London's modern Pooters, watching in pride as the clematis and wisteria slowly take hold on the 'antique' brick wall.

Farther up the hill is the church of St Stephen's built by Barry in 1868 but with none of the flamboyance of the College itself. The Governors expected their architect to play safe up here where speculative profit was at stake. New tenants were not to be subjected to stylistic innovation, least of all at church. This is where the conservative middle classes of a Galsworthy novel or a Granville Barker play would have worshipped.

At the summit we reach what is now no more than a memory of old **Crystal Palace**. Some relics of the original terracing remain overlooking the National Recreation Centre beyond. A collection of life-sized prehistoric monsters still inhabit the park beneath, where dinosaur and tyrannosaur stalk the south London undergrowth. Banquets were held inside them when they were first built. Schemes for the palace site itself have come and gone – of varying degrees of vulgarity. But for the present the ghosts of Sydenham past walk 'the Parade' undisturbed, dropping by for old times' sake at the sad shell of the Crystal Palace low-level station.

Sydenham Hill runs left out of the Parade, a comfortable road with some few reminders of its nineteenth-century glory and a number of twentieth-century oddities: for instance, a classical pillared colonnade beside No. 17; a Gothic stable block to No. 16; and a real log cabin tucked away in the woods at Dome Hill Park. Six Pillars in Crescent Wood Road is a demonstration exercise in 1930s modernism by the Tecton partnership and has already acquired a period charm. Opposite is the house in which James Baird conducted his early experiments in television, a most unassuming setting in which to plot a cultural revolution. Farther down the hill a path named Cox's Walk runs through some undergrowth into Lapse Wood. The wood is a rare example of virgin London *flora*, its jumbled trees and unkempt slopes a relic of wilder days in these parts. The barbed wire which now surrounds it, penetrated only by small boys in search of adventure, is sadly not for its protection. For a number of years, the Estates Governors have been seeking permission to develop the wood for housing and have recently sold it to the local council.

As we descend Sydenham Hill towards Lordship Lane an extraordinary edifice rises on our right. The **Horniman Museum** in London

Road is the sort of institution most Londoners leave to their children (open 10.30 to 6.00 Sundays 2.00 to 6.00). Certainly school-children seem to be its most ardent supporters. The collection is described as anthropological, but is really the sort of agglomeration one would expect to find in an eccentric explorer's attic. It is built round a collection given to the people of London at the end of the last century by the tea millionaire, F. J. Horniman. The architect chosen for the museum buildings was C. Harrison Townsend, a leading member of the Arts and Crafts movement and creator of the bold façades of the Bishopsgate Institute and the Whitechapel Art Gallery in the East End. The Horniman, opened in 1901, was Townsend's ultimate attempt to bring art to London's working classes.

The museum is one of the most striking buildings of the Edwardian period. The conception is baroque, with segmental pediment over entablature and frieze on the main façade, offset by a flowing flight of steps, an entrance arch and tower with turrets. But the execution is splendidly 'aesthetic': floral reliefs crown the tower like garlands, the ironwork is graceful *art nouveau*, and a large mural by Anning Bell portrays a classical wonderland of nymphs and muses. What on earth can Townsend's workers have made of such greenery-yallery?

Inside is a glorious mixture of treasure trove and junk room – all tossed at the visitor with immense gusto. No guide is feasible, or necessary. I can best convey an impression of the contents by listing the objects noted with enthusiasm by one small boy: a large stuffed albatross; a Peruvian mummy contorted into a bundle; a carved aboriginal boomerang; a Navajo sandpainting; a Spanish torture chair; a stuffed walrus; a glass harmonica; a sunset scene with dinosaurs; a domestic pigeon, cut open in formalin; an assortment of Buddhist household goods; and a huge apostle clock (not working). When I was last there the acquarium had sprung a leak and staff were crawling about on the floor looking for escaped amphibians. The Horniman Museum is a monument to serendipity. I can think of no better destination for the profit on a cup of tea.

South of the Crystal Palace the old road to Brighton ran up over the Purley Downs beyond the once-small town of Croydon. This road now swings to the west through the industrial landscape of Waddon. The downs themselves are covered in the expensive homesteads of Selsdon, Purley, Coulsdon and Banstead (with, tucked in beneath the latter, the pretty village of Carshalton, still hanging on to quaintness by its fingertips). But **Croydon** is a different matter. In the 1960s, a determined local council decided to go for growth as an 'off-centre office location'. The old Victorian town was largely swept aside and a mini-Houston of skyscrapers and flyovers was erected in its stead. This may have done wonders for the rate revenue but it is awful to behold at close quarters (slightly better lit up at dusk from the old Croydon aerodrome site along Purley Way). Buried in its bowels are the remains of the medieval **palace** of the Archbishops of Canterbury (selected tours on summer afternoons), with great hall, chapel and undercroft. To the north, just off Wellesley Road in Poplar Walk, is one of the finest Victorian churches in south London, J. L. Pearson's **Church of St Michael**. This building, in a soaring Early English Gothic (1880), ranks with Pearson's masterpiece of St Augustine's Kilburn. It raises the spirit far above the skyscrapers beyond.

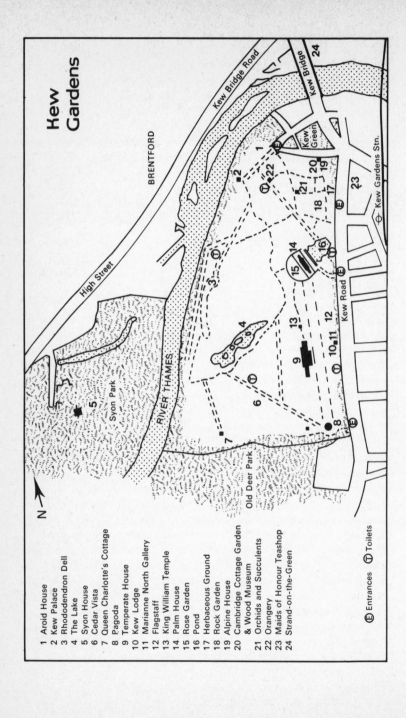

Kew Gardens

BRENTFORD

High Street

RIVER THAMES

Syon Park

Old Deer Park

Kew Bridge Road

Kew Bridge

Kew Green

Kew Gardens Stn.

Kew Road

N

1 Aroid House
2 Kew Palace
3 Rhododendron Dell
4 The Lake
5 Syon House
6 Cedar Vista
7 Queen Charlotte's Cottage
8 Pagoda
9 Temperate House
10 Kew Lodge
11 Marianne North Gallery
12 Flagstaff
13 King William Temple
14 Palm House
15 Rose Garden
16 Pond
17 Herbaceous Ground
18 Rock Garden
19 Alpine House
20 Cambridge Cottage Garden
   & Wood Museum
21 Orchids and Succulents
22 Orangery
23 Maids of Honour Teashop
24 Strand-on-the-Green

Ⓔ Entrances Ⓣ Toilets

CHAPTER FOUR

Kew

NOT having green fingers I have always entered Kew Gardens like an illiterate in a seat of high learning. All is well out on the Green. Old Kew Church and its quaint memorials hold no mysteries. And the ivy-hung walls of the Georgian cottages and town houses are old familiars. But as soon as I pay my ten pence (so recently just one penny) and enter the hallowed precincts, I am hushed and on tiptoes for fear of bruising so much as a snowdrop. This is the university of *pseudotsunga menziesii* and *sequoiadendron giganteum*, its precincts thick with scholarly spinsters, heads together and muttering Latin. It is a place of study as much as of pleasure, and its academic purposes must be respected even by the most casual visitor. But above all it is a place for the seasons. And though Kew in winter has its romantic charm there is nowhere better to observe London in spring, when the camellias and magnolias are opening, blossom is foaming on the trees and a carpet of every known variety of daffodil is spread underfoot. It is an experience which can so easily pass the city-dweller by. It makes the London winter worth enduring and renders uninhabitable any region, however balmy its climate, which has no spring.

The official map of the gardens, available at the entrance, is indispensable and, together with the excellent guidebook, helps unravel (and translate) the exhibits in Kew's three-hundred-acre museum. This chapter is therefore intended only as an introduction. The gardens began life as part of the Hanoverians' royal enclave which ran from Kew up the Thames to Richmond. George II lived at Richmond Lodge during his estrangement from his father, and his son, Frederick, lived next door at Kew House with his wife, the Princess Augusta. Two subsequent royal palaces were built at Kew, but both have gone. All that now remains is the earliest building, Kew House, renamed Kew Palace. This building had once been the home of the Capel family and it was Lord Capel who in the late

61

seventeenth century purchased the first trees for Kew: two mastics, orange trees, a herb garden and some hollies (at a price of £5 a bush). 'He had the choicest fruit of any plantation in England,' said John Evelyn after a visit in 1688, 'and is the most industrious and understanding in it.'

However it was Princess Augusta who, on Frederick's death began the major collection of what were known as 'exotics', or foreign plants, with William Aiton as her assistant. She also commissioned the architect, Sir William Chambers, to adorn her grounds with classical and oriental follies, while Capability Brown was landscaping the gardens of Richmond Lodge next door. On inheriting both these properties George III combined them and continued the work Augusta and Aiton had begun. The dictatorial Brown, however, was clearly the bane of his life; when he died, it is said the king exclaimed to one of his gardeners, 'Brown is dead – now you and I can do what we please here.' But it was not until Victoria came to the throne that the gardens were given to the nation (in 1841) and achieved their international reputation under the two great botanists, Sir William Hooker and his son, Joseph.

The gardens became – and remain – one of the finest monuments to the British Empire. Explorers such as Captain Cook and Charles Darwin would never return without 'precious specimens for Kew'. It was to Kew that the Amazon rubber saplings were smuggled, to be developed and sent out to the Far East to break the Brazilian rubber monopoly on British colonial soil. And while sheer spending power may have enabled other nations to steal a march on the National Gallery, the British Museum or London Zoo, they have never been able to equal the splendour of Kew. Its treasures have been two centuries in the making.

From the main entrance we can get our first drenching from the exotics by entering the **Aroid House**. This was designed by John Nash for Buckingham Palace (where its pair still stands), but was moved here in 1836. It is for plants used to the heat and humidity of tropical rain forests and visiting it is not unlike entering a sauna. Beyond it, along what was the old road to the Brentford ferry, stands **Kew Palace** itself, smallest and most domestic of all London's royal palaces. It was here that George III retired to enjoy a sort of tranquillity as his final madness approached, and here that his queen, Charlotte, lived until her death in 1818. It has not been inhabited since. The house dates from 1631 and is typical of the jolly Dutch

Renaissance mansions fashionable at that time. It is a feast of pediments – on gables, windows, blank walls even – with mini-rustication round the window openings. The walls are of warm brick laid in Flemish bond and offset by bright, white woodwork.

Inside (closed in winter) there is no sense of George's impending tragedy. He and Charlotte liked to stay here free of court and courtiers and with only a small staff of domestic servants. The rooms are handsome but modest, appropriate for a prosperous country gentleman, and therefore much to George's taste. They are furnished in the eighteenth-century style, though some still have their seventeenth-century ceilings. They contain an endearing collection of Hanoverian *bric-à-brac*, including royal toys and snuffboxes and the chair in which Queen Charlotte is reputed to have died.

Kew is a case of each to his own, but I have always started with the trees and ended with the flowers. This takes us in an anti-clockwise direction from the Palace, beginning with the eucalyptus, poplar and oak plantations which run along the river bank opposite the mouth of the Brentford arm of the Grand Union Canal. The path passes the rhododendron dell, laid out as a glade by Capability Brown but given its present flamboyance by the specimens brought back from the Himalayas by Joseph Hooker in the nineteenth century. Adjacent to it is the bamboo garden.

The lake at Kew might be that of any English stately home, surrounded by willows and conifers and populated with mallards and swans. Indeed Syon House can be seen across the Thames from its far end, looking for all the world as if Kew belonged to it. To its west, however, the trees merge into Kew's most cosmopolitan extravaganza: the pine, cedars and cypresses which surround the Cedar Vista with the Pagoda as its climax. The conifers now become grander, and beyond the water lily pond rise the great Californian redwoods, timeless sentinels from some primeval forest. Will these comparative saplings still be gracing Kew in four thousand years, as the parents from which they were propagated graced the American west that length of time ago?

Down behind the redwoods lies a momentary English diversion, Queen Charlotte's private garden with its *cottage orné*. This is believed to have been designed by a royal princess in 1770 as a summer house for the queen, the sort of woodland treat Hansel and Gretel might have eaten. It has high windows, thick ivy and a thatched roof; beyond it in spring are great clouds of bluebells.

The south-west corner of the gardens is dominated by Sir William Chambers' ten-storey **Pagoda**, surely one of London's oddest buildings, even without the eighty glass-covered dragons which once graced the corners of each storey. Chambers had travelled in China and brought back an enthusiasm for oriental gardening as an alternative to the grander landscapes of Capability Brown. The pagoda was built (along with a now vanished mosque and alhambra) for Princess Augusta in 1761, with pretty balconies by Chippendale providing a magnificent view over the gardens. Though it is now too unsafe to be open to the public, it remains a splendid symbol of Kew's eclecticism. A Japanese 'Gate of the Imperial Messenger' completes the oriental atmosphere nearby – presented by the Japanese government in 1910. Chambers also designed a number of temples, follies and a ruined arch which are dotted round the southern section of the gardens.

Crossing the Pagoda Vista we reach Decimus Burton's Temperate House, a large traditional greenhouse begun in 1860 and now in process of restoration. It is a handsome structure, which has suffered in public estimation through inevitable comparison with its elder sister, the Palm House. But immediately south of it, bordered by camellia and magnolia, is one of the true architectural gems of Kew, Eden Nesfield's **Kew Lodge**. Built in 1866 it is a very early example of the 'Queen Anne' style which, as Pevsner sardonically remarks, was 'supposed to have been created by Nesfield's former partner, Norman Shaw, about six years later'. Partial inspiration doubtless came from the Dutch Renaissance of Kew Palace but the steep roof, giant dormer windows, disproportionate cornice and colossal chimney seem the product of a wholly original sense of humour. We must drag our minds back across decades of Nesfield and Shaw imitations to realize what an impact building such as this must have made on a London of white Italianate terraces and ragstone Gothic churches. Next door to it is the **Marianne North Gallery**, filled with Miss North's paintings of plants and scenery. She toured the world collecting them and was the original, indomitable Victorian lady traveller. The rooms, decorated with rare panelling and original Victorian lettering are as much a part of the display as are the pictures.

Leaving the flagstaff on our right (two hundred and twenty-five feet high and made from a single British Columbian Douglas fir), we pass the shrub garden and climb the mound of the King

The Palm House, Kew: 'An eerie sensation of floating through a jungle.'

Bridging the Thames:
above The North London line *versus* Strand-on-the-Green;
below The view downstream under Richmond Bridge.

William Temple, with its plaques commemorating British military victories. Here can be had one of the most spectacular sights of London: the great **Palm House** seen across what in spring is a glacier of flowering cherry. Inspiration for the Palm House came from a visit paid by Queen Victoria to the Great Stove built by Joseph Paxton at Chatsworth in 1836. (Nineteenth-century conservatories were called stoves after their heating systems.) British gardening was at that time turning away from the naturalism of Brown and Repton. John Loudon and W. A. Nesfield (father of Eden) were laying out terraces, walks and vistas which reverted in style to the continental formalism of the seventeenth century. Herbaceous borders resembled fireworks displays. And heated 'stoves' were built to house the new exotics. None was grander than that of Kew.

Decimus Burton, architect to Kew Gardens and collaborator with Nash at Regent's Park, prepared initial designs for the Palm House, but the committee considered them too fussy, with 'too many columns'. Another scheme was presented by an Irish engineer, Richard Turner (who had built a number of greenhouses in Ireland), and it was this plan, modified by Burton, which was built. Though there are similarities with Chatsworth's convex profile, the modulation of the wrought iron ribs and the delightful clerestory makes the Palm House a wholly original structure, ranking with Harmondsworth tithe barn and Abbey Mills pumping station among the great (but neglected) secular monuments of the London suburbs. Burton's Temperate House looks temperate indeed alongside it and even Paxton's stolid Crystal Palace, designed six years later, seemed old-fashioned by comparison. Inside, a gallery runs the length of the building, enabling us to view the palm, banana, rubber and bamboo from above as well as below – an eerie sensation of floating through jungle.

The Palm House is adorned on one side by a vivid rose garden and on the other by terraces and the Palm House pond. Overlooking the pond are replicas of the ten Queen's Beasts carved by James Woodford for the coronation in 1953, reminiscent of those installed by Henry VIII at Hampton Court. They stare out at the far more fearsome Chinese Guardian Lions and at the equally bizarre swamp cypresses, which show their knees above the pond waterline. Opposite, Burton's Museum One contains a display of plants considered economically useful, as well as a collection of British moss.

Past the woodland garden, Kew becomes more academic. Through to the right is the Herbaceous Ground, where amateur and professional horticulturalists pore over row upon row of expertly tended plants. A rose pergola leads to the rock garden, its undulating banks of pastel shades forming a botanical Tower of Babel to the uninitiated. The iris, aquatic and alpine gardens follow, and at their eastern extremity a wall shelters one of Kew's most pleasant corners. **Cambridge Cottage** once belonged to the Duke of that name and is now a wood museum, but its old garden is a refreshing English homecoming after our botanical world tour. Or it is at first sight. On closer inspection, the familiar daffodils, hellebores and lilacs are interspersed with trees which boast a provenance in Persia, the United States and central China. Kew never lets up.

Turning north, we pass an extensive series of modern buildings housing the orchid and succulent collections, including the Sherman Hoyt cacti from California and the horrible carnivorous pitcher plants. Outside is a succession of rare individual trees: the elderly stone pine looking like a giant umbrella left leaning tipsily on the grass, the delicate oriental maidenhair tree and the dawn redwood, discovered in China in 1941 after having been thought extinct for a hundred million years. The lawn in front of Chambers' Orangery (now used as an exhibition centre) is a favourite spot for collapsing – and reflecting that within a week or two nature will rearrange the whole collection and insist we return.

The walk back across Kew Green takes us past a series of typical English front gardens, their owners clearly conscious of the critical eyes which pass them every day. One has resorted to a simple gesture by way of response: a paved patio with a single English rose as its centrepiece.

The Maids of Honour teashop, just down Kew Road from the Green, is a valiant survivor of a once-plentiful breed. It is usually bursting at the seams with sturdy ladies who spent the morning at Harrods and the afternoon among the herbaceous borders. The air is shrill with talk of fuchsias and peat.

Those in search of stronger ref.eshment should cross Kew Bridge and turn right to reach **Strand-on-the-Green** and its historic pubs, the City Barge and the Bull's Head. This enclave is one of the most attractive anywhere on the Thames, blessed with a footpath rather than a road between its eighteenth- and nineteenth-century cottages and the water's edge.

CHAPTER FIVE

Richmond

❧

THE view from **Richmond Hill** is the classic scene of the English picturesque: a river in a landscape, the dark green trees forming a patchwork with the softer shades of gardens and meadows, the setting enlivened by the white façades of great houses and their attendant cottages, people and cattle. The composition is framed by a hillside, steep but not rugged, on which figures recline against oaks, lost in admiration of the view. In 1772, Sir Joshua Reynolds commissioned one of the leading architects of his day, Sir William Chambers, to build him a house on the saddle of this hill, and from it he painted one of his few landscapes, 'Petersham and Twickenham Meadows', a painting full of the gentle light of the Thames valley in summer. Reynolds was not alone. De Wint, Knyff, Nicholls, urner and many others were captivated by the same scene, as were poets such as Pope, Thompson, Collins and Wordsworth. It is one of the most admired views in England.

The scene has changed little since Reynolds' day, apart from two tower blocks in Twickenham to the right. The Thames still snakes away towards Hampton, and London's ubiquitous trees camouflage the suburbs beyond. But for all its obvious good manners this is no tame landscape. I remember one evening standing on Richmond Hill watching the sun sinking into the Berkshire horizon. Ham and Twickenham were disappearing into the shadows and the river was turning from silver to grey. Suddenly, when all hope of day seemed gone, the sun appeared from beneath a cloud and shot a burst of flame straight at me. Instantly the Thames caught fire. The whole personality of the landscape was transformed. Here was a country through which medieval monarchs moved restlessly from one palace to another pursued by avaricious courtiers; a river up which Henry VIII would urge his boatmen as he plotted the overthrow of his chancellors and the murder of his wives; a shore along which Charles I's cavaliers fought a last desperate thrust towards London,

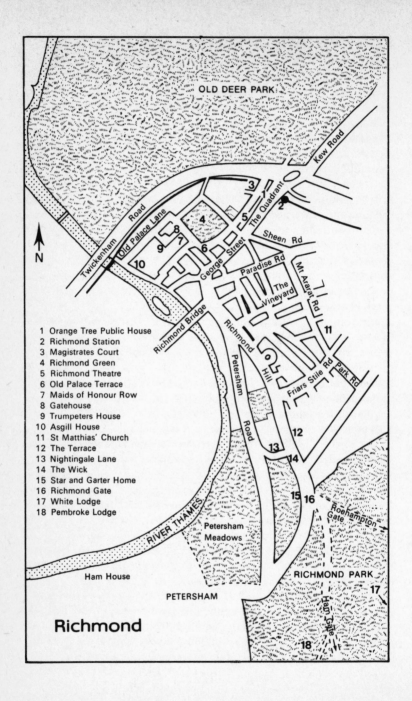

OLD DEER PARK

1 Orange Tree Public House
2 Richmond Station
3 Magistrates Court
4 Richmond Green
5 Richmond Theatre
6 Old Palace Terrace
7 Maids of Honour Row
8 Gatehouse
9 Trumpeters House
10 Asgill House
11 St Matthias' Church
12 The Terrace
13 Nightingale Lane
14 The Wick
15 Star and Garter Home
16 Richmond Gate
17 White Lodge
18 Pembroke Lodge

Kew Road

The Quadrant

Sheen Rd

Paradise Rd

The Vineyard

Mt Ararat Rd

Park Rd

Friars Stile Rd

George Street

Twickenham Road

Old Palace Lane

Richmond Bridge

Richmond Hill

Petersham Road

RIVER THAMES

Ham House

Petersham Meadows

PETERSHAM

RICHMOND PARK

Roehampton Gate

Ham Gate

N

Richmond

conquering at Brentford but baulked at Turnham Green. It was a river of blood in a landscape of nobility. It was never tame.

We shall return to Richmond Hill later. But first, the town. Richmond developed as the dependency of two royal palaces and retained this status long enough to be called 'Royal Borough' (with its London sisters of Greenwich and Kensington). But it has never seen itself as a suburb. It is an independent Surrey town which fiercely resisted incorporation into the Greater London Council in 1965. It has its own local newspaper group, owned by the Dimbleby family, its own distinctive politics (it elected a Liberal Council in 1974) and even, at one point, London's only private bus route.

Richmond's history began in the Middle Ages as the royal manor and palace of Sheen, and was important enough to witness the deaths of Edward III and Richard II's queen, Anne of Bohemia. Anne's death so shattered Richard that he had the old palace pulled down stone by stone. But Henry VII rebuilt it in 1501 and renamed it Richmond after his northern seat in Yorkshire. This palace, a shimmering Perpendicular castle of turrets, pinnacles and ornamental weather vanes, saw its most splendid years under Elizabeth, whose favourite residence it became. But monarchs seldom felt comfortable in the homes of their predecessors, and though the Stuarts patronized Richmond assiduously for its hunting they allowed the old palace to fall into decay. By the end of the seventeenth century its buildings had been demolished and private dwellings constructed in their place.

The town still retained royal custom. George II, when still Prince of Wales, took refuge at nearby Kew from the displeasures of his father, and Kew remained the chief residence of Queen Caroline throughout his subsequent reign. Meanwhile the beauty of Richmond's situation and its convenience *en route* to Windsor ensured that it became one of the most popular and aristocratic of Thames-side resorts. Ham, Petersham and Twickenham all basked in its reflected glory. Even in the present century, bombers and planners have caused it no more than flesh wounds. And its residents are as determined as any to protect it from harm.

We begin our walk where Kew Road joins the Quadrant. Richmond's main shopping area round George Street is, in the delicate words of one local historian, 'of little concern to the antiquarian'. Apart from a remarkable series of pubs, beginning with the excellent Orange Tree, only **Richmond station** is remarkable. It is the terminus for the North London Line, a relic of the Victorian railway companies' fight to get west London commuters into the City. This route ran 'round the back' through north London, in competition with the more direct line from Richmond to Waterloo. The north London trains still run into Broad Street Station in the City, their path through Kew, Acton, Brondesbury, Hampstead, Canonbury and Dalston offering an absorbing rear view of London's nineteenth-century suburbs. But take it soon – in its present form it is too anachronistic to survive for long. The station is appropriately bizarre for such a line, an authoritarian inter-war façade serving both railway and underground stations. One expects the station-master to goose-step out at any moment and harangue the assembled commuters. We now dive down behind the Orange Tree to Richmond's best modern building, the 1976 Magistrate's Court in Parkshot. It is a free variant on the familiar concrete and glass box, but small-scale, and managing to combine severity and accessibility, as befits its function. It is a rare good work from the G.L.C.'s architects' department.

However many times I used to visit Richmond in the past, I always managed to miss **Richmond Green** – which suggests one reason why the twentieth century appears to have missed it as well. Though it lacks church, cathedral or pond, it typifies the stately assymetry – the eye led from treetop to porch to lighted window to autumn bonfire – which is England's great contribution to the art of townscape. The Green is a place to listen to: not just the chatter of applause round a summer cricket match or the giggle of homebound secretaries, but the soft harmonies achieved by domestic builders who could sketch a façade or pencil in a doorcase with the same artistry as a composer might write a minuet.

The Green began life as a royal jousting place outside the Tudor palace, which spread out spaciously between it and the river. The demise of the palace in no way diminished its status, for it promptly sprouted houses for the courtiers associated with the new palace at Kew. Later, these houses would have been available for rent to rich Londoners eager to escape the pollution of the City at weekends. Horace Walpole was once surprised to see members of White's Club out from St James's, 'sauntering at the door' of a house they had taken to play whist at weekends. He remarked that surely they could play it equally well in London, as they did the rest of the week. He could only assume, 'It is so established a fashion to go out of town at the end of the week that people do go, though it be only into another town.' A century later Disraeli found the Green so unexpected a delight that he declared with finality, 'I shall let my house and live here.'

On the left as we enter from Parkshot are two oddities. The first is Richmond **Public Library**, built in 1881 and one of the first in London, 'with all the latest approved fittings and appliances'. These included a board on which the librarian indicated the books which were out on loan together with their expected date of return, an admirable time-saver which the number of books has now rendered impracticable. In the library's foyer the sub-culture takes over with notices of martial arts courses and vegetarian lectures (in Richmond, 'you are what you eat').

Next door is the terracotta façade of the **Richmond Theatre**. This was originally founded in the far corner of the Green by no less an impresario than David Garrick – another indication of Richmond's Georgian fashionability – and had Edmund Kean as its proprietor until his death in 1833. The present structure was built in 1899 by the theatrical architect, Frank Matcham, in a full-blown Edwardian Baroque with a green dome, to which someone has added a jolly *porte cochère* out over the pavement. The Orange Tree pub's theatre upstairs is now the home of Richmond's theatrical *avant garde*; but the old theatre still offers pre-West End runs, as well as standard repertory fare and Christmas pantomimes. Its lights blaze out across the Green as they always have done, shocking its Queen Anne neighbours with blowsy promiscuity.

The **houses** round the south and west sides of the Green mostly date from the late seventeenth and early eighteenth centuries. Any of them might be the Richmond Green setting described in Dickens' *Great Expectations* – 'a staid old house where hoops, powder and patches, embroidered coats, rolled stockings, ruffles and swords have had their court days many a time'. Of special note are No. 3 with its odd Gothic façade, Nos. 11 and 12 with floral doorcases, the cheerful Princes Head pub and the quaint paved court beside it. In the south-west corner is the square formed by **Old Palace Terrace** with the Green's three old ladies on its far side: Oak House, Old Palace Place and Old Friars. The basement of the last-named contains a warren of passages surviving from the medieval Convent of Observant Friars on the site. Indeed, scratch any wall or burrow into any cellar on this side of the Green and you may find a strip of floral fresco, a patch of wattle and daub or a Tudor arched door-way. In those pre-bulldozer days, no builder was averse to saving time and money by patching up an old wall instead of building a new one.

Maids of Honour Row is a splendid sequence of four redbrick houses each five bays wide and united by white string courses. It was built in 1723 on the orders of the future George II as lodgings for his wife's maids of honour. The famous 'maids of honour tarts' were a cheese delicacy made to a secret recipe believed to have been stolen from the royal kitchens and once reputedly 'on offer' for over £1000. The tart over which all the fuss was made is a modest creation, available today only at a bakery and teashop opposite the side entrance to Kew Gardens.

Next to the Row stands the last fragment of Henry's old palace, the **Gatehouse** leading into the old Wardrobe. The gate and its adjacent buildings are heavily restored but are clearly recognizable in outline from early drawings of the palace. The legend that it was in one of these upstairs rooms that Elizabeth I died is probably wishful thinking by local historians – though she did die at Richmond. But it could have been from one of the windows that a ring was dropped to the waiting Sir Robert Carey as a sign of her death, so that he could ride at once to James in Scotland to be first with the news of his succession. The palace was promptly emptied of courtiers scurrying north to curry favour with the new monarch, taking the last glory of the old palace with them.

Before entering the gateway, we can turn and take a last look at the Green itself. The remainder, on the north and east sides, is early Victorian. The semi-detached Pembroke Villas and the stuccoed Italianate Portland Terrace are both unobtrusive and suburban, the perfect foil for their more famous sisters across the Green. The only discord is the group to the north of Portland Terrace, built by architects Manning, Clamp in 1970. Modern architecture does no credit to an ancient setting by being indecisive. Here the apologetic bricks and pantiles keep nudging us, and shouting, 'Look, we're not really here!'

Under the Tudor gate and into **Old Palace Yard** we find three houses created from the surviving 'Wardrobe' block – the blue brick diapering of the Tudor walls just visible in places despite extensive restoration. One resident, the inter-war Lord Chancellor, Lord Cave, is proudly commemorated by a plaque with his coat of arms recalling that he 'lived in this house thirty-eight years'. His wife Estella was an enthusiastic historian of the old palace and of Richmond generally. The Wardrobe is apparently haunted by the ghost of Cardinal Wolsey, transformed into a spider. Lady Cave was always charming to any such creature she might encounter about the house.

Of the rest of the palace nothing is left. **Trumpeters House** across the court was built in 1701 and takes its curious name from two Tudor statues which used to adorn its façade. It is now divided into four flats. On the far side the house looks out over a lawn through one of the best porticos on the Thames west of Chelsea. A recorded argument between Sir Christopher Wren and a certain local builder suggests the great man might have had a hand in its design, though there is no other evidence. To the right of the house is pure Surrey, a modern group of town houses incongruously named Trumpeters Inn. They come complete with portico, bottle-glass windows, cobbles and Yorkshire terriers (1954–6 by C. Bernard Brown, according to Pevsner).

Old Palace Lane now takes us down to the banks of the Thames. The **river** at this point flows not east but almost due west on a serpentine which has always made it an inconvenient transport artery. Barges going up river in pre-steam days could nonetheless gain the benefit of the tide pushing up towards Teddington: the rise at Richmond averages three feet. On our right is the railway bridge built by the London and South Western Railway in 1848 in total disregard of its environmental impact, cutting off the old quarter of Richmond from the former palace grounds (or Old Deer Park) stretching down to Kew. A few hundred yards down this towpath there is a quaint late-Victorian iron footbridge over the river, complete with sluice gates to prevent barges being left high and dry on the Richmond mud at low tide.

George III ordered that this path should be closed to riders who were obstructing people towing barges. In one of the many engaging stories told of this monarch in Richmond, he was himself out riding one day when the gatekeeper, carrying out the order, refused him passage. The historian Walford takes up the tale: 'What, what, do you know who I am?' protested the king. 'No, sir, but if you were the king himself I couldn't open the gate for you.' 'King, king, but I am the king!' 'Oh, to be sure, sir,' said the man with a sarcastic grin, 'no doubt of that, but I can't let you through notwithstanding.' He added that the rule also applied to the 'Emperors of Chanay and Rooshey'. Only when a passer-by recognized the king and intervened on his behalf did the poor gatekeeper realize his mistake and hurry to open the gate – whereupon George refused point blank to go through: 'Won't go through, won't go through,' he said, much impressed by the man's sense of duty. He handed him a guinea so he might have 'a picture of the king' for future reference, and went back the way he had come.

Asgill House, to the left of Old Palace Lane, was built in 1758 by the architect Sir Robert Taylor for the Lord Mayor of London, Sir Charles Asgill. Asgill wanted a spectacular Palladian villa where his fellow aldermen could visit him on their private barges from the City. A central octagon, thrusting forward through a giant pediment, greeted visitors as they stepped ashore and stretched their legs on the lawn. The rusticated ground floor might be the entrance to an aquatic grotto, with a Coade headstone of Father Thames above its french window. The house has been restored by an American enthusiast and the trains which still clatter past its upstairs windows at least no longer shower it with soot.

The walk from Asgill House towards central Richmond was and still is one of the main **promenades** of the town. It passes the White Cross Hotel pub, pushing forward almost to the water's edge, and the early-Victorian Castle Assembly Rooms (where in 1973 the author addressed a stormy meeting of the Richmond Society called to save this river front from redevelopment). It is hard to imagine a more vulnerable sequence of buildings in London than those running from here to Richmond Bridge. Still threatened with demolition at the time of writing, they include the former Palm Court Hotel, defended by some vociferous squatters resisting demolition in the early 1970s. The group is patently crucial to the famous view of Richmond Bridge. But at least the Victorian Tower House, guarding the approach to the bridge itself, has been saved and rehabilitated.

Richmond Bridge is the oldest suviving Thames bridge in London – and the most beautiful. It was built in 1777 to a design by James Paine, but was altered in 1937. It remains, with Albert Bridge, one of the few London river crossings which are not mere extensions of roads but spring to life from each bank in a true elipse over the water. A toll of a halfpenny for pedestrians (plus a halfpenny for a barrow), and two shillings and sixpence for a coach and horses was levied to pay for its construction.

74

Now for the heights. We are here at the smart end of town – despite the extrovert façade of the Odeon cinema facing the bridge. It takes Richmond Hill at least two hundred yards to shake off the cluster of antique shops, bistros and boutiques which cling to its skirts, before it can strike out uphill towards the Park. We can either stride with it, or make a detour to the group of churches and almshouses of **The Vineyard**. Bishop Duppa's, Michel's and Queen Elizabeth's almshouses are all seventeenth-century foundations re-housed in Victorian buildings. The first was reputedly the result of a vow made by a local royalist clergyman named Duppa, saved from pursuing Cromwellian troops by a woman who put him to bed disguised as her daughter. It has an incongruous baroque arch as a centrepiece. The Vineyard's two churches make a curious pair, described by Walford as 'lovingly' next door to each other: the Congregational church of 1831 dressed in romanesque style, the Roman Catholic St Elizabeth's of 1824 in simple classical garb, though crowned with a gay baroque cupola. The result can be confusing. My father was minister of the Congregational church during the war and recalls a Polish serviceman hurriedly entering his church one afternoon and falling on his knees in prayer. When he looked up a puzzled frown crossed his face and he beat a hasty, un-ecumenical retreat next door.

Beyond the almshouses the hinterland of Richmond Hill is Victorian development at its best. On the south side of the Vineyard, for instance, is a terrace linked by a floral terracotta string course, the sort of decorative flourish rarely seen in domestic architecture before or since. Extending this detour, Mount Ararat Road brings us up to Sir Gilbert Scott's **St Matthias' Church**. Its tall misshapen spire is the dominant feature of Richmond and its decorated gothic façade is robust and confident. The nave has been partitioned and half has become a hall, with the old Victorian pews recycled as panelling. When I voiced my dismay to the verger he assured me that the architect had 'sat alone gazing at the old nave for hours' before breaking it up. Park Road to its north is a unified sequence of Victorian semi-detached villas, each topped by its own Dutch gable and excellently restored by residents who clearly take their domestic architecture seriously. Friars Stile Road brings us back to the Hill.

The view from Richmond Hill has already received its eulogy. But how gratifying that the houses of **The Terrace** should complement

75

it so well – no suburban terrace this, but townhouses of a quality we might expect to find in Berkeley Square, each with a personality of its own. Best-known is No. 3, possibly by Sir Robert Taylor, the architect of Asgill House. It has pedimented windows, a rusticated ground floor and a scroll frieze, an urban palace in miniature. George III once remarked on the house as he rode to the Park. On being told it was the home of the royal card-maker, a man named Blanchard, the king replied genially that 'all his cards must have turned up trumps'.

At the corner of Nightingale Lane stands The Wick, designed by Robert Mylne in 1775 in a style clearly akin to Adam. It has all the accessories of the perfect London villa: arched lamp-holder in front of handsome doorcase, large conservatory, bow window to the rear overlooking the Thames and a classical summerhouse in the garden. It was until recently occupied by the actor, Sir John Mills, and his family. Next door is Wick House, built for Reynolds by Sir William Chambers, though much altered since. Reynolds reputedly never spent a night in the house, travelling down from London for the day with his friends to enjoy his beloved view. A row of eighteenth-century houses opposite has been converted to form the Richmond Gate Hotel, looking as if it might have dropped in from some south-coast seaside resort.

Towering over Richmond Hill – and indeed over the whole Thames valley at this point – is the huge pile of the **Star and Garter Home** for disabled war veterans. It stands on the site of one of London's most famous hostelries, which prospered in the nineteenth century and went bankrupt at the onset of the twentieth. It was finally demolished in 1919. (The name of the old hotel was transferred to the equally extravagant though less obtrusive Victorian hotel down Nightingale Lane, now restored as the Petersham.) The present building, designed by the neo-classical architect, Sir Edwin Cooper, was erected in its place. The Home is in a style which can only be termed High Queen Anne Revival – or 'Wrennaissance' – with giant orders mounting to a steep pitched roof punctuated by dormers and tall chimneys. Despite its mass, it is not an offensive building and there can have been few lovelier spots in which to recover from the horrors of Mons and Ypres.

In front of the Star and Garter, a small whirlpool of traffic announces the entrance to the Park at Richmond Gate. It is guarded by Ancaster House, partly by Robert Adam and built in 1772 for

Sir Lionel Darell, a friend of George III (was there no end to Richmond's summer villas?). The house became famous locally when Sir Lionel's daughter left his study locked for sixty years after his death. It was exactly as he had last seen it, with hat, stick and *The Times* for the day of his death.

Richmond Park is one of the wonders of London. It is a survival of the open woodland which once covered much of England, across which herds of deer would drift like clouds on a sunlit meadow and a man could ride for miles without meeting a fence. Its two thousand acres were first enclosed by Charles I as a royal hunting park. The citizens of London seized it during the Commonwealth but returned it to the Crown after the Restoration. In the eighteenth century Sir Robert Walpole had one of his sons, (not Horace) made Ranger and drained it to indulge his love of beagling. But it was the next Ranger, Princess Amelia, who precipitated the most famous event in the Park's history. By banning the public any right of access to the Park, she provoked a local brewer, named John Lewis, to sue for entry. To the delight of the local people, he eventually won his case, the judge insisting that a ladder be erected easy enough for old women to climb over. The Ladderstile Gate on the Kingston side of the Hill is a memorial to this victory. The Princess promptly resigned the Rangership in a huff.

We can now either retrace our steps down Richmond Hill and George Street or press on across the Park (the gates close at dusk). Each approach to Richmond Park has its own character. Roehampton Gate is like reaching the end of the metropolis, with rolling acres to the horizon beyond. Richmond Gate is a sudden release from the noisy struggle up the Hill. But my favourite is Ham: a scramble up a hillside of bracken and scrub, dotted with deer and horses, and with falling streams adding a touch of the picturesque. At the summit the whole of London is suddenly spread before us – small wonder so many English monarchs loved to hunt with this view securely on the horizon.

The terrain of the Park is rough and often marshy, with its grass cropped close by the deer. These animals have roamed the Thames valley since – and doubtless before – the Middle Ages. They are now carefully conserved at some two hundred red deer and four hundred fallow and the annual culling still yields venison for royal and ministerial dinner tables. A price has to be paid for their decorative presence: the wooded enclosures must be stockaded and individual trees surrounded with neat fences. But if Richmond as a result lacks some of the sylvan mystery of Epping or Hampstead, it makes up for it in the dramatic arrangement of its spaces. As we walk across it, woods, hills and vistas seem to move round us like stage scenery shifting to some pre-ordained plan. Though Capability Brown never laid hand to Richmond, nature (with some help from the Ranger's staff) has done the job as well.

The most famous of the Park's residences, the **White Lodge**, was built by George II in 1727 as a Palladian hunting lodge of the grandest sort. It became a favourite retreat for his wife, Caroline, when she tired of her palace at Kew. The house was later occupied by Lord Sidmouth, on whose dinner table Nelson drew in wine his battle plan for Trafalgar. In the nineteenth century it was the home of the Duke and Duchess of Teck, parents of the future Queen Mary, wife of George V. The Tecks were assiduous participants in local affairs and Richmond responded enthusiastically to their patronage. When a Teck daughter married one heir to the throne and then in 1894 gave birth to another, both at White Lodge, Richmond was, said a local newspaper, 'in high glee and pleasure, the whole town being draped in its gayest hues'. When Queen Victoria came to visit the child (the ill-fated Edward VIII), she was so delighted with the reception the town gave her that she knighted the mayor forthwith, a man rejoicing in the name of Szlumper. The White Lodge is now the home of the Royal Ballet School and is open to visitors only during August (2.00 to 6.00).

The Lodge looks out to the distant towers of London (on a clear day) and also to the grimmer blocks of the Alton Estate in Roehampton. No visitor to the Park can avoid them. Built by London County Council architects in the late 1950s, the towers were world-famous as an application of the collectivist principles of Le Corbusier to an English landscape setting. Confrontation would be a better word. They are characterless, dreary and have won a string of architectural awards. Their apologists claim to find them 'sculpturally exciting' and even 'classical'. How we fool ourselves at the expense of those we seek to house! A party of Russians were proudly taken to see them by the architects and professed themselves much more interested in the terraced suburban houses they saw *en route*. They had plenty of Altons back in Moscow.

On the west side of the Park is **Pembroke Lodge**, once the home of the Victorian statesman, Lord John Russell. It began life as a molecatcher's house – an occupation of state importance in royal hunting parks where pot-holed terrain could lead to riding accidents and political crises (the death of William III, for instance). Today it is a modest Regency building used for refreshments in summer. But there is no finer spot than its garden in which to spend a late summer evening, with a mist rising from the Thames towards Windsor and the rolling greens of Petersham and Ham spread out at our feet.

Richmond's little sister, **Wimbledon Common**, is altogether more domestic. From Tebbets Corner, where highwaymen's corpses once swung from gallows, it progresses over pleasant heathland towards the famous windmill and the old village strung along the crest of the hill. **Wimbledon Village** is an attractive ensemble. Like its north London companion, Highgate, it has an open aspect with a tall spire pinning it to its hill (seen behind television shots of the tennis championships). The Green contains Eagle House (of 1613) as well as the equally ancient Rose and Crown Inn. It is doubtful if Caesar ever set foot in 'Caesar's Camp' near the golf course. But the place is picturesque enough without him.

Beyond South Wimbledon is the small garden suburb of **Merton Park**, developed in the late-nineteenth century by John Innes, of potting compost fame, who bought the local manor in 1867. In a style too late for Bedford Park but too early for Metroland, the district intersected by Melrose and Mostyn Roads contains cosy cottages and houses which form a distinctive architectural enclave in a rather dull area. Their front gardens are clearly tended by ardent Innes enthusiasts.

CHAPTER SIX

Petersham and Ham

☙

PETERSHAM has always been an offspring of Richmond, but an offspring which has grown up pretty and married well. As with so many Thames-side villages, it was the Restoration which elevated it from medieval hamlet to fashionable retreat. At least six major houses were erected within its boundaries in the 1660s and 1670s, overlooked by the home of Charles II's Secretary for Scotland, the Duke of Lauderdale, at Ham. Ever since, Petersham has sat out the dance of time, holding tenaciously to its status, fighting housing estates and gritting its teeth against the traffic of the main Kingston Road hurtling through its narrow high street. Only once did this torrent dry up: for a brief moment in 1979 when the mains were being relaid and the road was closed. Mud and leaves accumulated over the tarmac. Girls on horseback clattered past pineapple gateposts. And elderly ladies walked down the middle of the street with flowers to decorate the church. Petersham was its old self again, but not, I fear, for long.

The village sits at the foot of Richmond Hill a mile upstream of the bridge. Cars are best left at its boundary, by the neo-Tudor Dysart Arms. Just past this pub, a lane leads down to the sixteenth-century tower of **St Peter's Church** and to one of those extraordinary farms which manages to survive in the interstices of London's suburban development. The church is one of the few pre-Victorian places of worship in this book which merit the hunt for the key (usually available at Reston Lodge over the main road opposite). It still has a set of box pews and galleries complete enough to rival the marvellous interiors of St Mary's, Whitby, and Minstead in Hampshire. While most English churches had space to spare in the late seventeenth century, those of the Thames valley found themselves in the midst of a population boom and made the best of it. Pews yielded rents and were crammed into every corner of the building. Petersham even added a new transept, later enlarged in

Richmond on guard:
A buck with does in
Richmond Park and
left A mid-Georgian
porch on the Green.

The Duke and Duchess of Lauderdale, who began their conversion of Ham House in 1672. He was 'rough and boisterous and very unfit for Court', she 'a woman of great beauty...but restless in her ambition, profuse in her expense'.
(Painting by Lely at Ham.)

Left Ham House river façade.

the nineteenth century. On weekends when 'all England was ruled from Peterhsam' (when the CABAL met at Ham), a private pew in the church must have been a coveted acquisition. Prince Rupert of the Rhine was married here in 1664. In 1672 Elizabeth, Countess of Dysart came to this altar with the then Earl of Lauderdale, and two centuries later the Earl and Countess of Strathmore, parents of the present Queen Mother, were also married here.

Two memorials are worth noting. One is the jolly seventeenth-century monument in the chancel to George Cole (died 1624) and his wife Frances, lying on their sides in black alabaster, one above the other and guarded by figures symbolizing death and the resurrection. The other can be found on the west wall, where a plaque commemorates Captain George Vancouver, who sailed with Captain Cook and later discovered and charted the west coast of Canada. He spent the last three years of his life in Petersham, just managing to complete the journal of his voyage before his death in 1798. The city which now bears his name gave funds for the repair of the church after the war and an annual service is still held here in his memory. His tomb is in the graveyard outside.

The main houses of Petersham are clustered round the dogleg in the main road just west of the church. A collector's corner of seventeenth-century architecture, they are too grand to be called town-houses yet are not quite country mansions. They were seldom permanent residences, being used as summer retreats by the London rich, and they are less ostentatious than the Palladian villas which followed them upriver half a century later. The first is **Petersham House**, built about 1674 for the keeper of Richmond Park, Colonel Thomas Panton. Panton's attachment to the house cannot have been great. He was a notorious gambler and owner of Piccadilly Hall off the Haymarket, where Restoration rakes were prone to lose their fortunes. However, he married well, gave up gambling and wisely took to property development instead – hence Panton Street in the West End. The most delightful feature of the house is its circular domed porch supported by Ionic columns, presumably an eighteenth-century addition. Across the road, behind a large wall and a magnificent set of iron gates, stands **Montrose House** of about 1670, built for the Recorder of the City of London. It was altered in the eighteenth century and owes its present name to the Duchess of Montrose, who lived here at the start of Victoria's reign. In 1850 a lawsuit was fought by the Tollemache family as Lords of the Manor

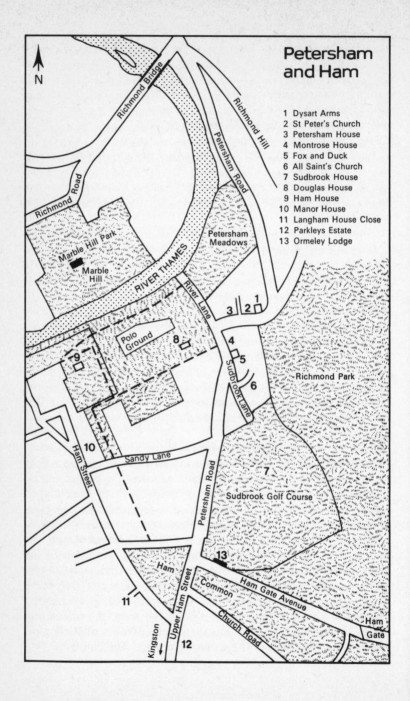

Petersham and Ham

1 Dysart Arms
2 St Peter's Church
3 Petersham House
4 Montrose House
5 Fox and Duck
6 All Saint's Church
7 Sudbrook House
8 Douglas House
9 Ham House
10 Manor House
11 Langham House Close
12 Parkleys Estate
13 Ormeley Lodge

to acquire some of the Montrose House garden to improve the dangerous corner in the road. To judge by the battered state of the present wall they did not acquire enough. Local planners have been fighting a similar battle ever since, but a Petersham by-pass would apparently require the loss of one hole of Sudbrook Golf Course – an unthinkable sacrifice. For the moment the house is occupied by the singer, Tommy Steele, the one resident likely to generate enough noise to drown the traffic. **Rutland Lodge** opposite was the first of the Restoration arrivals built for Sir William Bolton, Lord Mayor of London, in 1666, the year of the Great Fire. A more recent conflagration gutted its interior, which is now divided into modern flats.

Turning left past the Fox and Duck (an ancient local institution now irredeemably modernized), we reach Sudbrook Lane and a charming sequence of old houses, a cut above the normal Surrey village back street. But what is this in Bute Avenue? An Italian *campanile* in romanesque terracotta and brick suddenly shoots up from its surrounding yews and hollies for all the world as if this were a Catholic convent in the Castelli Romani. **All Saints Church** is in fact Anglican and was presented to the village, complete with hall and vicarage in the same style, by a Mrs Lionel Warde in 1908. What local rivalries can this have instilled? The older church appears to have had the last laugh: a notice on the door recently directed communicants back across the traffic to St Peter's – a penance which the notice pointed out, 'teaches us to distinguish between theology and convenience'.

It is believed – or at least fervently hoped by local residents – that Charles Dickens wrote *Nicholas Nickleby* while staying at Elm Lodge on the main Petersham Road. Accordingly, at the end of Sudbrook Lane stands an estate of modern villas named after characters in his novels. Directly ahead, a handsome pair of gates announces Sudbrook Golf Course, surely the only one in the country with its clubhouse designed by James Gibbs. **Sudbrook House** was built in 1717–20 for the second Duke of Argyll, grandson of the Duchess of Lauderdale who, despite his title and tempestuous military career, was born at Ham and died at Sudbrook. (His is the monument which towers over Poets' Corner at Westminster Abbey.) The house now sits magnificent among the trees, the undulating greens of the links merging into the rising contours of Richmond Hill beyond. But beware the scurrying golfers. The club is private and they are more interested in the fairway than the view; they may defend their privacy with a fusillade of balls.

We now retrace our steps to the Fox and Duck and enter Ham House grounds past Douglas House and the polo ground – a pandemonium of thundering hooves in summer but eerily deserted the rest of the year. **Douglas House** on the right was built about 1700 as the summer home of the eccentric Duchess of Queensbury, patroness of John Gay. There she continued to wear in old age the clothes and hairstyles in which she had been so admired as a girl, while Gay looked on in dutiful admiration. It now houses the London German School, whose not-so-discreet modern extensions peer out of the trees behind.

Now for **Ham House**. Of all London's great buildings Ham is my favourite. Its seventeenth-century interiors exemplify a period which managed to combine gaiety with grandeur in perfect proportion. But in addition, its rooms, closets and corridors are, more than anywhere I know, animated by the ghosts of those who created them. Chief among these was Elizabeth Murray, Countess of Dysart and Duchess of Lauderdale. Elizabeth was daughter of William Murray, a Scotsman who was whipping boy to Charles I and rose through this doubtful honour to acquire both an earldom and the house and estate begun by Sir Thomas Vavasour at Ham in 1610. Shortly before Murray's death in 1651, his daughter married a Suffolk baronet named Sir Lionel Tollemache. She was already a remarkable beauty, painted by Lely with strong features and sharp, wilful eyes – in contrast to the kindly face of Tollemache in a joint portrait which hangs in her old bedroom at Ham. Tollemache was never the equal of his wife, who had inherited all her father's courtly ambitions and social agility. She soon became the lover of the rising star of the Royalist cause, the Earl of Lauderdale. She interceded with Cromwell on his behalf after his capture during the Civil War, and in later life most improbably claimed Cromwell as a lover.

Even before Tollemache's death in 1669, Elizabeth and Lauderdale were openly consorting together. When they finally married in 1672 he was at the height of his political power as Secretary for Scotland and member of the CABAL ministry, to which acronym he contributed the final L. Elizabeth dominated him as she had Tollemache. By then she was in her forties, but still a remarkable presence. The contemporary historian, Bishop Burnet, who had once been infatuated by her, now gave a more sober assessment: 'A woman of great beauty but of far greater parts; had a wonderful quickness of apprehension and an amazing vivacity in conversation; had studied not only divinity and history, but mathematics and philosophy; but what ruined these accomplishments, she was restless in her ambition, profuse in her expense and of a most ravenous covetousness ... a violent friend and a much more violent enemy.' Her public image was not improved by the brutality of her husband's reign in Scotland. Burnet has him 'large, his hair red, his tongue too big for his mouth, and his whole manner rough and boisterous, and very unfit for a Court'.

By the time of his fall from power and death in 1682, both Lauderdale and his wife had become deeply unpopular. Yet it is hard to credit the monstrous picture which the eighteenth century painted of them as we walk round the more intimate of their private apartments. Despite her social ambitions, the Duchess could not afford to rebuild completely her father's Jacobean house. Like him, she was engaged in a constant struggle of make-do-and-mend, and Ham is thus a counterpoint between her courtly aspirations and the architectural material on which she had to work.

The **house** which Elizabeth inherited from her father was still a traditional Jacobean H-plan, with a renaissance frontispiece above the central door. Like his daughter, William Murray had seen architectural innovation as the concomitant of advancement at court. He was an ardent collector and he made extensive alterations to the house in 1637. These included the insertion of features similar to those which Inigo Jones had introduced at the Queen's House in Greenwich. None of this, however, was sufficiently radical for the Lauderdales. When they set up home at Ham in 1672 they determined to alter the more embarrassingly old-fashioned aspects of Murray's legacy.

Two architects appear to have been involved in this work: Sir William Bruce, Elizabeth's cousin and Lauderdale's surveyor-general in Scotland, and a local gentleman-architect named William Samwell. The turrets on the angle blocks of the river façade were removed, as was the projecting frontispiece bay over the main door. Certain casement windows were replaced by sashes, and round niches were inserted above the ground floor of the entrance front to contain classical busts. The hall was a major problem, set off-centre in the cross-bar of the H-plan in the medieval manner. (This was not solved until the eighteenth century, when its ceiling was knocked through into the dining room above to double its height. However, a new set of rooms was inserted into the southern recess of the H overlooking the gardens, forming what can seem from a distance a separate Restoration mansion sandwiched between two Jacobean wings.

To our great benefit, Ham has remained virtually untouched since the Duchess completed her work in the 1680s. When it passed from her Tollemache descendants into the hands of the National Trust in 1948, it came with an inventory of 1679 showing that most of the contents were also intact. The Victoria and Albert Museum, who are in charge of the house and contents, have since put most of them back as they would have been in the Lauderdales' time.

The interior is open daily except Monday (2.00 to 6.00, 12.00 to 4.00 in winter), and is best appreciated as a contrast between the Jacobean informality of its overall plan and the ostentation of the Dutch and Italian work inserted by Murray in the 1630s and the Lauderdales in the 1670s. Thus the front door leads directly into the **Great Hall**, a medieval touch the Duchess was unable to eradicate. But the room itself is austerely classical, the oval balcony leading the eye to the ceiling put in by William Murray in 1637, clearly echoing Inigo Jones' work at Greenwich. The statues of Minerva and Mars over the fireplace are believed to represent Murray and his wife – further evidence of their classicist enthusiasm. The walls are hung with portraits, mostly of eighteenth-century Tollemaches, including a magnificent Reynolds of Horace Walpole's niece, Charlotte. It was her fate to endure one of the bleaker periods in Ham's history as wife to the stingy fifth Earl of Dysart (a stinginess which probably saved Ham from eighteenth-century emasculation). Excusing her betrothal, she wrote to her sister, 'If I was but nineteen, I would refuse point-blank. But I am two and twenty, and am likely to be large and go off soon. It is dangerous to refuse so great a match.' Love sacrificed for immortality on a Reynolds canvas – though her portrait sugggests she was far from 'going off'.

The **Marble Dining Room** is one of the range of rooms inserted by the Lauderdales. Although those on the ground floor were intended for domestic use rather than for entertaining, the dining room was decorated lavishly. The floor was originally of black and white marble, the walls are covered in gilt-embossed leather and every detail of panelling and framing is richly carved. The furniture in this and most of the other rooms at Ham represents the latest in Restoration design; chairs with cane seats and twisted 'barley-sugar' uprights, black lacquer tables and cabinets imported into Europe from the Orient by Dutch East Indiamen. Over the mantelpiece is a copy of the famous Danckerts painting of Charles II being presented by his gardener, Mr Rose, with the first pineapple to be grown in England. The house in the background has never been identified.

The set of rooms to the right of the dining room were the Duke's and those to the left the Duchess's. At some stage they switched bedrooms whilst keeping the same closets, which must have been as confusing for them as it is for us. The joy of these rooms is their intimacy: the sun streaming across a long perspective of doorways, reflecting from parquet floors on to rich carpets and panelling. Their ostentation is discreet in such details as the carved moulding, round windows and fireplaces and the artificial graining of the wall. They might be calm backdrops for a Vermeer or a de Hooch. It is hard to envisage Lauderdale crashing through them in a rage, or his wife dismissing grovelling courtiers with a bossy retort.

The **Duchess's Bedroom** (though it would then have been the Duke's) contains four superb seascapes on panels in the walls. They are by the younger Van de Velde, painted shortly after his arrival in England in 1673. They have the same sense of drama as his paintings at Greenwich, though the artist can hardly have been pleased to see them placed almost out of sight over the doorways.

The **Duke's Closet** beyond is hung in black and gold damask with an exotic writing cabinet in elm and ebony with silver mounts. It makes an extravagant contrast with Thomas Wyck's two paintings of an alchemist's studio above, studies in scholarly chaos. We return by way of the dining room to the Duchess's quarters. Her bedchamber has been repainted a vivid yellow which the Victoria and Albert assures us is the original colour. The room was at one time used for the Duchess's collection of caged birds. There follow two small closets for her private use. The first is the beautiful **White Closet** with a dashing Italian ceiling by Verrio and a painting, attributed to Danckerts, of the Duke and Duchess in front of Ham, surrounded by bowing servants and guests admiring their collection of classical statuary. It is a delightful evocation of a house-proud couple. Also in this room is a writing cabinet with an exquisite oysterwork veneer. The private closet beyond contains a set of japanned tables dating from the seventeenth century, on which the Duchess and her ladies would take tea. (Here began the pseudo-genteel custom of the ladies withdrawing from meals before the men.)

At the foot of the main staircase lies the **chapel**, its smallness regarded by her enemies as a clear sign of the Duchess's irreligion – though it is hard to imagine what she would have done with a larger one or where she would have built it. The V and A's guidebook remarks on the rarity of the altar hangings, very few surviving from this period in England. Equally rare are the armchairs outside in the Inner Hall, upholstered in woollen cut velvet and in a remarkable state of preservation. On the wall is a portrayal of the Battle of Lepanto (1571) attributed to Cornelius Vroom, and an early portrait of the Earl of Lauderdale with William, Duke of Hamilton, painted in 1649 when Lauderdale was thirty-three.

The carved balustrade panels of the **staircase** were made for Murray in 1637. They are unusual in being representational rather than geometric, portraying arms and trophies of war. Their only parallel in London is on the staircase at Cromwell House in Highgate. We are led from the top of the stairs into a small suite of rooms used by Lady Maynard, the Duchess's sister, now decorated as they appeared in the early nineteenth century. Apart from the rich marquetry frame to the looking glass, the rooms are chiefly remarkable for two early works of John Constable – copies of portraits by Reynolds and Hoppner executed when Constable was staying in Ham in 1812. In the Cabinet of Miniatures across the landing is a lock of the Earl of Essex's hair, one of many which appear to have been taken from him on the morning of his execution. Next to it is a delightful Hilliard miniature of Elizabeth I, whose tortuous relationship with Essex led in part to his downfall.

The **Round Gallery** (then the dining room) is the first of the sequence of state rooms created by the Duchess and intended to lead through drawing room, picture gallery and antechamber to culminate in the royal bedchamber. It was a ritual progress which came to dictate the layout of great English houses in the eighteenth and early nineteenth centuries, but at Ham great ingenuity was needed to fit it into the fabric of a Jacobean structure. The ostensible purpose of 'state rooms' was to receive the sovereign – in this case Charles II's queen, Catherine of Braganza. But the underlying motive was to signify the status such a visit conferred on a house and its owners.

The gallery contains two famous Lelys of the Duchess, first as a girl and later at the height of her political influence. Despite Lely's habit of portraying all his ladies as typical Restoration beauties – heavy-lidded eyes, strong nose and pale skin – these two pictures make a fascinating comparison of innocence and maturity. In the one, the young Elizabeth is fresh-faced, poised and vulnerable, a sprig of oak above her head. In the other, she sits beside and slightly in front of her husband, plumper, her face more deeply shadowed. 'Both ye Graces in One Picture' was how the inventory described them, with perhaps a tinge of sarcasm.

The **North Drawing Room** dates from William Murray's time. It is a fine example of an interior of the Jacobean period, again with a Jonesian ceiling. But the focus of the room is the fireplace, an astonishing baroque creation by a German, Francis Cleyn, copied for Murray from part of Raphael's cartoon of the healing of the lame man at the temple (now in the V and A). The painting was in the possession of Charles I, and was much imitated by aspiring courtiers. The motif which most caught Cleyn's attention was the twisted pillars of the temple. They appear here as pilasters topped by gigantic scrolls and clambering *putti*, all heavy with gilding and a far cry from the more delicate marble and wood surrounds of the later Restoration rooms at Ham. One can envisage the Duchess pressing her visitors to move swiftly through to see 'her' rooms – though not before they had admired the Mortlake tapestries on the walls, illustrating the seasons of the year.

The **Long Gallery** likewise dates from the Jacobean period and again demonstrates Murray's Jonesian enthusiasm – a series of Ionic pilasters rising to the ceiling on both sides of the dark panelled room. Between them, twenty-two portraits gaze down from their original gilt frames which, so the inventory tells us, cost the substantial sum of 70 shillings each. Most are by Lely or by the schools of Lely or Van Dyck. They make an impact more by the flamboyance of their presentation than by their individual merit. An 'after Van Dyck' of Lucy, Countess of Carlisle, is worth noting: she pre-dated the Duchess in combining amorous activities with political influence. She contrived to be an intimate successively of Strafford and Pym. 'She felt a woman's pride in attracting to her the strong heads by which the world was ruled,' said a contemporary, '... but she plays with love as a child – naturally, she hath no passion at all.'

Here also are portraits of William Murray, Charles I and Charles II and one of Colonel John Russell by John Wright. The latter was one of the few artists of this period who was truly English. Indeed, in the whole of Ham there is scarcely a lick of paint on wall or canvas that was not applied by a foreigner. In the Gallery itself is a superb cosmopolitan ensemble: a Japanese lacquer cabinet decorated with oriental scenes on a Dutch table composed of four voluptuous mermaids and holding a display of blue and white Chinese ceramic ware.

Adjoining the Long Gallery are two rooms illustrating the emergence of cultural virtuosity as a gentlemanly attribute in the seventeenth century. Both Murray and Lauderdale might seem crude men to us, but their enthusiasm for philosophy, the arts and languages would put many modern politicians to shame. The **Green Closet** at Ham, dating from the 1630s, is one of the earliest in England designed specifically for the display of works of art. The ceiling was painted by Cleyn, Murray's artist in the adjacent drawing room, and is packed with scenes of classical allegory. The walls would have been covered with up to fifty paintings and miniatures, fitting in like a jigsaw wherever there was space. They were for wondering at, rather than inspecting.

On the other side of the Gallery are the two **Library Rooms**, dating from the 1670s. They were installed by Lauderdale to house his prized collection of books – including some printed by Caxton. It is the oldest surviving country house library in England. Mark Girouard suggests it may once have had backstairs access from the Duke's private closet below, giving him what amounted to a private wing where he could escape the constant coming and going of the rest of the house.

We now enter the series of state rooms added by the Lauderdales in the 1670s and intended to compensate in opulence for what they lacked in scale. The Queen's Bedchamber is preceded by an **antechamber** filled with oriental furniture – lacquer work inlays, japanned chairs, a beautiful Chinese miniature cabinet. The carving over the fireplace (by John Bullimore) contributed a dash of English naturalism in a style soon to be perfected by Grinling Gibbons. The **bedchamber** itself was altered in the eighteenth century to become what the Georgians called a saloon – the original bedroom is recreated in a model downstairs. The room has a mid-Georgian atmosphere, largely due to the Watteau-esque tapestries covering the walls, depicting a dainty lifestyle far removed from the flamboyant laxity of the Restoration. The fire irons were much ridiculed by later generations for their silver mounts – 'silvery dogs, pokers, bellows, etc., without end', remarked Walpole on a visit. The embossed fire tray would not have lasted long beneath a roaring blaze. The room was designed on an axis through the traditional seventeenth-century garden and plantation to the main gates on to Ham Common, the route down which the Lauderdales' visitors would have approached the house.

Next to the bedchamber, the **Queen's Closet** is the jewel of Ham, a miniature throneroom with encrusted decoration. It has an arched screen, raised dais and 'sleeping chair' with an adjustable back, upholstered in the same silk as covers the walls. The ceiling is attributed to Verrio and paintings are inset over the fireplace, which is itself surrounded by some of the earliest English *scagliola* work (a composition of plaster, stone and marble fragments, bonded with glue and polished). Both fireplace and marquetry floor contain the initials 'J & EL', lest the royal visitor forget whose hospitality she is enjoying. This is the inner sanctum of the state apartments, and though servants and intimates would have had access beyond, the V and A is anxious we should approach such architecture with proper deference. We must therefore return (bowing?) the way we came in.

The **grounds** of Ham have recently seen a struggle between authenticity and nature. The National Trust have, since 1975, been painstakingly restoring the gardens to their seventeenth-century formalism, an operation which involved relaying the rectangular lawns and paths and clearing the 'wilderness' plantation, which to the delight of local residents had started to live up to its name. Together with the loss through disease of the great elms in Ham Walks, this has deprived Ham's surroundings of much of their former romance. Especially in winter, I feel as did Queen Charlotte on a visit in 1809: 'The place remaining in its old style is beautiful and magnificent, both within and without, but truly *melancholy*.' Still, the garden will revive a long-neglected style, and the trees will grow again. And in summer the stables provide us with an uncommonly well-served tea on the lawn.

The village of Ham is now reached along Ham Street to the west of the house. In among the tidy new estates can still be found the Manor House, almshouses and farm cottages dating from days when a whole community depended on one family. **Ham Common** itself is a triangular country 'common' of rare charm. We might be in deepest Sussex: a villagescape open to the skies with each point of the triangle leading us off to Petersham, Ham and Kingston, and each side a perfect composition of houses, trees, gates and flowers, one of the most unspoiled in London. Despite the sequence of grander Georgian houses on the west side (including Forbes House in a clever 1936 pastiche) nothing upsets the balance of the whole. Continental planners would have had to design such an effect; in England it merely happens. Tucked in behind the common to the west are two intriguing examples of 1950s architecture: Eric Lyons' Parkleys Estate of 1954, and Stirling and Gowan's Langham House Close of 1958. They are beauty and the beast. The latter is much admired by modernists for its gritty brutalism and lack of compromise in the use of exposed concrete. It already looks tawdry. Parkleys is a different matter. Lyons was at this time architect to the Span estates company and this was the first of their major projects (now owned by a housing association). As at Blackheath, Lyons worked in a domestic tradition stretching directly back to Norman Shaw, his eye on his client rather than his professional critics. Parkleys is clearly a modern estate – witness the 'Festival of Britain' porches with spindly supports, glass panels in pastel colours, even some 'Modern Movement' columns in the foyers. Yet the two- and three-storey scale is never overpowering and the brick and tile-hung façades have weathered perfectly, as they have on English houses since the Middle Ages. Eric Lyons' disciple, Ian Nairn, said of Parkleys, 'It will be worth a visit when many other modern buildings look like last week's joint warmed up.'

The road back to Petersham runs past a medieval timbered house dating from 1487. It was transported lock, stock and barrel from Kent in 1925, a gesture of faith in interwar 'Tudorbethan' worthy of the good citizens of Pinner. A more ambitious walk lies across the southern section of Ham Common which runs up on to Richmond Park. Passing the eighteenth-century front of Ormeley Lodge, it leads us into the sandy, birch-and-bracken terrain of the western slopes of the hill. At the cluster of cottages which mark Ham Gate, we are in real country, with dogs barking in the distance and horses and deer appearing through the trees. From here up to the park, along to Richmond Gate, down the hill to the river and back across Petersham Meadows is about four miles, and one of the finest walks I know.

The road south out of Ham Common leads directly into **Kingston-upon-Thames**. This once handsome Thames-side town suffered even more than its northern and southern sisters, Enfield and Croydon, from unsympathetic post-war redevelopment because it had more to lose. If ever a town did not *deserve* to be visited it is Kingston. But it does contain one splendid set piece, a **market square** worthy of the old county capital of Surrey. The grouping of Italianate market hall, Tudor-to-Victorian houses and shops and perpendicular church tower is offset by narrow lanes (notably Harrow Passage), old inns and the small Apple Market to the south. The traffic does a swirling waltz round the outside, orchestrated by Kingston's lunatic local council. But for a while people are supreme. A precious survival.

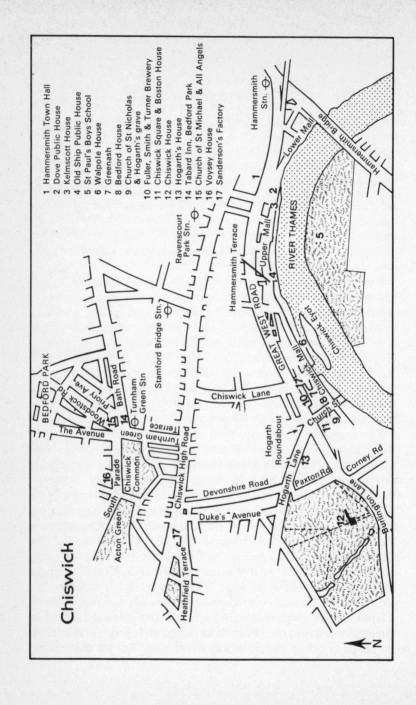

Chiswick

1 Hammersmith Town Hall
2 Dove Public House
3 Kelmscott House
4 Old Ship Public House
5 St Paul's Boys School
6 Walpole House
7 Greenash
8 Bedford House
9 Church of St Nicholas
   & Hogarth's grave
10 Fuller, Smith & Turner Brewery
11 Chiswick Square & Boston House
12 Chiswick House
13 Hogarth's House
14 Tabard Inn, Bedford Park
15 Church of St Michael & All Angels
16 Voysey House
17 Sanderson's Factory

CHAPTER SEVEN

Chiswick

THE old County of London came to an end just above Hammersmith Bridge. From there on its creators assumed the riverside villages of Middlesex could watch the Thames flow by, blessedly free of the metropolitan embrace. Both counties have long since disappeared, but a few of the villages still put up a spirited resistance. And the first of these is Chiswick.

Despite its curious name – derived from 'cheese-village' – Chiswick's prosperity came first from fishing, and then from seventeenth- and eighteenth-century Thames-side development spreading upstream from Chelsea. But for most Londoners today, Chiswick has a different connotation. Since the M4 motorway was led into its Hogarth roundabout in the 1960s it has become the unofficial gateway to the capital, the point at which Heathrow airport travellers finally touch down in London. For them, Chiswick means revving engines, belching lorries, screaming children and fuming drivers, the most concentrated cacophony of internal combustion in London.

The section of the Great West Road known as the Cromwell Road Extension is a post-war creation. Originally the route west from London led north along Chiswick High Road, whose wide carriageway and set-back buildings suggest a proper Victorian thoroughfare. A new road to the south was pushed through in the 1950s, cutting some houses incongruously in half and neatly destroying the civic centre planned by Hammersmith Council to run from their new town hall across lawns to the river. The hall itself, 1930s Georgian with what I can only call neo-Aztec touches, now gazes out across the traffic as if waiting for Fernando Cortes to alight from an airport bus at its steps. The road itself has squeezed the old village of Chiswick on to a tiny isthmus beside the river, so much so that a freak combination of high tide and colossal traffic jam threatens one day to rip it from its moorings and carry it downstream to the sea or off up the motorway to oblivion. But for the present, we shall head for the byways rather than the highways, and discover a Chiswick of which the passing millions are mercifully unaware.

The malls which line the Middlesex river bank between Hammersmith and Chiswick began life lined with country homes for wealthy Londoners to use at weekends or in summer, well situated for both river and road communication. They have miraculously survived the transformation of their parent villages into suburbs and comprise one of the pleasantest Thames-side promenades. Seasoned walkers can approach Chiswick from Hammersmith Bridge. A shorter route is to turn left off the main road at Black Lion Lane (or walk down from Ravenscourt tube station) and turn downstream into Upper Mall before going upstream along Chiswick Mall. **Upper Mall** contains two of London's more famous pubs – the Dove and the Old Ship – both recently restored and, praise be, not spoiled in the process. The Dove used to be a coffee-house and claims many literary associations – or as the splendid Walford puts it, 'teems with reminiscences of poets, men of letters and artists: let us therefore softly tread; 'tis hallowed ground'. Prince Augustus Frederick, son of George III, so liked the place he bought part of it as a private smoking box in which to contemplate the Thames and plot his campaigns against the slave trade. It claims Ernest Hemingway and Graham Greene as more recent patrons, and is still approached by a 'narrow path winding through a cluster of houses', as was noted in a guidebook of 1860.

We are here deep in Arts and Crafts territory. Next to the Dove, the printer Cobden-Sanderson established the Doves Press in 1900. At Sussex House opposite, Sir Emery Walker worked on typography and engraving for the Morris group and the Kelmscott Press. While upstream at Kelmscott House itself, Morris spent the last years of his life, hectoring, bullying and inspiring his followers, holding socialist meetings in the stables and Arts and Crafts parties in the garden. He took pride in the fact that the same Thames that flowed past his Mall gate also watered the land round his country house at Kelmscott in Oxfordshire. The house is now the William Morris Centre.

Upstream and adjacent to the Old Ship a lookout point has been constructed from which we can survey **Chiswick Reach** and inhale the scents of the river, sweet on the ebb but reeking of London on the flow. To the left rises the outline of Sir Joseph Bazalgette's Hammersmith Bridge, its cumbersome suspension looking more

Chiswick House: The Blue Velvet Room by William Kent with portraits of Alexander Pope and Inigo Jones.

William Hogarth
(1697-1764), self-portrait
with his dog. Hogarth's
patriotic writings and
engravings were filled with
satirical scorn for the
Burlington school, whose
masterpiece was Chiswick
House (*below*).

graceful from a distance but marred by the bulk of Charing Cross Hospital behind. On the Surrey bank opposite, a long row of trees screens (at least in summer) the buildings of the new St Paul's boys school. And on the river beneath the occasional oarsman can be seen avoiding the tide-race, skimming over the water like an exotic bird. To the right, we catch sight of trees of Dukes Meadow and the curious muddy hump of Chiswick Eyot, with its squabbling population of ducks, swans and seagulls. At low tide we can clamber down to the foreshore and along the back of Hammersmith Terrace, each garden wall topped by davits, some even with boats in them. After nightfall and with the babble of voices from the Mall pubs in the distance, we might almost be on board an ocean liner during a night of revelry.

Hammersmith Terrace itself is an oddity, its stern Doric porches facing inland like disapproving aunts imported from Bloomsbury. Two plaques record the residences of Sir Emery Walker and of Edward Johnston (d. 1944), 'master calligrapher'. None records the house of the Georgian painter and quack physician, Philip Loutherbourg, who could attract three thousand patients at a time to try his barley-water remedies in the 1790s – and almost as many to protest their ineffectiveness afterwards. Nor is there record of the fact that at No. 12 lived that inveterate lover of the Thames, Sir Alan Herbert, author of *Misleading Cases*. 'A.P.H.' was one of many lawyers who have enjoyed satirizing their profession. Unlike most, he practised what he preached as one of the last independent M.P.s. He was for fifteen years Member for Oxford University, surrendering his seat only when university M.P.s were abolished in 1950. Herbert habitually travelled by boat to the House of Commons and knew every detail of river lore and navigation. He was a ceaseless but largely unsuccessful campaigner for the greater commercial use of the Thames and for the care of its bankside. After reading one of his more impassioned pleas, I once took a trip down to Greenwich with the master of an old 'water bus' based at Twickenham, and mentioned Herbert's enthusiasm to him. 'Yes, I read him too,' the waterman replied, 'and I've been trying to make sense of what he says all my life. But except for tourists on a sunny day, the river can never beat road or rail. A.P.H. is a century out of date.'

Chiswick Mall now leads us past a sequence of attractive houses, only partially spoiled by the plate glass parapets to their front garden

The Gothick Gallery in Horace Walpole's Strawberry Hill. Mostly designed by Thomas Pitt and completed in 1763, its impact was such that one of Walpole's friends 'hoops and holias and dances and crosses himself a thousand times over'.

walls. These have been built to keep out the river, which regularly bursts its banks. Buildings to note include Norfolk and Island Houses, of 1840, complete Victorian riverfront villas with bow windows overlooking the Eyot, a small loggia and twin pediments to stand out when seen from passing boats. Farther along, Strawberry House of 1700 has a pretty iron balcony and perfectly proportioned wisteria. Grandest of all is Walpole House, home in the seventeenth century (though its façade is later) of Barbara Villiers, 'fairest and lewdest of the royal concubines' of Charles II. She shared with Nell Gwynn, her equally scandalous successor in the king's affections, links with an improbable number of residences round London. But undoubtedly she lived here until her death in 1709, aged sixty-eight. By then she was a sad figure, rejected by court and society alike. But as she promenaded along the Mall, she must have carried with her some trace of the romance of a glittering era and a popular monarch. Charles had made her Countess of Castlemaine and Duchess of Cleveland and her royal bastards were created dukes. When she died, she was buried without memorial in the local fishermen's church of St Nicholas – but two dukes and two earls came to Chiswick to act as pallbearers.

The tall whitewashed house named Greenash was built by the neo-baroque architect, J. J. Belcher, in 1882 for the naval designer Sir John Thorneycroft. The latter's sculptor father lived in Chiswick and it was here that the young boatbuilder first tested the weapons and hull-shapes that led to his invention of the torpedo and motor torpedo boat. So successful were Thorneycroft's designs that his Chiswick munitions works were moved to the Solent in 1906. Some at least of Chiswick's residents must have sighed with relief.

At the far end of the Mall, Bedford House took its name from the Russell family, Earls of Bedford, who in the sixteenth and seventeenth centuries were the major landowners of the neighbourhood. They owned Corney House, a hundred yards upstream, at a time when the old Jacobean Chiswick House was occupied by the impoverished Earl of Somerset. In the 1630s, a Russell heir (later 5th Earl of Bedford) fell in love with Somerset's daughter, Lady Ann Carr, a match disapproved of by the Russells on the grounds of Somerset's poverty. Eager for his daughter's well-being, Somerset mortgaged Chiswick as well as his plate and jewels to raise the dowry of £12,000. The suit was successful and the couple were happily married. But the mortgage remained and Chiswick House had to be sold, passing to the Boyle family, Earls of Burlington. Bedford House today is a marvellous concoction of motifs: pediment, Venetian window, bow window, coade headstones. It was recently the home of that prolific theatrical family, the Redgraves.

The **Church of St Nicholas** is hidden from the river by a row of warehouses. It is one of those Middlesex churches which age has bruised beyond recall. It was a medieval foundation, expanded in the Tudor period with buttressed tower and lantern to guide local fishermen. But it was rebuilt in the 1880s by J. L. Pearson in a dull neo-Perpendicular. If you can find a way of getting inside and penetrating the gloom there is a fine monument in the Lady Chapel to Sir Thomas Chaloner and his wife, facing each other in prayer.

Outside the church towards the river is the tomb of William Hogarth, whose house we shall see later. It is a handsome stone casket topped by an urn and inscribed with an epitaph by David Garrick: 'Farewell great painter of mankind/Who reached the noblest point of art/Whose pictured morals charm the mind/And through the eye correct the heart.' Poor Garrick suffered much for this homage. Dr Johnson wrote to Garrick before it was engraved, criticizing it word by word and suggesting it be rewritten. Johnson even offered an alternative epitaph of his own. But Garrick was clearly having none of this interference. In the same graveyard are buried Sir James Thornhill, Hogarth's father-in-law and painter of the Greenwich Hospital ceiling, and J. M. Whistler, whose admiration for Hogarth was such that he asked to be buried next to him at Chiswick.

Church Street now leads inland from the river, one of those London lanes which can easily slip by unnoticed. The street curves out of sight as all good streets should. Ahead is the former Burlington pub, which claims fifteenth-century origins. Round it is an orderly clutter of Georgian houses, cottages and alleyways: here an old mews, there a solid Doric porch, above is the outline of the Griffin brewery, and behind is the grey church guarding our exit, with its smart white vicarage and old Father Thames beyond. The whole composition cocks a snook at the tourists thundering down their tarmac runway not a hundred yards to the north. To the right of the Church Street junction runs the long façade of Fuller, Smith and Turner's brewery. Fuller's and Young's were the only two breweries which upheld the independent tradition of 'real' beer production during the 1960s and 1970s when the major national chains (which meant virtually all pubs) sold only top-pressure bitter, treated with chemicals. Fuller's Extra Special Bitter, available chiefly in their 'locals' in this part of London, is (or was at time of writing) the strongest bitter in Britain. It is prepared, stored and served with the sort of attention the French give to their wine. And be warned: it *is* strong! Just beyond the brewery wall is the Fox and Hounds pub in Mawson Terrace at the end of Chiswick Lane. In this heavily restored row of late-seventeenth-century houses, the young Alexander Pope lived with his parents before moving up river to Twickenham. Here he produced part of his famous translation of *The Iliad*.

Left out of Church Street lies **Chiswick Square** and Boston House. This is a remarkably complete William and Mary group, which most people will have noticed from the Hogarth Roundabout flyover passing directly in front of and above it. The glass-wall façade of the Cherry Blossom shoe polish factory stands opposite. It must be the most seen but least regarded building in West London. Behind it in Burlington Lane is the entrance to the grounds of Chiswick Park (they can also be approached from the Great West Road itself). And here, close to the road but mercifully shielded from it, lies Chiswick House.

Chiswick House is architecture in the raw. It does not possess the idiosyncrasies of Greenwich, the domesticity of Ham or the splendour of Hampton Court. It was never a house to be lived in but a stylistic essay, designed to shock and be admired. As a result I have always found it a building hard to like. Whether peeping apologetically through its trees in summer or standing stark amid bare branches in winter, Chiswick has always seemed out of place. Unlike other foreign imports into British architecture it has refused to learn English. Unmistakably, it speaks Italian.

Chiswick was largely designed by Richard Boyle, 3rd Earl of Burlington, and begun in 1725. It was a pavilion gallery linked to the old Jacobean mansion of the same name which had been bought by the first earl in 1682. Burlington was thirty years old when he started Chiswick, but he was already a generous patron of the arts and architecture. His reputation was built on two visits to France and Italy – a precursor of what was to become the Grand Tour enjoyed (or more often endured) by many young noblemen. Burlington was determined to recreate in England what he regarded as the true spirit of the Renaissance. This he saw as derived in direct line of descent from the classical architectural writer, Vitruvius, through his sixteenth-century Italian exponents, Andrea Palladio and Scamozzi and their English disciple, Inigo Jones. In this respect he set himself firmly against the emerging eighteenth-century baroque of architects such as Sir Christopher Wren, Hawksmoor and Vanbrugh, best expressed in Vanbrugh's extravagant pile then under construction at Blenheim in Oxfordshire. He accordingly took under his wing a number of artists eager to rebel against this establishment and excited to find a patron willing to import novel designs from abroad and spend money executing them. One of these was William Kent (1685–1748), an architect, painter and designer ten years Burlington's senior, whom he had met in Italy. Kent brought a more eclectic approach to the classicism of the Burlington school, including a romantic sense of landscape and a feeling for the voluptuousness of Italian baroque interiors.

Already in 1715 Burlington had commissioned his friend Colen Campbell to redesign Burlington House in Piccadilly on Palladian lines. Campbell was author of a book, *Vitruvius Britannicus*, which contained drawings of English buildings which he regarded as properly Vitruvian or Palladian – notably by Jones and Webb. At Chiswick Burlington conceived a Palladian villa, filled with works of classical art and set in an Arcadian landscape of temples, statues and formal vistas. He worked on the designs himself and took as his model Palladio's Villa Capra (or Rotunda) near Vicenza, as well as other villas by Palladio and his follower Scamozzi (many an architecture thesis has sought to discover which). The result is what a musician would term a variation rather than a copy: the theme being the square plan round a central dome, the variations a portico and double staircases front and back, Venetian windows and a row of abrupt obelisks concealing the chimneys. An avenue of statuary once led to the main entrance and another, flanked with cedars, framed the view to the rear. The composition has a magnificent sense of proportion – portico to roofline, staircase to window, window to wall – and the lessons of the master, Palladio, are clearly well-learnt. But it has an awkward precocity, as if teaching its grandmother how to suck eggs. Note, for instance, those fussy angular staircases: Inigo Jones at Greenwich was not ashamed to make his steps curve seductively in a flourish of baroque.

101

The **house** (open daily, 9.30 to 7.00, but see p. 228 for winter) is entered by a simple doorway beneath the main portico, which leads not to the *piano nobile* but to the ground floor beneath it. Here a grid of small rooms reflects the plan of the main floor above. In the centre is an octagonal hall leading into an oval room with two circular rooms off each end, forming what was Lord Burlington's library (or at least his Chiswick one). It is an intimate set of chambers, now bare of furniture but used to display plans, prints and drawings of the history of the house and its grounds. As if to emphasize the privacy of these quarters, the route upstairs is by an almost secret spiral staircase in the corner of one of the rooms.

At the top Chiswick takes on a completly different personality. It is as if the classical purity of Burlington's ideas provided an inadequate setting for the splendour of his eighteenth-century lifestyle. The central **Domed Saloon** is the hub of the composition, octagonal with four pedimented doorways separated by busts of classical figures and topped by large old master paintings. The octagonal theme is repeated in the dome itself, with each panel diminishing as it ascends towards the apex – a baroque device creating an illusion of greater height. The paintings include a copy of a Van Dyck of Charles I's family and a Reni of 'Liberality and Modesty'. The main gallery is, like the library beneath, divided into three parts, the central room a richly ornamented chamber with niches and an apsidal door at each end topped with gilded half domes. The ceiling is painted by Kent himself and is not a distinguished work. The two smaller rooms are five-finger exercies designed to set and solve different problems; one is circular, the other octagonal. The circular room, though small, is an architectural *tour de force*, with six doorways, ornate fireplace and window opening.

Either side of the saloon are the Red and Green Velvet Rooms, so named because of their original wall-coverings, now replaced by flocked paper. These rooms, encrusted with gilt and rich colour, are full of the joys of life. As with so much of Chiswick, they demonstrate that English ability to hide great passion beneath a placid exterior. In the smaller, **Blue Velvet Room**, Kent abandons all restraint. Here is his most daring ceiling: large gilded console brackets starting out from the walls and sweeping up to support painted ceiling panels including, as a centrepiece, the personification of Architecture. On the walls are portraits of Inigo Jones and Alexander Pope, Burlington's muse and poet laureate respectively.

The effect is wholly un-Palladian – fluid, personal, almost expressionist, the pyrotechnics of an architect born under a Stuart rather than a Hanoverian sun.

Following Burlington's death in 1753, Chiswick House passed by marriage into the Cavendish family, Dukes of Devonshire, who in 1788 demolished the Jacobean building next door and extended the villa itself to make it properly habitable. The architect, James Wyatt, designed matching wings to the left and right of the portico façades in keeping with the Palladian of the original. The house experienced a glittering revival during the Regency, under Georgiana, Duchess of Devonshire. As evidence of its status, both Charles James Fox and his political opponent, George Canning, died at Chiswick, in 1806 and 1827 respectively. And it was to Chiswick that Walter Scott came in 1828 to a garden party which 'resembles a picture by Watteau ... the scene dignified by the presence of an immense elephant, who under charge of a groom wandered up and down giving an air of Asiatic pageantry to the entertainment'. By the end of the last century, however, the Devonshires had tired of the place and it was leased as a private lunatic asylum. This it remained until 1928 when it passed into the hands of the local council. The wings were demolished after the war and it was restored to its original Burlingtonian purity in 1952.

The **gardens** at Chiswick were no less influential than the house itself – and for England they were considerably more innovative. Again borrowing from France and Italy, Burlington and Kent turned against the formal seventeenth-century layouts (best illustrated upriver at Ham), seeking naturalism rather than symmetry. Water flowed through lakes and cascades, no longer disciplined into formal canals. Trees clustered, patios wound, vistas were unexpected. Among them were scattered an assortment of statues and follies, including a temple, an obelisk and a 'rustic house', mostly designed by Kent himself. It was a style which Kent carried to greater effect at Rousham and Stowe and which Capability Brown developed into a fully-fledged naturalism towards the end of the eighteenth century. We are now so steeped in that naturalism that Chiswick gardens can seem hesitant, almost half-hearted by comparison, and the effect is not improved by recent dilapidation. However, the main vistas have been restored and repopulated with statues and follies. And on a hot summer's day, with a phalanx of Italian tourists doing the rounds, the Borough of Hounslow (who run the gardens) can just persuade us we are really basking in the Valley of the Brenta.

In homage to his hero, Inigo Jones, Burlington placed one of the master's classical arches just north of the house near what is called the summer parlour. It is the former gateway to Beaufort House in Chelsea, moved here to act as final punctuation to Burlington's textbook. As Alexander Pope wrote in its honour:

> Erect new wonders and the old repair;
> Jones and Palladio to themselves restore
> And be whate'er Vitruvius was before.

For those like myself who need an antidote after a visit to Chiswick, there is none better than to step out on to the Great West Road, turn right towards the Cherry Blossom factory and duck into a small Queen Anne house which cowers beneath its wall. Here lived the man who stood for all Lord Burlington was not: for simplicity, hard work, militant chauvinism and, towards the end of his life, a fierce moralism. William Hogarth (1697–1764) hated Burlington and his circle with a consuming passion. And his engraving tool was merciless in its attack. He savaged not just the morals and manners of Hanoverian society in general but those of Burlington and his friends in particular. In the Kitchen Room of the house is his response to the goings-on over his garden wall – an etching entitled 'The Man of Taste' with Burlington portrayed as fancy, pompous and absurd.

Hogarth's House (11.00 to 6.00, 11.00 to 4.00 but closed Tuesdays in winter, Sundays 2.00 to 6.00, 2.00 to 4.00 in winter) was used by him as his summer residence. His studio, now vanished, was in the garden and from the first-floor bow window he must have looked out over the fields to Turnham Green and Acton beyond. From the mulberry tree in the garden (still standing) his wife, Jane, would make tarts for him to take to the children at the Foundling Hospital, whom he used as models. The rooms are now filled with his engravings, the 'Roast Beef of Old England', the 'Harlot's Progress', 'Marriage à la Mode', the 'Election' and his final tragic work, 'Finis', in which Father Time himself lies dying, the tools of his trade – and Hogarth's – lying broken about him.

Hogarth's was a turbulent and pugnacious personality at odds with the times and with those about him. 'Other prints we look at; his prints we read,' said Charles Lamb. Yet his eye for the character of the human face and the foibles of human behaviour is unrivalled in British painting. Hogarth was the great London artist. It is sad that his memorials should be out here in Chiswick rather than in the rough and tumble of Soho or Covent Garden, where his ghost could have mingled with the Londoners he painted.

Hogarth's house sits beside the main road like an architectural stray. Its proximity to Chiswick House led William Gaunt to write of the pair of them: 'Like the placid aftermath of controversy, in brick and Portland stone the two houses so near together ... witness to the opposite aims and natures of their original owners.'

Half a mile north of Hogarth's House lies Turnham Green and another, later reaction against the classical revival. Here at **Bedford Park**, the favourite architects of the mid-Victorian establishment created a model from which a hundred suburban developments took their cue. Coming upon it in the 1880s, the traveller Moncure Conway could not believe his eyes. After charting the white stuccoed Italianate of South Kensington, he cried: 'Angels and ministers of grace! Am I dreaming? Right before me is the apparition of a little red town made up of the quaintest of Queen Anne houses!' So imitated and so debased had Bedford Park become that this amazement seems incongruous today. Although some of the most important early houses have been demolished and 'mock-Tudor' has crept up on the Tabard Inn, most of Bedford Park is as the Victorians left it – and is fiercely guarded as such by its proud residents.

The suburb was initiated in the mid 1870s by Mr Jonathan Carr, a wealthy radical who had aquired land in the district by marriage (the name Bedford Park shows we are still in Russell territory). Carr's brother, Comyns Carr, was a director of the Grosvenor Gallery where the Pre-Raphaelite movement were showing their work. The estate on which Carr embarked was to be in the latest style, 'Queen Anne Rivival', already much in vogue on the Cadogan Estate in Chelsea. E. W. Godwin designed some of the first houses, but it was Richard Norman Shaw, now one of the style's leading exponents who became architect to the estate in 1877. Shaw produced a number of basic designs for individual owners and builders to choose from. He was also architect of the church, inn and shops. The houses were intended to be of the 'latest convenience, at moderate rents, good construction with attention to artistic effect, coupled with the most complete sanitary arrangements'.

By artistic effect, Shaw meant the steep gables, tile-hung façades, elaborately carved eaves and porches, red brick and white-painted woodwork which were his hallmarks. The sunflower, symbol of the Victorian aesthetic revival, was much in evidence. In accordance with the new sanitary wisdom, none of the houses had basements and most of them were limited to two storeys. The houses were not large – by Victorian standards they were almost poky and their gardens minute. But each tried to be different. Residents were encouraged to choose wallpapers and furnishings from the firm of William Morris. The local school was to be co-educational and there was a club house and an art college (now demolished). Even Shaw's **Church of St Michael and All Angels** was in keeping with the prevailing style, one of the first outwardly 'Queen Anne' churches in the country (of 1879). Its interior, however, has a more perpendicular feel and there is Gothic tracery in the windows. (It was a characteristic of nineteenth-century developers to play safe in their churches, however daring their houses or schools might be; the ecclesiastical Goths, having defeated the classicists in the 1830s, held on to that victory deep into the twentieth century.) Shaw's inn was a self-conscious attempt to contrast the rurality of Bedford Park with the notorious gin palaces of London. It was quaint and old world, decorated with work by Walter Crane and William de Morgan, whose tiles still adorn the entrance. Original advertisements portray locals in smocks sitting outside it. The whole ensemble, which originally included a row of shops beyond, was graced with the Chaucerian name of The Tabard.

Bedford Park attracted the sort of artistic almost-rich who later flocked to such places as Hampstead and Highgate. It was too far out of town to be grand, so it became special instead – a 'colony' or a 'quarter' rather than a suburb. One early visitor commented that at Bedford Park, 'they dress not for dinner but for parties'. Mark Girouard, in his essay on the suburb, describes one artistic resident 'steering his friends on a tour of inspection in which he would comment on the abundance of children, point with pride to their good looks and condition, and explain they came of parents "who married like himself, young and in love and imprudently"'. The *Lady's Pictorial* was more brisk; in 1882 it remarked that in Bedford Park, 'the odour of pot pourri supercedes that of eau de cologne'. G. K. Chesterton satirized it as Saffron Park.

Although the development made little or no money for its

initiator, Carr handing its management over to a local company in 1881, it was a great success on its own terms. Its residents were to include the architects May and Voysey, both of whom worked on the estate, the painter Jack Yeats and his brother W. B., and the playwright Sir Arthur Pinero. Bedford Park even had its own revolutionary, Sergius Stepniak; he was run over and killed by a local train when he was reading his notes too attentively on a walk. (It is important to keep one's eyes up if the revolution is to succeed.)

The best way to view Bedford Park is to strike north from Turnham Green station past the Tabard and along any of the roads which radiate north and east – Priory Avenue, Woodstock Road, Queen Anne's Gardens. The point at which Shaw stops and his Acton imitators begin is not easy to discern. But peep through the windows on a winter evening and you can see modern Bedford Park quietly reverting to type. As the Scandinavian modernism of the 1950s and 1960s passes out of fashion, the new residents are blossoming once more into William Morris furnishings, Kate Greenaway children and an abundance of 'pot pourri'.

A final detour for connoisseurs of the work of Charles Voysey, who started in the Norman Shaw tradition but developed as one of Britain's first unmistakably twentieth-century architects. At 14 South Parade (running due west of the station) is his emphatic 1889 response to the redbrick cosiness of Bedford Park: simple overhanging eaves, small stone-mullioned windows and white rendering covering the façade. (I see a later resident has taken his revenge on Voysey's modernism by putting a carriage lamp outside the entrance extension.) And tucked away behind Turnham Green, off Chiswick High Road, is the factory Voysey built in 1902 for the Sanderson wallpaper company. It is an extraordinary rectangular box in white tiles with strong black bands, but its most noticeable feature is the undulating rhythm given it by Voysey's roofline. The building can be regarded as essentially classical, with pilaster piers, cornice and parapet, all in the stately modulation of a Greek temple. Yet its windows and roofline could as well be the product of 1920s *art deco*. Despite its comparative antiquity, Voysey's Sanderson building glows like a creature from another planet set down in the surrounding tawdriness of modern Chiswick.

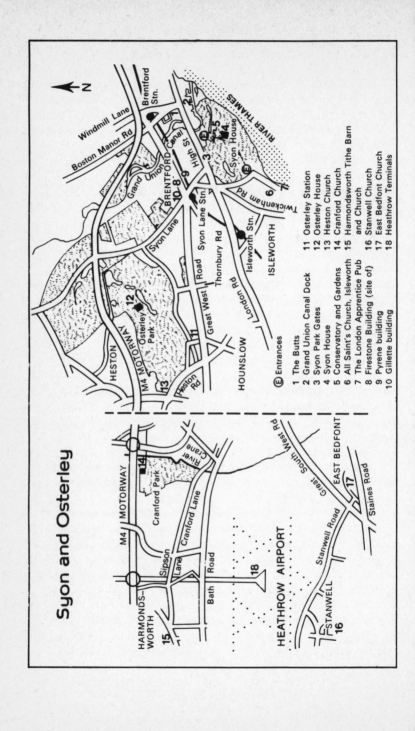

Syon and Osterley

Entrances ⓔ

1 The Butts
2 Grand Union Canal Dock
3 Syon Park Gates
4 Syon House
5 Conservatory and Gardens
6 All Saint's Church, Isleworth
7 The London Apprentice Pub
8 Firestone Building (site of)
9 Pyrene building
10 Gillette building
11 Osterley Station
12 Osterley House
13 Heston Church
14 Cranford Church
15 Harmondsworth Tithe Barn and Church
16 Stanwell Church
17 East Bedfont Church
18 Heathrow Terminals

CHAPTER EIGHT

Syon

☙

THE approach to Syon could not be less encouraging. Brentford, once capital of Middlesex and guardian of the western reaches of the Thames, has all but vanished as a distinct entity. It used to be a place of roughneck highwaymen, watermen and horse thieves. It was the scene of a celebrated skirmish in the abortive Royalist advance on London in the Civil War. Later, in the 1760s, it entertained the riotous London mobs who poured in to ensure the election of their hero, John Wilkes, as Member of Parliament for Middlesex after his prosecution for seditious libel. But no trace of this glamorous past remains. As the High Street leads us from Kew Bridge roundabout, we find a steam engine museum (open weekends) housed in the former Grand Junction waterworks and a piano museum in a Victorian church, engagingly nicknamed St George's-by-the-gasworks. Up Half Acre in The Butts stands an attractive sequence of eighteenth-century houses set round the square in which Wilkes' election rallies were held. But what could be a dramatic as well as historic open space has been turned into a municipal car park. Continuing down the High Street, we cross the Brentford arm of the Grand Union Canal. After traversing half England, it finally makes its rendezvous with the Thames in this last flight of locks.

Then comes the surprise. Incongruously facing a tedious housing estate is an old brick wall of the sort which in England often hints at great works beyond. Set into this wall is a gateway topped by a stone lion, through which we glimpse an extraordinary rural tableau of trees, meadows and grazing cattle. The gate itself looks more suited to a West End drawing room than a suburban highway. It has delicately enriched pilasters, columns with thin fluted capitals and an entablature filled with classical motifs. It is balanced immaculately with a screen and gatehouses to either side. But this is no isolated folly. For the gate is a foretaste of one of the richest interiors in all England, Robert Adam's Syon.

Syon House is reached by turning left down Park Road towards Isleworth. The land on which it sits was once that of the Bridgettine nuns, who wandered across Europe after the Dissolution but eventually returned to settle in Devon (at a place now also called Syon) where they still remain. The monastery passed to the Protector Somerset, who built a house on the site basically in Syon's present form. But on gaining the throne Elizabeth I granted it to the Percy family, Earls of Northumberland, and it has been owned by that family ever since. Indeed the house is now the last major house in the London area still in private ownership (a status demonstrated by its relative inaccessibility).

Although Syon was later refaced in ashlar and the river front topped by the Percy lion from old Northumberland House at Charing Cross, demolished in 1874, its **exterior** is still Tudor in appearance and very plain. It has a square plan round a small courtyard, with projecting corner turrets and a crenellated parapet. There is a seventeenth-century colonnade on the river front. Only the toy-like gatehouses across the front lawn – their windows too small for their parapets – suggest we are approaching anything other than a rather daunting prep school.

The **interior**, however, is another time and another world. Adam came to Syon in 1762 fresh from his researches in Italy, the fount of inspiration for so many of the houses in this book. In four years, from 1754–8, he measured and drew classical ruins in Rome and Spalato (Split) in Dalmatia, where the remains of Diocletian's great palace still lay unsurveyed. He had left for Italy a junior member of his father's architectural practice in Edinburgh. He arrived back in London at the age of thirty determined to establish a national reputation. He hurled himself at his work, revelling in his own eclectic brilliance. He wanted to cast aside what he saw as the dogmatism and stodginess of the Palladian tradition. As he and his brother exuberantly stated in introducing their work: 'We have introduced a great diversity of ceilings, friezes and decorated pilasters, and have added grace and beauty to the whole by a mixture of grotesque, stucco and painted ornaments. We flatter ourselves we have been able to seize with some degree of success the beautiful spirit of antiquity, and to transfer it with novelty and variety through all our numerous works.'

Adam's chief rival was William Chambers, five years his senior, who had returned from the continent three years earlier and was already picking up lucrative country house commissions. Chambers could never conceal his distaste for Adam's innovations, which he regarded as entirely 'affectation' and persistently kept him out of the Royal Academy. Fortunately for all concerned, Chambers was soon diverted into public commissions such as Somerset House by his appointment as surveyor-general to George III. (Adam shared this appointment but gave it scant attention.)

Adam's practice expanded swiftly, early works including Harewood in Yorkshire and Kedleston in Derbyshire. But in Hugh Percy, newly-created Duke of Northumberland, he found the perfect client, rich, metropolitan and influential. Northumberland was a close adviser to the king and a traditional aristocrat: enlightened and civilized on his country estates but an incompetent political meddler whenever he came to town. He was a firm opponent of Wilkes, and was once forced to drink his health when besieged by a mob in his London house. His extravagance was constantly ridiculed by Horace Walpole. Indeed, with Walpole upstream at Twickenham and Wilkes downstream at Brentford, it is a wonder the duke and his wife spent any time or money at all on rebuilding their Syon home.

Yet spend they did. Adam was exultant: 'The idea was to me a favourite one, the subject great and the expense unlimited.' Although he was wrong about the expense – a rotunda intended to fill the central court was never built – the five principal rooms he completed at Syon remain his most brilliant work, testament to his virtuosity as both architect and decorator. They are, as Sacheverell Sitwell says, 'among the greatest works of art in England'.

The house is open only from Good Friday to the end of September from 12.00 to 5.00 but is closed on Fridays and Saturdays. The front entrance gives directly on to the **hall**, a large room begun in 1762 and full of cool colours, its details picked out in soft shades of white, cream and pale blue. Pillars flank each window and door, and statues of classical figures fill the wall spaces, as if quietly warning us of tempests to come. One end is giant apse, its ceiling rosettes diminishing in size to give added perspective. At the other end, a flight of steps enabled Adam to turn the uneven floor levels of the old house to dramatic effect: 'to increase the scenery and add to the movement'. In front of these steps is a large bronze of the Dying Gaul, his head bowed as if in awe of the majesty round him. A diamond pattern crosses the ceiling, in plasterwork so delicate it might be made of icing sugar. This work is by Joseph Rose, whose firm executed most of Adam's commissions and did so with such skill that the line between designer and craftsman must often have been blurred. Yet the hall at Syon is still essentially traditional, a harking back to the palladianism from which Adam was so dramatically to depart.

The greater is the shock of the **anteroom**. Adam's trick here is simple: a rectangular box thirty-six feet by thirty feet deftly converted into a square by the insertion of a screen of columns carrying the full entablature round as a fourth side and leaving a six-foot alcove beyond. But this is mere geometric flourish. The character of the anteroom at Syon lies in its content. Huge columns line each wall, covered in a veneer of *verde antica* marble, some of it classical fragments dredged from the bed of the Tiber specially for the duke. In the wall spaces are trophies of Roman swords and shields. Whereas at Osterley similar panels are in plaster, here Joseph Rose covered them in gilt. Indeed Rose's gilding drips from every corner of the room, from the anthemion flower patterns in the turquoise entablature, from the Ionic capitals of the columns, from the twirling fronds of the ceiling and, above all, from the statues gazing out from atop the columns, each frozen in some athletic pose. The floor is *scagliola* at its most versatile. When an evening sun splashes over it from the park outside, its blues, browns and yellows leap into life and people the room with shadows. We can only echo Sitwell: 'as superb as any Roman interior in the palaces of the Caesars'. It is surely one of the most brilliant rooms ever built.

Yet no sooner has Adam dazzled us than he switches his colour tone once more. In the **Dining Room** he reverts to whiteness. Apart from the statue niches (in maroon) and the gilding used to pick out each item of decoration, everything is white. And the white and the gold seem to dance together. This is gilding not laid on with a trowel, as Kent and the Palladians would have done, but gently folded into place. An apse at either end – pillars in delicate Corinthian instead of stately Ionic – stretches the room and establishes a remarkable tension with the rectangular pattern of the ceiling. On this ceiling, Adam's arabesques, fans and flower motifs can be studied in abundance. In the panel over the fireplace is a marble of the three Graces, the cold material making them look particularly naked amid all this richness.

These three rooms are from Adam's earlier hand, perhaps with just a glance over his shoulder at Chambers. By 1764, when he came to design the **Red Drawing Room**, the more characteristic features of the later Adam style were emerging. The duchess's guests have now processed and eaten and are about to relax and gossip. Red silk covers the walls, statues are supplanted by pictures, including a fine Lely of Charles I and the Duke of York. The fireplace and door surrounds are in lower relief, less architectural, their pilasters beaded and enriched with ormulu so delicate it might almost be filigree (indeed the cynical Walpole derided it as such). The ceiling is a daring throwback to the Renaissance, to Raphael's ceiling in the Villa Madama. Its deep coving and central panel are entirely covered with a repeating pattern of octagons and squares, decorated with foliage and containing medallions of classical scenes painted by Cipriani. This design was much criticized on the grounds that the medallions were too small to be seen properly. Chambers called them dinner plates shied on to the ceiling; art become mere decoration. But the overall effect is of a sparkling canopy of golden colours. It is as if Adam had disregarded all the lessons of Palladio and taken his cue instead from Wolsey's closet in Hampton Court or Henry's Field of the Cloth of Gold.

The room is lent further lustre by the carpet woven by Thomas Moore – like Joseph Rose, a master craftsman present in many of Adam's finest interiors. Though the pattern (most unusually for an Adam carpet) owes nothing to that of the ceiling, it is executed in the same warm yellows, pinks and greens. Next to the windows are two sideboard tables displaying mosaics recovered from the Baths of Titus in Rome and with startling ram's head capitals to each of the legs. Adam seemed able to toss off such masterpieces almost as after-thoughts to his rooms.

Last comes the **gallery**. This is not Georgian but a relic of the Jacobean room from the old house. Here Charles I's minister, Strafford, paced up and down trying in vain to persuade the 10th Earl of Northumberland to join the king's cause against Parliament. And here the same king's children were later brought while their father was briefly imprisoned at Hampton Court. From these windows, generations of Percys have looked out across the Thames to Kew Gardens beyond, enjoying one of the least altered eighteenth-century views in London.

Adam's intention was to redesign the gallery so as to afford

Syon House: the Anteroom, designed by Robert Adam in 1762 with gilded plasterwork by Joseph Rose. 'As superb as any Roman interior in the palaces of the Caesars.'

'variety and amusement' to the ladies after they had withdrawn from the dining room to a sufficient distance not to be disturbed by raucous male voices. He sought to widen the room's tunnel-like proportions by an optical illusion on the ceiling. The lozenge patterns are 'bled off' at the point where they meet the walls as if, in the words of Adam's biographer, Geoffrey Beard, 'one could pop one's head through a door and see them emerge at the other side'. The decoration of the gallery has all the familiar Adam signatures: gaily painted pilasters, arabesque frieze, urns, drops and assorted *putti* interspersed with inconsequential little pictures and, yes, even some books – though I sense Adam could barely restrain himself from redecorating their bindings. These themes are repeated in the furniture, much of it also by Adam. Tables are inlaid with the most ravishing marquetry and chairs and sofas demonstrate the English style in its noblest period, released from William Kent's heavy-handedness but not yet reduced to the spindley eccentricity of the Regency.

Then suddenly it is all over. Adam has done with us, and lets us down with a bump. The **Print Room** was decorated in the nineteenth century and contains some seventeenth-century furniture, an eighteenth-century bed and numerous Percy portraits, including a Gainsborough of Adam's patron, the first duke. An **oak passage** is all we see of the north range, never rebuilt by Adam. Today it is hung with portraits of the sort crammed into most English stately homes, though seldom in such profusion. Here, from dado to cornice, is a procession of English faces: pallid medieval kings, haughty Elizabethan knights, florid Restoration noblemen. There is a Gheeraerdts of the young Charles I looking extraordinarily unwell, a Tudor lady in an extravagant black dress and a hideous portrait of the Duke of Lauderdale.

At the far end of the passage, however, is a gem: a **pictorial map** of the Hundred of Isleworth, painted in 1635 by Moses Glover and splendidly illustrating many of the places described in this book as they would have been before the Civil War. The town of Brentford nestles at the foot of the picture, with above it Syon and Isleworth looking across to Sheen manor and the gilded vanes of Richmond Palace. Upstream an old sailing barge passes Ham on its way to Twickenham and Hampton Court, which dominates the far horizon amid the woods of Bushy. To the north, travellers can be seen making their way down the Bath Road across Hounslow Heath, where their lives and purses would be at risk until they reached the distant towers of Windsor Castle. Farther round we can make out the turrets of Osterley and its surrounding lakes. Trees, fields, windmills and streams are all picked out meticulously. The picture is framed by old Middlesex oaks and by the shields of the county's great families. It is the cartographer as artist as well as social historian.

The **grounds** at Syon can lay claim to being the oldest horticultural gardens in England, older even than Kew. They were begun by the Protector Somerset in the sixteenth century with the import of mulberry trees from the continent. But again it was the 1st Duke of Northumberland who transformed Syon Park into the landscape we see today. His designer was the ubiquitous Capability Brown, who worked at Syon at the same time as Adam, eventually graduating to work for George III at Kew. Brown characteristically swept away the neat walls and *parterres* of the existing Tudor gardens and replaced them with long fairways of grass, clumps of trees and two lakes. Those surrounding the main drive to the house are now almost agricultural in character. But to the north, where the main tree and shrub collection is laid out, the gardens are more formal. They are open to the public daily from 10.00 to 6.00, or dusk if earlier.

The gardens are entered past Charles Fowler's Great Conservatory, built in 1827 with a graceful glass dome rising above what might be a miniature Palladian mansion, complete with quadrant wings and pavilions. Though the interior may seem modest compared with the splendours of Turner's Palm House across the river, Fowler predated Turner by over a decade. The levity of his design and the inventiveness of the cast iron mouldings answers well to Adam's sense of gaiety. We might be in Bath or even Brighton. (Fowler built the central market in Covent Garden in the same year, clearly with some of the same patterns in mind.)

The ornamental gardens are if anything richer than those at Kew. The specimens of trees and shrubs are thicker on the ground and in spring the rhododendron bank displays the most breathtaking botanical promiscuity. Best of all is the view from the head of the lake. Here a set of iron railings in an Adam anthemion pattern frames a perfect English tableau: tall oaks and beeches descending through azaleas to the lilies at the water's edge, where a weeping willow softly dips into its own reflection.

For those impelled to emulate Brown and his successors, Syon now boasts a garden centre, including what must be one of the largest gardening supermarkets in the country. This is supplemented by a rose display, containing some four hundred varieties, on the far side of the house. If even this is not enough Crowther's Yard, back on the London Road, sells everything from garden *putti* and Neptune fountains to complete eighteenth-century interiors. Syon's fantasies now come both table d'hôte and takeaway.

Beyond Syon, the village of **Isleworth** still clings to the Thames where the river turns on the fulcrum of All Saints Church and the London Apprentice pub. The old church survived wartime bombing only to be burned down in 1943 by two local schoolboys (who also destroyed Hounslow church the same night). Its modern successor, attached to the original tower, was designed by Michael Blee with a disconcertingly open courtyard on the site of the old nave. But the church itself, with a wooden roof in what might be termed ecclesiastical vernacular style, is warm and intimate and contains a number of monuments from the former building. A tiny Joshua chapel has been added overlooking the river.

The walk from the church to the pub passes the neo-Gothic pastiche, Butterfield House, designed as recently as 1971, as well as some attractive Georgian houses and cottages. The pub commemorates the apprentices who rowed or sailed upstream from the city on their days off. Their successors, City clerks and West End salesmen, still come (albeit by car). They can be observed of a summer evening, shouting funny stories at each other along the parapet or watching children fishing from the foreshore while the shadows of the Old Deer Park lengthen across the river. Here is unchanging London.

CHAPTER NINE

Osterley

𝒟𝓈

POOR Osterley. It has been fated since birth to be overshadowed by its rich sister, Syon. Like Syon it has a noble pedigree, but not quite so noble. Like Syon it has a magnificent park, though not quite so magnificent. And like Syon it is an outstanding example of the work of Robert Adam though, it must be said, not quite so outstanding. It has no Thames flowing by, and since the war the Furies have visited on it both the main Heathrow flight path and the M4 motorway less than a mile from its walls. Anywhere else but blasé west London, Osterley would be a major attraction. As it is, the old place can only wait patiently for its few faithful visitors, and hope to outlast the twentieth-century chaos surrounding it.

Osterley has already outlasted the extraordinary set piece by which it is normally approached, the Great West Road. This road, together with the Western Avenue to the north, were the twin arteries of the new industrial London planned in the late 1920s as symbols of pollution-free private enterprise. These were the factories of the future: household appliances, cosmetics, safety razors, car accessories, aeroplanes, wireless sets, pharmaceuticals. And they are made and sold from buildings worthy of Hollywood film sets. From Brentford to Osterley a great avenue stretched into the future (in the form of Heston Aerodrome), landscaped with trees and flowers and lined with factories which were clean and prosperous. At Christmas time, I remember, the trees were even filled with coloured lights. Many of the factories are now empty and inevitably threatened with demolition. Their preservation as the most remarkable collection of 1930s industrial architecture in Europe is imperative.

The estate begins rather nervously in the shadow of the Chiswick Flyover with such modest exercises in modernism as the Fiat and Alfa-Laval buildings. Its confidence increases as the M4 veers off to the right with a neo-Georgian curio, Rank Audio-Visual, and the Trico windscreen wipers factory. And the climax is reached with the Pyrene building on the left and Firestone on the right. Both are by the firm of Wallis, Gilbert and Partners, masters of the application of *art deco* motifs to essentially revivalist forms. Colourful decoration, said Thomas Wallis to the RIBA in 1933, 'is not money wasted. It has a psychological effect on the worker, if he is a good worker, and good workers look upon their business buildings with pride. A little money spent on something to focus the attention of the public is not money wasted, but is good advertisement.'

The Firestone building was the demonstration of this thesis. Built in 1928, three years before the same firm's famous Hoover Building on Western Avenue, it was the last stylistic flourish of British architecture before its avant garde succumbed to the unadorned abstractions of the German Bauhaus school. The façade is a variant on a classical temple, ten attached columns beneath a flattened pediment containing a mannerist clock and the name of the firm in Gothic lettering. Capitals and bases, however, are Egyptian in style, in green, blue and orange tiles. The doorway is surrounded by vivid blue, topped by an F monogram with horns on either side, reminiscent of a Red Indian headdress. These horns are repeated in the coping of the steps and round the tops of the excellent *art deco* lamp-standards. The whole structure is faced in white tiles, which have weathered noticeably better than the concrete and cement aggregates which superseded them in architectural fashion. The long flight of steps across the front lawn is, as the *art deco* historian Bevis Hillier points out, a masterstroke, 'instilling awe into the visiting commercial rep, not unlike the set for a procession in a film by Twentieth Century Fox'.*

A year later Wallis, Gilbert produced the Pyrene building opposite (and like Firestone, now empty). It is less exotic in its decoration but has the same stylistic independence of spirit: fan corners above the central block, baroque double-staircase up from the road, abstract ironwork on the main doors. The Great West Road now loses some of its punch. A lesser Wallis, Gilbert work is the former Coty building, west of Pyrene on the left. And at the junction with Syon Lane is the Establishment's reply. The Gillette building, designed by the architectural historian Sir Banister Fletcher eight years after Firestone, has none of the same panache, though its tower heralded home for millions of weekend drivers returning

* Firestone was demolished in August 1980, shortly before its listing for preservation.

118

in their Fords and Morrises up the old A4. Its brick façade and blue-painted panels are half-hearted where Wallis was bold; its entrance is modest where Wallis was triumphant. The whole building is a stylistic blind alley (but no demolishers, please).

The more reason to appreciate the still small voice half a mile farther up the road and just beyond the turning for Osterley – one of Charles Holden's excellent underground stations built in the early 1930s for London Transport. As with all his Piccadilly Line work, notably at Sudbury and Arnos Grove, Osterley station shows Holden's quiet professionalism in adapting the English classical tradition to modern needs. Here his typical curving brick walls are capped by a splendid joke, an elongated pinnacle encased in lighted panels, like a weapon from *Star Wars*. It would have been a beacon, offering escape to the warm heart of the city from the lonely isolation of those inter-war suburbs.

From the station, however, we turn up Thornbury Road into a different world. The ranks of semi-detached Heston break step and retreat. We are suddenly in old Middlesex, in a landscape of tall trees, ancient fields and rich earth beneath our feet. Here it was that Sir Thomas Gresham, founder of the Elizabethan Royal Exchange in the City, came to enjoy the fruits of his wealth as a country gentleman. He built himself a new house substantial enough to entertain Queen Elizabeth when she visited him in 1576. During her visit, he ordered his masons, in the middle of the night, to build a new wall across the central courtyard after she had suggested at dinner that it might 'appear more handsome' that way. Thomas Fuller commented cynically on this lavish gesture that 'money commandeth all things'. After Gresham's death the house passed through a number of hands, including those of the Restoration property developer, Nicholas Barbon, until it was bought in 1711 by the banker, Sir Francis Child. Since he never lived in the house himself, it has been suggested he bought it for the capacious vaults beneath the courtyard, suitable for storing his cash and bullion. Child died in 1713 but by the end of the century **Osterley** had been transformed by no fewer than five of his heirs, three sons and two grandsons.

The remodelling of Osterley took some thirty years, from 1750 to 1780, and was carried out by the two leading architects of the mid-Georgian era, first Sir William Chambers, then Robert Adam. We do not know for sure why Chambers dropped the commission

119

in the late 1750s, eventually giving way to Adam in 1761. Was it a status-conscious City family eager to switch from the more austere classicism of Chambers to Adam's novel Italian refinements? The Childs' neighbour, the Earl of Northumberland, was employing Adam to redecorate Syon. Or was it as the guide suggests, that Chambers was simply too busy with official commissions as surveyor-general to give more than passing attention to this work? At any rate, Adam did not have an easy time of it. His first design, now on display in the house, was for a new Palladian mansion round four sides of the old Elizabethan courtyard. Shortage of money, or more probably the transfer of the house from one grandson to another in 1763, led to this design being modified. The original three ranges of the Elizabethan house, together with its corner turrets, had to be retained. As at Syon, Adam had to squeeze the quart of his Italian eclecticism into an English pint pot.

Of Chambers' work, little survives beyond the gallery. Most of the interior is by Adam, whose work at Osterley was completed by the end of the 1770s. Since then the house has remained unaltered, with the furniture Adam designed for it also intact – a remarkable testament to the custodianship of the Child family whose descendants, the Earls of Jersey, left it to the nation in 1923. It is now owned by the National Trust and cared for by the Victoria and Albert Museum, whose staff have been engaged in trying to recreate the Adam decoration. The house is described somewhat ominously as an 'experimental station' by Peter Thornton of the V and A in the official guidebook. And it must be admitted that experiment sometimes gets the better of atmosphere.

In remodelling the **exterior**, Adam's final plan took the Elizabethan original as its base: a three-sided house with prominent corner towers round a central raised courtyard. The garden front was adorned with a simple shallow pediment and curving double-staircase (perhaps by Chambers?). But the master stroke was the entrance front, a double portico linking the north and south wings to make a quadrangle. Adam had at first planned to fill this space with a Palladian front with a four-column portico. Forced by the Childs to retain the original corner towers, he decided to increase the strength of his portico to six columns, double it and leave the courtyard open behind, tying these elements together with a bold balustrade.

Some critics have argued he *could* have pushed the portico forward to give it still greater emphasis against the jutting towers; he need not have jammed the end columns quite so close to their adjacent brick walls; and guests must have been drenched reaching the entrance across the open courtyard in the rain. But critics be damned. The entrance front at Osterley is an original masterpiece. Its portico has all the rolling drums and crashing cymbals of Baroque without resorting to baroque tricks to accomplish it.

The **interior** of Osterley (2.00 to 6.00, 12.00 to 4.00 in winter, closed Mondays) is less a historic house than a museum of Adam decoration. No detail – the proportion of a triglyph, the colouring of a ceiling scroll, the turning of a doorhandle, the grain of a piece of marquetry – was too small for his attention. Child's neighbour down at Twickenham, Horace Walpole, watched the progress of the work at Osterley and was much impressed. After his first visit in 1773, he wrote that it had become 'a palace *sans* crown, *sans* coronet [a reference to Child's commoner status] but such expense! such taste! such profusion! ... It is so improved and enriched that all the Percys and Seymours of Syon must die of envy.' Although the interior today has little of the contents and intimate paraphernalia which give most English houses their special charm, those which remain were part of Adam's original design. Not until the growth of the Arts and Crafts movement in the 1880s were English furniture and architecture to achieve such a marriage.

The layout of the house is remarkably simple: a central hall with long gallery beyond and a sequence of formal rooms turning back along each of the two wings. The family apartments were on the first floor. The entrance across the courtyard leads directly into the **hall**, a room decorated with characteristic Adam refinement. Low-relief wall panels portray the trophies of war – a relic of days when halls were hung with real armaments – and niches at either end contain classical statues. The marble floor responds to the pattern of the ceiling. It is cool but luxurious, lacking only a dozen or so liveried footmen to bring it fully to life.

The hall leads into the **gallery**, which clearly predates Adam and, was almost certainly designed in 1759 by Chambers. His greater robustness can be detected in the Palladian details of the door and chimneypiece friezes, close in years but far in spirit from the Adam motifs of the other rooms. Adam's contribution to this room is confined to the *girandoles* (mirrored candle brackets) between the windows and the two sofas at each end. The full-length portraits on loan to the house include two stern Hoppners, of the Duke and Duchess of York, facing each other down the length of the gallery.

The first of the rooms in the north wing is the **Eating Room**, with a rococo ceiling filled with the most appetizing detail, its geometric pattern intertwined with grapes, ivy, vines and Bacchic emblems. Round the walls are the lyre-backed chairs and ormulu mounted pier glasses which Adam designed for each of his rooms at Osterley. Each pattern was a variation, the 'strings' of the lyre-backs sometimes so fine one could almost pluck them. Next comes the **staircase**, guarded by a screen of two columns on each floor and decorated by large-scale Adam cup and scroll reliefs. The whole composition was designed as a frame for its ceiling, which was covered by a large work by Rubens, 'The Apotheosis of a Hero'. Sadly the painting was taken down by the Jerseys before they relinquished the house and has since been lost in a fire.

We now reach the **library**, one of the two virtuoso Adam performances at Osterley. The walls are lined with bookshelves, filled with white and tan leather bindings so elegant as to be almost part of the decoration (though they are lent by the Athenaeum Club and St Paul's School). Above them are inset paintings by Antonio Zucchi, who also worked with Adam at Kenwood. But the glory of the room is once again in the ceiling. Here fans, swags, acanthus leaves, beasts and many other old friends from Adam's notebooks join hands to form one vast symmetrical work of art. The V and A have struggled valiantly to rediscover and recreate the original colours for this ceiling, based both on his own drawings and on fragments of paint from the ceiling itself. The result may not be to everyone's taste. A modern eye used to regarding 'Adam' as a style of faded pastel shades may well be shocked by these bright yellows, blues and greens in close proximity to each other. It is colouring reminiscent of cheap Italian pottery in a Venice market, and visitors can be heard to exclaim 'What *have* they done!' Yet it is colour, more than anything, which separates the fashions of the centuries. The shocking impact of this library ceiling is the price of authenticity. The furniture in the room is by John Linnell, again with lyre-patterns on the chair backs and using the most intricate veneers.

The **Breakfast Room** at the end of the north wing is more plain, possibly by Chambers, but with a bold rococo ceiling. It illustrates one principle of mid-Georgian design: if a Palladian treatment of the wall produces too severe an effect, then the ceiling should be

122

used to compensate. Here the Adamists have studiously recreated a colour of turquoise blue on a bilious yellow background – not something I would want to face at breakfast time.

We now return through the gallery to the south wing, which contains the main 'state rooms', though no head of state ever visited them (the Childs never equalled Gresham's status). When Walpole first set eyes on the **Drawing Room** he described it as 'worthy of Eve before the Fall'. A great sunflower bursts from the centre of the ceiling, its ostrich-feather rays bathing the surrounding panels in soft greens and golds. This sunflower was taken by Adam from Robert Wood and James Dawkins' *Ruins of Palmyra*, published in 1753; it was imitated on tens of thousands of Regency and Victorian drawing room ceilings. 'Pea green silk damask' covers the walls and the same colour is reflected back from the carpet beneath. Here Adam's associate, the weaver Thomas Moore, takes up the sunflower theme in yet softer tones, its leaves and flowers dancing a minuet across the floor. On one wall is a painting of a fearsome English blood horse, on another a rich Italian landscape, while two Reynolds portraits gaze calmly down at us from beside the fireplace. Not one inch of door, window, wall or floor seems to have escaped Adam's attention. The huge pier glasses came from France – the guidebook rightly wonders what horrors the carriers must have experienced transporting them over primitive eighteenth-century roads. The marquetry commodes, with rosewood medallions also by Adam, are equally splendid. As a crowning glory, the view from the windows out towards the lake is shaded by a green umbrella of mature cedars, planted in 1764 to celebrate the birth of a daughter to the house. Green is seldom an easy colour to handle. Here, man and nature have together brought it into perfect harmony.

Beyond is the **Tapestry Room** about which Walpole was equally enthusiastic. It was designed to display the tapestries specially made for it at the French Gobelins factory to designs by Boucher. The chairs and sofa, probably by Linnell, are upholstered from the same source. However magnificent, the colours of these fabrics are so vivid as to clash with subtler tones of Adam's ceiling and carpet. Nor do Boucher's garlands and *putti* sit happily alongside Adam's delicate fronds and classical profiles. Voluptuous, yes, but also a bit of a mess.

The **State Bedchamber**, next door, is chiefly remarkable for its bed. This is an astonishing fourposter with a canopy topped by a dome and a bed-head of small boys cavorting on dolphins above bare-chested maidens. It is described as 'one of Adam's most elaborate and ambitious pieces of furniture'. It has a lightness of touch not normally associated with these monuments to regal slumber, but one still expects a posse of Nubian slaves to march in at any moment and carry it on stage for an aria from *Aïda*. The walls of the room are of pleated silk.

Last we reach the **Etruscan Dressing Room**, the best-known room at Osterley because the most revolutionary. It was described by Adam himself as differing 'from anything else hitherto practised in Europe' in its attempt to adapt Etruscan motifs to the decoration of a complete chamber. The result is certainly odd: an army of Greek and Roman characters march up and down the wall and across the ceiling, linked by sinuous fronds and garlands, all coming together on the chimney-board as if at a loss for company. Walpole did not like it at all and spoke dismissively of 'going out of a palace into a potter's field' – a reference to the enthusiasm with which Josiah Wedgwood had taken up the Etruscan craze at his Etruria works in Staffordshire. The room lacks the panache of the rest of Osterley, but is nonetheless a fascinating exercise. And the attention to detail is still faultless. Note how the chair backs respond to the pattern on the wall immediately behind them. Woe betide anyone who 'pulls up a chair' in an Adam room.

Osterley **park** is one of the largest estate parks surviving in London – larger even than Kenwood – but marred both by its flat, featureless character and by the M4 cutting it in two. Yet the vicinity of the house is still totally rural, with an ornamental lake on one side and the surviving Elizabethan stables and clocktower on the other. These stables may once have formed the old Osterley manor house; they look substantial enough, with the renaissance door arches and staircase towers in the angles of the wings. Behind the kitchen garden are two summer houses, one a semicircular orangery designed by Adam, the other a Temple of Pan, facing it across the lawn. The latter is earlier, and contains a delightful classical interior, possibly by Chambers. Through the woods beyond, a path leads to Heston old church a mile away. This used to be a real country walk, but someone has allowed the local council to build high-rise flats overlooking it. When London planning re-enters the age of civilization, someone should pull them down.

*

The land west of Osterley was once some of the richest farmland in England. The villages of Heston, Harmondsworth, Stanwell and Bedfont were composed of prosperous farms and smallholdings from before the Norman conquest right up to the last war. Their churches were graced with handsome Tudor towers and their monuments and brasses testified to the wealth of the local gentry. This was not the courtly society of the Thames valley. It was true country, with only such coaching towns as Colnbrook (on the Bath Road) and Uxbridge (on the Oxford Road) hinting at proximity to the metropolis.

Ironically, the arrival of London's latest 'port' at Heathrow in the 1950s brought this cluster of villages a measure of protection. Under the crashing flight paths and towering hangars of London Airport, combine harvesters still roam over fields declared unsuitable for housing and old farm buildings snooze in semi-retirement. They are full of happy surprises for anyone with an hour to spare on the way to catch a plane. Nowhere is the surprise greater than at **Cranford Church**, tucked away in a bed of evergreen, right under the Feltham exit from the M4 (and accessible from it, perish the thought). The stables and clocktower of old Cranford House abut on to the motorway and the church has good memorials and a splendid view south along the banks of the River Crane.

At the far end of Cranford Park, a small lane turns right through what feels like deep Middlesex countryside (eight hundred yards from the main runway!). After two miles, the village of **Harmondsworth** is reached, blissfully unconcerned at the monstrous Post House hotel looming over it. Here stands one of the noblest monuments of English secular building, the tithe barn constructed by the Bishops of Winchester in the early 1400s. I once visited the barn with Sir John Betjeman and doubted whether he could negotiate the broken doors and hay in order to clamber inside. At the first sight of its massive roof, his unsteady legs lost their lameness. He sprang across the yard, leaped through a crack in a door and let forth a flood of Betjemania: 'Ah, hallowed roof, Ah, pillared hall – O Harmondsworth, O Middlesex!'

The Manor has since been sold to someone who has padlocked the gate and deters sightseers with Alsatians. The barn is losing its farmyard setting as well as being inaccessible. I can only record that this building is a cathedral in all but name, a hundred and ninety feet long and thirty-six feet high and wide. Two rows of columns divide it into nave and aisles, and the braces, tie-beams and kingposts of the roof are as brilliant an illustration of the builder's art as any Tudor fan-vault or Victorian bridge span. It makes the jumbo-jet hangars of Heathrow look puny by comparison.

Next door is a pretty group of village green, pub and church, the latter with a Norman doorway and Tudor tower. In its grave-yard lies Mr Richard Cox, a Victorian farmer who produced from these fertile meadows the Orange Pippin apple which has immortal-ized his name. There is no lovelier spot to administer first aid to anyone suffering from a bad attack of Heathrow.

A circumnavigation of Heathrow continues from Harmonds-worth to **Stanwell** in the south-east of the outer perimeter – a church with a rare Middlesex spire and a splendid monument to Lord Knyvett inside – then round to **East Bedfont** church on the south-east, with its thirteenth-century wall paintings, weather-boarded tower and topiary peacocks guarding its graveyard. Rumour has it they were cut by a local man whose offer of marriage had been refused by two local sisters. He said they were 'proud as two peacocks'.

Now a final nod in the direction of **Heathrow** itself. The airport has received few kind words ever since it was first laid out in 1939 and obliterated the only iron-age temple colonnade in England. It opened as a civil airport in 1946, and the Queen's Building, de-signed by the archetypal post-war public architect, Frederick Gibberd, was completed in 1955. The three terminal buildings, how-ever, are not bad illustrations of the architecture of their respective decades and are worth a second look.

The Intercontinental Terminal Three with Stefan Knapp's garish murals, was opened in 1961 when airports were still conceived of as glorified railway termini. Terminal One (1969) is in a clean, clinical sixties style. It could be a hospital, a new university or a multi-storey car park – and is largely the last. But the new additions to Terminal Two are an extraordinary tumescence. Moulded plastic shapes in bubblegum colours have been applied to the old Queen's Building in a style suggesting a children's space comic. Gibberd's original brickwork peers over it like a wing-commander spluttering through his moustaches, 'I say, chaps, hold on a bit!' But it makes a diversion from the pandemonium of internal combustion taking place on every side. And there is a fourth terminal on the way!

CHAPTER TEN

Twickenham

POINT of departure for the Thames-side village of Twickenham is the apex of the elliptical footbridge connecting its embankment with the tangled community of Eel Pie Island. It is a curious spot. Upstream we can still make out the cedars and willows overhanging the curving Middlesex bank, above which Alexander Pope and Horace Walpole sited their villas in the eighteenth century. Downstream is the comfortable wooded embankment beyond York House terrace towards Marble Hill. Yet all round us is an Arthur Ransome bustle of boats and boathouses, children, dogs and sailors. Twickenham is the last place on the tidal Thames where the river still seems master of the town. Skiffs from the local rowing club skim across the current. Private cruisers, with names such as *Cheryl* and *Suzy*, jostle old canal longboats up from Brentford for a refit. The banging of a carpenter's hammer rises and falls over the drone of an outboard.

It was here that old Walter Caisley ran his Thames Launches, in its day the largest fleet of pleasure boats on the river. When I last visited him in 1971 his Twickenham boatyard (now the Poseidon Works) was rebuilding a gunboat for a Middle East potentate. There was no money left on the Thames, he said sadly. His firm is now in other hands and the summer cruise boats no longer even stop at Twickenham. Yet his spirit lives on in the busy clutter of this stretch of the Thames. Ever so faintly, Twickenham still has about it the tang of the sea.

The village has been a prosperous resort ever since Francis Bacon first noticed the beauty of its serpentine sweep of river and came to live at Twickenham Park opposite Richmond in 1592. By the eighteenth century, its proximity to the palaces of Richmond, Hampton Court and Windsor made it a flourishing dormitory for assiduous courtiers and when, in 1719, Alexander Pope invested the profits from his Homer translation in a move upstream from

127

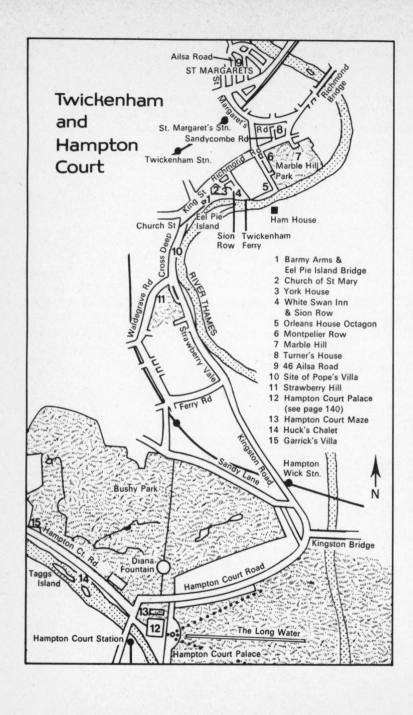

Twickenham and Hampton Court

Ailsa Road
ST MARGARETS
St. Margaret's Stn.
Sandycombe Rd
Twickenham Stn.
St Margaret's Rd
Richmond Bridge
Richmond Rd
Marble Hill Park
King St
Eel Pie Island
Church St
Sion Row
Twickenham Ferry
Ham House
Cross Deep
Waldegrave Rd
Strawberry Vale
RIVER THAMES
Ferry Rd
Kingston Road
Sandy Lane
Hampton Wick Stn.
N
Bushy Park
Kingston Bridge
Hampton Ct. Rd
Diana Fountain
Taggs Island
Hampton Court Road
Hampton Court Station
Hampton Court Palace
The Long Water

1 Barmy Arms &
  Eel Pie Island Bridge
2 Church of St Mary
3 York House
4 White Swan Inn
  & Sion Row
5 Orleans House Octagon
6 Montpelier Row
7 Marble Hill
8 Turner's House
9 46 Ailsa Road
10 Site of Pope's Villa
11 Strawberry Hill
12 Hampton Court Palace
   (see page 140)
13 Hampton Court Maze
14 Huck's Chalet
15 Garrick's Villa

Chiswick, Twickenham's status as summer capital of literary London was assured. Later the same century another newcomer, Horace Walpole, found himself enraptured: 'We shall be as celebrated as Baie or Tivoli ... nothing is equal to the fashion on this place. Mr Muntz says we have more coaches here than there are in half France.' It was, said Walpole, 'the Muses' favourite seat'. Apart from Pope and Walpole, Twickenham's residents have included Francis Bacon and the Earl of Clarendon, the Countess of Suffolk and Lady Wortley Montague, Sir Godfrey Kneller and J. M. W. Turner, Henry Fielding, Charles Dickens and Lord Tennyson. The Middlesex shore above and below the village boasted a succession of villas with gardens running down to the water's edge. No sooner had one illustrious resident left than another, equally renowned, moved in. Bacon's mansion of Twickenham Park passed through fifteen owners, almost all noblemen, between 1600 and its demolition in the 1820s. Yet only one of them, Lord Berkeley, was buried in the local church. The resort's glory was strictly a seasonal one, and when London encroached in the nineteenth century, that glory swiftly fled. Today only three of some two dozen major houses survive.

Eel Pie Island itself is a London original. It first came to fame as an angling resort, taking its name from the pies sold to Victorian day-trippers coming up from London on the steamers. The tavern which dispensed them was successively rebuilt, transforming itself from picnic inn to pub to smart hotel to jazz centre. It ended its days in the 1960s, spectacularly squatted by a group of hippies. The hotel met its nemesis when it was demolished to make way for ugly townhouses. The rest of the island has remained determinedly native. Houses, shacks and boatyards have sprung up on all sides, connected to the mainland only by paths to the footbridge. A sign firmly declares its privacy and it still has about it the scruffy independence of a seaside village – old bits of rope, broken paddles, a smell of tar and a refreshing absence of planning conformity. A scheme to connect the new townhouses to the Surrey shore by roadbridge has been thwarted: those who want roads should not live on islands in the Thames.

The old **waterfront** of Twickenham village was badly damaged by a stick of bombs in the last war, and the Twickenham and Richmond councils have been striving ever since to demolish whatever the bombs left standing. But enough odds and ends of seventeenth- and eighteenth-century buildings remain to provide a sort of ragged frame to the picture. Church Street is a battle-weary example of a London village street fighting off competition from a neighbouring highway of multiple stores (in this case the horrific King Street). Behind a veil of 'To Let' signs it nervously awaits each new twist in retail fashion: antique and craft shops are apparently strong at present. Long may it prosper and keep the demolishers at bay. Back on the foreshore, oarsmen, cruiser skippers and tourists can refresh themselves at the extraordinary 'Barmy Arms', with its upside-down playing card inn sign. 'Barmy' is believed to refer not to the sign but to the ancient word for beer froth. Equally odd is the stocky **Church of St Mary**, fastening the scene to its bank like a tent peg. It was rebuilt in 1714 by John James (architect of St George's Hanover Square) and is a bold pedimented box tacked incongruously on to the former fifteenth-century tower. The western pediment rises up behind the tower almost as if the latter did not exist – or perhaps James was anticipating its demolition. St Mary's is another locked church with no mention of a key and a notice blandly suggests visitors come back another time.

Those lucky enough to gain entry will see that the interior of St Mary's was deprived of much of its Georgian character when it was stripped of its box pews in 1860. The reason for this is graphically conveyed in an account left by the in-coming vicar, the Reverend G. S. Master, in 1859: 'The entire area of the church was in the possession of a small number of families, and the poor were practically excluded altogether; a few uncomfortable brackets placed sideways in the central passage being the only accommodation provided for them.' Master did at least retain the monuments, some of which are remarkable. Francis Paulton and his wife clasp hands across a skull, presumably one of their children, on a memorial dating from 1642 – a gloomy relic of that year of civil war. And Alexander Pope's name crops up on all sides, despite his Roman Catholicism. A monument to his parents, in Latin, can be found on the east wall of the gallery, and a plaque on the floor of the main aisle commemorates his own death. More poignant is a tablet on the outside of the east wall erected by Pope to his old nurse, Mary Beach, who died in 1725: 'In gratitude to a faithful old servant'.

Beneath the medieval tower, the eight ropes (or 'sallies') of Twickenham's church bells wait silently for the change-ringers to pull them to life. On the walls are plaques reflecting the longevity of this peculiarly English tradition. The first records a three-hour session of what enthusiasts understandably call 'the exercise' in 1749. The most recent is from 1969 when '5040 changes of Grandsire Triples Parkers twelve part' were rung in three hours seven minutes, seven minutes longer than it took to ring the same peals in 1932. For the first time a woman is mentioned as having taken part – Anne Horsford on bell No. 3. The tumbling peals of these old bells (rung on Sundays at 6.00) can strip away the centuries from a Middlesex suburb and return us to a world of meadows and lanes and autumn bonfires. Change-ringing is the true music of the English village.

Next to the church stands **York House**, used as a summer residence by the Lord Chancellor, the Earl of Clarendon, when Charles II was at Hampton Court. It took its name from the Duke of York, Charles' brother and the future James II. It was by him that Clarendon's daughter Anne became pregnant in 1660, leading to a secret and scandalous marriage a month before the birth of a boy who might in time have become king of England. The marriage turned out to be a lasting one and though all its male offspring died in infancy, it produced two queens, Mary II and Anne. The house itself was rebuilt in 1700 and passed through the hands of the eighteenth-century Austrian statesman, Prince Stahremberg, the Comte de Paris, a grandson of Louis Philippe, and the Indian iron and steel tycoon, Sir Ratan Tata (who died in 1918). It was finally bought as offices by that omnipotent plutocrat, the local borough council.

Restored William and Mary architecture can look so much like twentieth-century 'neo-Georgian' that York House passes almost unnoticed from the main road. But its **gardens** are open to the public during office hours and are a pleasant surprise, leading us past a water-garden over a footbridge to a terrace fronting the river. Tucked in beneath the terrace is an evergreen walk culminating in one of London's most extraordinary follies: the fountain installed by Sir Ratan, adorned by seven extremely nude nymphs and crowned by Venus revealing a large posterior to the upstairs windows of the vicarage next door. Was this some private joke on Sir Ratan's part? The terrace of York House garden offers a tranquil view of the Twickenham waterfront. The tip of Eel Pie Island with its boatyards, inlets and straggling trees, might be on the Norfolk Broads.

Immediately below York House runs the half-mile of **riverside** towards Marble Hill. This lane is no stately progress along an

ornamental bank, but a game of hide and seek with the river, darting
in and out of a winding passage flanked by old brick walls. Twickenham was meant as a private resort, not a public one, and its villas
were careful to keep their garden skirts well above the waterline,
leaving the locals to endure the regular flooding of the lane below.
The record high-water mark of 1774 is indicated on the churchyard
wall, and is well above our heads. A hundred yards downstream
is **Sion Row**, an urbane Georgian terrace oddly out of place in what
seems deepest Middlesex. Though built in 1721, its houses still have
the overhanging eaves supposedly outlawed as a fire hazard by the
1707 Building Act. Presumably it was a case of out of town and
out of sight. The White Swan Inn, next door, is in the fine tradition
of Thames-side pubs – compare the Dove at Hammersmith and
the London Apprentice at Isleworth – unspoilt and with a sunny
terrace overlooking the water. Opposite runs, or is supposed to run,
the Twickenham ferry to Ham. All attempts on my part ever to
find the ferryman, and thus combine a visit to Marble Hill with
one to Ham, have been disappointed. Enquiries at the White Swan
receive a splendidly Dickensian roar of laughter and the remark
that the ferry runs 'when it suits the ferrymen'. This, I am told,
is like the pub itself a great London tradition.

We now enter the grounds of what was once a cluster of villas
opposite Ham, with such exotic names as Mount Lebanon, Rag-
man's Castle, Orleans House and Marble Hill. The first two have
long vanished, and of **Orleans House** only a corner pavilion remains
from the mansion erected by William III's Scottish Secretary, James
Johnstone, for his retirement. The house derived its name from its
nineteenth-century owners, the French Orleanist royal family. Many
of them lived in Twickenham in exile from 1815–17 and they
maintained the house as a useful London bolt-hole after that – wisely,
as many returned here again in the 1860s. The shipping magnate,
William Cunard, demolished most of it in 1926 – a particular tragedy
since this was reputedly the finest of the Twickenham mansions
– but the Octagon pavilion was saved at the last minute by the
intervention of a Mrs Levy (who later became Mrs Ionides, both
names hinting at ample resources). She bequeathed the property
to the local council on her death in 1962.

The **Octagon**, with its modern extensions, looks more like a folly
than a home. Johnstone added it to his existing property in 1720
to receive Caroline, Princess of Wales. He was a great favourite of

hers and the pavilion has some of the flavour of the Hanoverian palaces she would have known in Germany. Designed by James Gibbs, its breezy Baroque makes a refreshing contrast to the sober style of Marble Hill next door. The interior (open 2.00 to 5.30 daily, including Sundays, closed at 4.30 in winter) is effectively an ante-chamber to the former house. It comprises a domed room with three doorways and a chimneypiece, executed with theatrical bravura and decorated with stuccowork of almost edible delicacy. The latter is by Gibbs' faithful Italians, Bagutti and Artari, who worked with him on St Martin-in-the-Fields. Coming upon it through the trees from her residence at Kew, the Princess must have been delighted at such a reception. Johnstone was also an enthusiastic gardener with 'the best collection of fruits of any gentleman in England'. The gardens included his own vineyard on these slopes, from which he produced a substantial quantity of wine each year. Of all this, nothing visible remains.

The road now curves inland to reach **Montpelier Row** one of the best early-Georgian terraces outside central London (finer even than Hampstead's Church Row). Developed in the early 1720s, it illustrates a period in which all the builder's ingenuity and learning were concentrated in the one feature on which he was permitted stylistic licence – the door surround. Montpelier Row is a museum of such surrounds: No. 10, Ionic pillars with pediment; No. 12, simple rusticated opening with neither pilaster nor pediment; No. 15 (Tennyson's house for a brief period), delicate 'Queen Anne' scroll brackets beneath a hood; and at No. 30, South End House, a final mannerist flourish of tapering fluted pilasters. This last idiosyncrasy so horrified the arch-Palladian, Robert Morris, that he used it to illustrate his thesis that in the baroque doorcase 'fancy alone has had the superiority over truth and reason in the extravagant address of the composition'. A Doric pillar, he said, was the proper guardian of an honest house. No. 25 Montpelier Row is a modern addition built by Geoffrey Darke for himself in 1969. Designed to the scale of its neighbours, but a fraction bigger, it manages to be deferential to its forebears without being obsequious.

We are now at **Marble Hill**, last relic of Twickenham's golden age. It was begun in 1723 by the mistress of the future George II as a security against old age. The lady, Henrietta Howard, later Countess of Suffolk, was an engaging individual. She and her husband, an impoverished dragoon officer, had decided to seek their fortune by attaching themselves to George's court when he and his father were still living in Hanover. She managed to secure for herself a post as woman of the bedchamber to Princess Caroline. On George's arrival in England in 1714 and his subsequent banishment by his father to Richmond Lodge at Kew, Henrietta joined the circle of 'maids' to Princess Caroline which were such a feature of that court. Here her 'good sense, good breeding and good nature' soon brought her to the attention of the Prince. She was clearly the model mistress from everyone's point of view. She was simple and charming, rather than a great beauty. There is some doubt as to whether she had a physical relationship with George, though he would sit up half the night chatting amiably with her and even gave her husband a pension to remove him from the scene. Horace Walpole concluded that she was 'sensible, artful, agreeable but had neither sense nor art enough to make the king think her more agreeable than his wife'. Therein must have lain Henrietta's secret, for she was tolerated by the queen and retained George's good favour throughout his life. In 1723, at the age of thirty-five, she felt secure enough to seek funds from him for a house of her own. £12,000 was provided, together with an earldom for her husband, and two friends of George's were appointed trustees, the Earl of Ilay and Henry Herbert, the future Earl of Pembroke. Ilay duly bought a site at Marble Hill, near to his own property and convenient to Kew.

Herbert was an amateur architect and enthusiastic follower of Lord Burlington, and his sketched plans were executed by his friend, the Palladian Roger Morris (relative of Robert, above). The building appeared in Campbell's *Vitruvius Britannicus* and Campbell may even have played a part in its design. The result is a classical box of three storeys, five bays wide, with Ionic pilasters and a pediment on the front façade and an identical pediment on the back. The whole building is stuccoed. The effect is handsome rather than exciting, a conversation piece for a Burlington dinner party.

The house (open 10.00 to 5.00 except Fridays, closed at 4.00 in winter) was designed with two purposes: as Henrietta's private house and as a showpiece in which she could cut an aristocratic dash when entertaining friends. The result is the subordination of the plan to a main reception room, the **Great Room**. This is Herbert's one trumpet blast at Marble Hill. It rises through both upper storeys, clearly taking its cue from Inigo Jones' Single Cube Room at Wilton,

Herbert's country seat. Shortage of funds denied Herbert a triumphal staircase up the outside of the house in the manner of Chiswick; guests had to enter the room from the living quarters beneath. But the room itself is tremendous, twenty-four feet cubed, with white walls and heavy gilt swags round the cornice and entablature, rising to a steeply coved ceiling. Two monstrous gilt cherubs lie languidly across the chimneypiece pediment, above an inset painting of Venus and Adonis by Thornhill. The paintings on the walls are school of Van Dyck, in frames similar to those holding real Van Dycks at Wilton. The whole room has a vibrancy excellently recaptured by the Greater London Council in its 1966 restoration.

The other rooms at Marble Hill are unremarkable, though pillared screens regularly inject a touch of splendour appropriate to the career of a royal mistress – notably in the Countess's bedroom adjoining the Great Room. The screen in the breakfast parlour on the ground floor is a florid creation with scroll brackets and other motifs supposedly copied by Herbert from works of Inigo Jones. They seem a curious Palladian doodle.

Despite the Great Room, Marble Hill is sadly neglected by the public. 'Not a good year' was the comment of the doorman when last I asked after his attendances. Certainly it could do with more furniture and pictures: some paintings are currently on their way from the G.L.C. collection at Kenwood and a sublime Thames scene by Richard Wilson already hangs in the bedroom. But the place lacks a theme. Perhaps since it was built by one royal lady and later rented by another (Mrs Fitzherbert, no less), it could become a museum of such regal liaisons. There is no shortage of suitable material from the mansions of the Thames valley.

Marble Hill's **grounds** were originally sketched for Lady Suffolk by Alexander Pope and laid out by Charles Bridgeman. Pope was naturally eager to welcome so famous a resident to his Twickenham set and equally eager that she should espouse the new Palladian 'naturalism' which he was demonstrating in his own garden a mile upstream. Pope's naturalism seems oddly formal when compared with that of, for instance, Capability Brown later in the century: a print of Marble Hill in 1749 shows serried ranks of trees marching down to the water's edge. Little remains of Pope's design today, but the old stables in the grounds are worth a visit and provide a passable tea in summer.

Beyond Marble Hill, the dedicated suburban explorer will turn up Sandycombe Lane where, surrounded by jovial Victorian terraces, stands the only known work of architecture by J. M. W. Turner. It is the Italianate lodge which he designed and built for himself between 1810 and 1814 for his visits to Twickenham, and which he subsequently passed to his father. On past the roaring torrent of Chertsey Road, we reach St Margaret's, a leafy estate of the sort of Victorian villas long ago demolished on the heights of Sydenham and Tulse Hill. And at 46 Ailsa Road is a stark white Modern Movement creation with a bold zigzag pattern on the door. Complete with silver birch in the front garden it looks more like an artist's impression than a real building. It might almost be a stage set for Jacques Tati's *Mon Oncle*.

One Twickenham secret remains: Strawberry Hill, masterpiece or curiosity depending on one's point of view. This is the house built by the man who succeeded Pope as presiding genius of the Twickenham set in the mid-eighteenth century, Horace Walpole. To reach Strawberry Hill, we must return to the centre of town and walk, or drive, half a mile upriver, past a ponderous Egyptian super-cinema and the site of Pope's villa on Cross Deep. Of this villa nothing remains; it was demolished in the 1820s to the fury of residents who were beginning to prize any links, however tenuous, with their vanishing literary past. In its place arose a fantasy chalet built for a tea merchant and described as 'Elizabethan half-timber and Tudor Renaissance, with the addition of Dutch and Swiss and Italian and Chinese features'. This example of rampant eclecticism forms the core of the present convent. Immediately beyond it, the gardens of Pope's neighbour, Lord Radnor, are now open to the public. Their weeping willows dip into the Thames and lend a touch of limp gentility to the suburban development pressing in on all sides.

The house which Horace Walpole acquired as a mere 'plaything' in 1749 stands upstream of the site of Pope's villa in Waldegrave Road. It is now almost submerged in the campus of St Mary's College of Education, and is only to be seen by prior appointment with the principal's office. Tours are held on occasional Wednesdays and Saturdays guided, rather slowly, by one of the students.

More than any house in London, **Strawberry Hill** continues to express not only its owner's social and artistic ambitions but also his bizarre psychology. He was the younger son of the Prime Minister, Sir Robert Walpole, and was himself for a time a Member of Parliament. But from the moment he left Eton and went on the Grand Tour, he found his true vocation in art, letters and literary gossip. Though no match for Pope as a writer or critic – Walpole wrote little fiction, apart from his Gothic romance, *The Castle of Otranto* – he was certainly his equal in fastidious bachelor snobbery. He held court at Strawberry Hill, clothed in velvets and silks, with his kittens and poodles about his feet. Friends would be summoned, lectured, quarrelled with and dismissed. And his social conquests would be written down in one of the most voluminous and enthralling correspondences in English literature.

Walpole had a family fortune behind him and wanted Strawberry Hill to be both cultured and unusual. His desire for pre-eminence in the dilettante society of eighteenth-century Twickenham led him to consult all and sundry. He chose the Gothic style for his villa in what was a radical departure from the prevailing Palladianism, not to shock his friends but because he regarded it as more suitable for a small house in the country. To help with the interior he recruited a group of friends, including the poet Thomas Gray, with whom he had been at Eton, John Chute and Richard Bentley. This group he pompously dubbed his 'committee of taste'; they scoured the churches and abbeys of northern Europe for inspiration, with the same zeal as that shown earlier in the century by Burlington's Palladians.

Each room is thus a variation on some existing Gothic model, with particular emphasis given to the fireplaces, most of which were copied from English and French tombs. Yet the overall effect is not sombre but light, almost frivolous. Bentley's work especially is much nearer the levity of the Rococo than the ecclesiastical revivalism of Walpole's nineteenth-century successors. Indeed when we reach the Victorian extension to Strawberry Hill, added by Lady Waldegrave in 1869, we can see how ponderous these successors could be. The contrast is best observed from the gardens, where the ogival windows of Walpole's villa are gentle and delicate against the heavy neo-Tudor stonework of the later buildings.

The tour of the interior begins with the entrance down an open passage between 'the castle and the priory': on one side a castellated façade and on the other a cloistered wing with a Gothic screen beyond it. This assymetry, reflected in every aspect of Strawberry Hill, was not new – see Vanbrugh's Castle at Greenwich – but it must have seemed an exotic innovation in the classical Arcadia of eighteenth-century Twickenham. (Walpole was perpetually besieged with sightseers, to his feigned dismay.) The dark entrance hall is surrounded by domestic rooms, all with pretty wallpaper and pointed doors and windows. The **staircase** was meant to be mysterious and gloomy (Walpole had a taste for the occult) but is executed by Bentley with a masterful lightness of touch. Walpole loved it: 'It is so pretty and so small that I am inclined to wrap it up and send it to you,' he wrote. The staircase rises to an armoury at the top, a memorial to Walpole's much-researched but probably fake Crusader ancestor, Sir Terry Robsart. Robsart's bust pops up in one room after another.

From here on, Horace Walpole never looked back. Bentley soon broke with him, as did most of his associates at various times. But the fantasy moved constantly forward. Bentley's design for the **library** was rejected by Walpole's 'committee' and it was created instead by John Chute. It is an astonishing room, its Decorated Gothic bookcases taken from the screen in old St Paul's Cathedral and its fireplace from the tomb of John of Eltham in Westminster Abbey. The **Holbein Chamber** has a tripartite ogival screen borrowed from that of Rouen Cathedral, and a rock-hard horsehair mattress. It was in this room that Walpole claimed he had the nightmare which formed the basis of *The Castle of Otranto*; it is not hard to see why.

Most dramatic of all is the **gallery**. When Walpole's friend, Montague, first saw it he 'hoops and hollas and dances and crosses himself a thousand times over'. It was designed by Thomas Pitt, another of Bentley's successors, after the fan vault of Henry VII's chapel in Westminster Abbey. Yet its bays, recesses and mirrors, glittering with Gothic fretwork, are so light it seems to float away from us over the garden. When I last visited the house an American lady was busy photographing each detail to give to her interior decorator 'back home' – at Strawberry Hill a case of *plus ça change* . . .

Off the gallery is the **cabinet**, decorated by Walpole to simulate a chapel. He never consecrated it and used it as a showcase for his religious pictures and other works of art. Though loosely modelled on the Chapter House of York, its atmosphere is firmly secular. Finally, at the far end of the gallery, is the **Beauclerk Room** with a fireplace borrowed from the tomb of Edward the Confessor at Westminster. The room is the work of Robert Adam, working, as was normal at Strawberry Hill, to Walpole's instructions. J. Mordaunt Crook calls it 'the most outrageous piece of motif-mongering in the whole house'. Walpole wrote that 'The tomb of the confessor has been improved by Mr Adam and beautifully executed in *scagliola*,' while the ceiling is a free version of the great rose window of old St Paul's. Adam's tiny acanthus-leaf frieze can, however, be detected in the cornice: a Walpole design, or Adam getting the last laugh?

Hampton Court

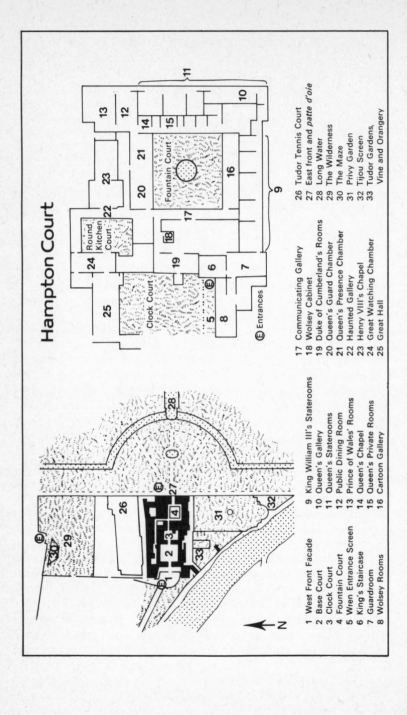

1 West Front Facade
2 Base Court
3 Clock Court
4 Fountain Court
5 Wren Entrance Screen
6 King's Staircase
7 Guardroom
8 Wolsey Rooms
9 King William III's Staterooms
10 Queen's Gallery
11 Queen's Staterooms
12 Public Dining Room
13 Prince of Wales' Rooms
14 Queen's Chapel
15 Queen's Private Rooms
16 Cartoon Gallery
17 Communicating Gallery
18 Wolsey Cabinet
19 Duke of Cumberland's Rooms
20 Queen's Guard Chamber
21 Queen's Presence Chamber
22 Haunted Gallery
23 Henry VIII's Chapel
24 Great Watching Chamber
25 Great Hall
26 Tudor Tennis Court
27 East front and *patte d'oie*
28 Long Water
29 The Wilderness
30 The Maze
31 Privy Garden
32 Tijou Screen
33 Tudor Gardens,
   Vine and Orangery

CHAPTER ELEVEN

Hampton Court

൧

Why come ye not to Court?
To whiche Court?
To the Kynges Court,
Or to Hampton Court?
Nay to the Kynges Court,
The Kynges Court should have the excellence,
But Hampton Court hath the pre-eminence.

WITH these teasing lines the Tudor satirist, John Skelton, introduced his public to the splendour of a palace which has come to typify the grand alliance of history and architecture more than any building in England. Hampton Court is a museum of English characteristics; of English ambivalence towards dictatorship and licence, of English ability to snatch passing styles out of the wind and make them our own, of English ability to guard and cherish the beauty of the past. It is often compared with Versailles. Mercifully there is no comparison. Hampton is incurably human, flawed and miscellaneous. In the 1690s a foreign monarch, William of Orange, thought to demolish the place and build a structure of continental grandiloquence. Time and money ran out on him. Later monarchs treated it instead with the preservationist balm of benign neglect. Unaltered since the Hanoverians rejected it in favour of Windsor and Kew, Hampton Court is arguably Britain's most important, and loved, national monument.

The palace's public reputation is largely due to its being the setting for the saga of Wolsey, Henry VIII and his six wives. Of this saga the hero must be Wolsey. The son of an Ipswich butcher, he rose to become in 1507 chaplain to Henry's father, Henry VII, when he was still in his early thirties. Eight years later, with the younger Henry on the throne, he achieved the highest rank in the land, Lord Chancellor and Cardinal of the Church of Rome. A year earlier he had, on the advice of his physicians, bought the manor of Hampton as an appropriate site for a cardinal's palace. The location was as much strategic as therapeutic: most of the king's riverside palaces were within easy reach and the Thames provided fast access to Westminster and the City of London.

Wolsey intended nothing but the best for Hampton Court. A complex conduit was built for water from Surrey. Landing stages were constructed for royal barges. And a sequence of courts, halls, kitchens and stables were built to house a retinue which at times rose to more than five hundred people. In 1526 the French ambassador brought a party of two hundred and eighty to Hampton Court and marvelled at his reception. The palace may not have been embellished with quite the renaissance lavishness of Francis I's new Loire palace of Chambord, but it was unquestionably bigger. Wolsey's reign was brief. The ambition of which Hampton Court was the most public symbol brought about his eventual downfall. Already nervous of his position Wolsey had in 1525 formally assigned the palace to the king. But it was not enough to assuage the envy of that monstrous monarch. Four years later, with Henry desperate for a divorce from Catherine of Aragon to which Wolsey was bitterly opposed, the creator of Hampton Court was arrested. He died while on trial for treason in 1530.

Henry emphasized his victory by seizing the palaces of Hampton Court and York Place in Westminster, as well as all Wolsey's works of art. He immediately set about the rebuilding of the former, determined to outshine even Wolsey in magnificence. The hall and chapel were demolished and reconstructed. New courts were added, together with a tiltyard and tennis court. And an ornamental path was laid to link the landing stage with the house, flanked by heraldic beasts. Henry's Hampton was the largest house in England (much larger than it is today) and only his gilded folly of Nonsuch equalled it in richness.

Much scholarship had been expended on disentangling Henry's work at Hampton from that of Wolsey's day. But for most visitors this academic debate is irrelevant. The fascination of Hampton Court lies in the tension between the surviving Tudor palace as a whole and the new buildings begun by Christopher Wren under William III but never completed. Though the guidebooks will refer to Wolsey's palace as renaissance and Wren's as baroque, it is better to think of the former as the climax of the English medieval tradition

– the last fanfare of castle, keep and great hall – and the latter as an advanced example of European classicism by one of its finest exponents.

Hampton Court was a river palace and was meant to be approached from the river. This is still possible in summer on a day trip from Westminster: up in the morning, back in the late afternoon. Car visitors can park at the far end of the Green, and those coming by train will approach from the battered terminus of the old London and South-Western railway (Waterloo) on the Esher bank, as did thousands of Londoners after Queen Victoria first opened the palace to the public in 1838. The station was intended to give tourists a first taste of 'Tudor' architecture as they stepped from the train – though the service was initially so poor they sometimes discovered that the carriages were drawn by horses! The bridge over the river was designed by Edwin Lutyens in 1925 and is a strong but inoffensive foil to the palace beyond. From its apex is the first exciting glimpse of the dominant feature of the Tudor buildings, the Great Hall towering over Wolsey's courts and surrounded by a forest of twisted chimneys.

Hampton Court is first and foremost an essay in **brick** and any appreciation of it involves an understanding of this excellent building material. At the time when Wolsey was commencing work, most noblemen's houses in England were built of stone. In the Thames basin this had to be imported from as far away as the North Downs (at Reigate) or even Caen in France. Bricks on the other hand offered swifter construction – Wolsey was a man in a hurry – great adaptability and the opportunity for new-fangled decoration. Given a ready supply of clay and of skilled labour to manipulate it, the resulting buildings were well-insulated and modern in appearance. Wolsey's master builder at Hampton, as elsewhere, was Henry Redman, and his early bricks were smaller, darker and less refined than the later work. They were laid in English bond – alternate rows of 'stretchers' (long) and 'headers' (short) – into which were set vitrified black or purple bricks to create a decorative effect known as diapering.

Henry's masons, working a decade later under John Molton, used slightly larger and redder bricks, still in English bond. But by the time of Wren, bricks were being brought from farther afield than the Middlesex clay beds. They were now rubbed and dressed and laid in the new Flemish bond with stretchers and headers alternating in each row, producing a more even and refined effect. Bricks became pinker and their mortaring thinner. But it is the wayward character of the early-Tudor brickwork which gives Hampton Court its special appeal. Each brick has its own individual shade, depending on the length of firing and the impurities in its clay: soft pinks, crimsons, russets, plums, purples, the sand or grit crystallized into a sparkle or crumbling to reveal a tiny fossil from some prehistoric tidal surge. Rebuilding has made the discovery of such brick a difficult treasure hunt, for only recently have restorers appreciated the importance of matching brick for brick. Thus even so important a structure as the West Gate Tower has erupted into a jarring pink Flemish bond (the original work can be seen at the base of the left-hand tower). Unravel their story, however, and the bricks of Hampton Court can be its most intriguing guidebook.

Wolsey's **west front** façade is renaissance only in the symmetry of the ranges flanking the gateway and the terracotta medallions of Roman emperors set into the walls. These were the work of the Italian, Giovanni da Maiano, and were a decorative innovation both in theme and in material. Otherwise, this is a medieval façade nostalgic for a past of moats, guard-towers and machicolations. Only once was Hampton Court fortified, when the Protector Somerset anticipated a revolt against the young Edward VI. But he soon withdrew to the more easily defensible fortress of Windsor. The tower was then two storeys higher, but was reduced in 1770. The stone dressings to the windows and the mythical beasts clambering along the coping have all been heavily restored, while the 'king's beasts' guarding the bridge are twentieth-century copies. The projecting corner pavilions are part of Henry's additions to the palace, as is his coat of arms on the gate-tower.

Through the gateway we find ourselves in Wolsey's **Base Court**, a wide grassy quadrangle reminiscent of an Oxford college. From here Hampton Court's chimneys perform their star turn, shooting up like rockets above every roof, twisted, studded, chevroned, honey-combed, their crowns battlemented or cusped. Thus did a Tudor grandee show off the lavishness of his modern heating system and provide his brick carvers with a public gallery for their skill. The court itself has the same spacious assymetry as Wolsey's Tom Quad at Christ Church, Oxford, though here we have the west end of Henry's Great Hall towering over it. The rooms have been let out as grace-and-favour apartments to court retainers ever since the palace ceased to be a royal residence in the eighteenth century.

We now pass through Anne Boleyn's Gate into the **Clock Court**. The gate, which led to the Great Hall, has Henry and Anne's initials intertwined in the bosses of its vault. Catherine of Aragon was still in residence when the king moved his new mistress into the palace. But no sooner had Anne's presence been recognized architecturally than she was on her way to the Tower and hasty adjustments had to be made to receive Jane Seymour. Masons who had so recently obliterated the emblems of the late Cardinal must have needed an acute political hand to keep their carvings up to date.

We are now in the heart of Wolsey's old palace, and each side of the courtyard demonstrates a phase in the palace's history. Only the west wall is a true relic of Wolsey's day, though its colourful astronomical clock, manufactured in France and built in 1540, postdates him. Apart from giving such measurements as the time of day and the phases of the moon, it marks the time of high water at London Bridge – a useful detail for those having to row or sail the whole way back to the City. To our left rises Henry's major insertion into Wolsey's fabric, the massive south wall of the Hall, with elongated buttresses rising to gilded weathervanes and a tall bay window at its east end. Completed in 1536, it must then have seemed a structure of giant ostentation, the ultimate gesture in out-Wolseying Wolsey. Ahead is the east range, its upper storeys altered by William Kent for George II in the 1730s and a curious incursion of eighteenth-century Gothic in this part of the palace.

On our right is the first taste of Wren. He introduces himself modestly: a simple baroque colonnade to provide a covered approach to the king's staircase inside, the columns paired and thrusting up into the balustrade to give the composition a sense of rhythm. But through into **Fountain Court**, all is Wren – or almost all. Wren, then still a young man, was never quite his own master at Hampton Court, with both William himself and William's Dutch architect, Daniel Marot, involving themselves directly in the designs. The exteriors bear many traces of Marot's palace recently built for William at Het Loo and the strangely squat cloister of Fountain Court was so criticized by Wren's contemporaries that William felt constrained to take the blame for it himself. The original plan had been to demolish all of Henry's palace with the exception of the Great Hall, but the deaths first of Mary then of William himself combined with shortage of money to leave the building half-completed. Wren found himself, as in his work in the City and Greenwich, unable to complete a grand baroque design and forced to contribute instead to a historical miscellany. His loss is our gain.

The interior of Hampton Court calls for a patient nerve and a strong shoulder, for this is the mainstream of world tourism. It is open daily from 9.30 to 6.00, Sundays 2.00 to 6.00 (closed at 4.00 in winter) and is approached through Wren's colonnade in the Clock Court. It is usually packed. The main **State Rooms** are those designed by Wren, though a few Tudor rooms and Henry's hall, chapel and kitchens are also open (at least in summer). The contrast between them is not just one of style and scale but also of the philosophy of kingship they represent. To Henry a palace was still a medieval home, the symbols of office being the magnificence of dress and ornament with which king and courtiers were alike surrounded. A century of Stuarts, however, and the example of Louis XIV turned monarchs almost into gods. Palace architecture accordingly had to express the distance between king and people, and did so in long *enfilades* of reception rooms and adulatory murals.

The reign of William and Mary was a double one, Mary having refused to take the crown after the Glorious Revolution of 1688 unless her husband became king as well as consort. Wren therefore had to design two reception suites of equal prominence at Hampton Court, lending the building both splendour and confusion. The king's apartments face out over the Tudor garden, with his bedroom as their climax. The east range, facing the Long Water and with its own formal staircase, contains the queen's rooms. Since we enter through the king's staircase, we approach the Queen's rooms in reverse order, a technically unsatisfactory arrangement which involves us coming on the queen's throne from behind. The rooms themselves are large and cold, like many Wren interiors, and their dark panelling and plain mouldings give them an institutional atmosphere which not even a scattering of Grinling Gibbons carvings can quite relieve. Hampton Court, however, was not created by Wren alone and is full of surprises.

At the top of the staircase (tedious murals by Verrio, ironwork by Tijou), we enter the **guardroom**. Here some three thousand pikes, swords, muskets and pistols are arranged in pretty patterns on the walls, to delight children of a military bent. Ancient drums can be spotted in the gloom above the windows. Down to the right is a small suite of rooms surviving from the Tudor palace, referred to as the 'Wolsey rooms'. The first two have linenfold panelling on the walls and the farthest looks down on the tiny garden knot, which was intended to be seen from this height. The ceiling is richly decorated with reliefs of Wolsey badges.

The **paintings** at Hampton Court are something of a disappointment. They include many fine works from the royal collection, though largely from what might be termed its second division. Nor is there any guide to the often changing selection put on display, and as many of the attributions on the pictures themselves are doubtful this adds to the difficulty of appreciating their importance. I can only indicate the approximate location of the better-known works. The first of the Wolsey rooms contains a collection of Hapsburg portraits, all with the famous lower lip. There is also a survivor of Henry's set of anti-papist pictures, this one showing a pope being stoned to death (attributed to Girolamo Treviso). The far room has a splendid group of Tudor portraits, including a full-length painting of the ill-fated Edward VI, his frailty contrasting with a tough 'Holbein' of his father, Henry VIII, and the cold, white face of his sister, Elizabeth. A large Gheeraerdts of a woman in an embroidered dress is on the east wall, portraying what must have been a *tour de force* of Tudor needlework. Over the fireplace is a gloomy picture of Hampton Court in 1640, showing the height of Wolsey's gatehouse and the extent of Henry's old palace before the Wren demolitions. This must have seemed a dark year for the ancient retainers of Hampton, those who could recall the glittering years of Good Queen Bess amid the gathering storms of civil war. We return to the Guardroom past a magnificent 'Barbarini' tapestry depicting scenes from the scriptures. Dating from the seventeenth century, it is in a remarkable state of preservation, full of soft golds and strong blues.

We now enter King William's state rooms: two presence rooms, audience room, drawing room and bedroom. The bedroom would have been the scene of the morning *levée*, though the king's private rooms continue beyond. Here the chief delight is Gibbons' carving, which seems to bring all the naturalism and gaiety of the countryside to these sombre surroundings – like whistling a popular tune in church. Gibbons' signature was a pod of peas hidden somewhere in his composition, its size indicating his satisfaction or otherwise with his payment for the job. The king (or Wren) appears to have paid him well.

The **First Presence Chamber** contains William's chair of state together with a huge painting of him on horseback by Kneller. This artist was to the courts of Mary and Anne what Lely has been to Charles II, a sort of photographer royal. In this room normally hang Kneller's 'court beauties', commissioned by Mary to rival those painted by Lely for Charles II, which now hang in the Communicating Gallery. Mary was unlucky in either her ladies or her artist, for there was no comparison. As one critic wrote of the Knellers, if these were the beauties, God preserve us from the rest. In the **Second Presence Chamber** is a Tintoretto of 'Esther before Ahasuerus', jewellery glittering amid his typically heavy shadows, contrasting with Bassano's robustly rural 'Adoration' on the wall opposite. Two Tintorettos adorn the **Audience Room**, the 'Knight of Malta' and 'Nine Muses'. Here too is a magnificent Titian of 'The Lovers', hidden away in a far corner. It is a strangely timeless painting, one man has his hand tucked erotically inside the girl's dress while another gazes over her shoulder. What Venetian intrigue or Hapsburg court rivalry can have been its inspiration?

The **King's Drawing Room** contains more Italian masters: Titian's powerful 'Head of a Man' and Tintoretto's 'Head of an Old Man', the latter with the depth and serenity of a Rembrandt. The room also contains more rollicking Bassanos and works by Andrea del Sarto, Correggio and Lorenzo Lotto. But what are we to make of the **Bedroom**? Here William held his *levées*, alive with raucous Dutch voices, beneath a ceiling of supreme silliness. Verrio, an ardent Stuart, was always a reluctant painter for William and Mary, and Horace Walpole even suggested that he deliberately 'painted down' to them. Here William is regaled by Endymion asleep in the arms of Morpheus, while over the mantelpiece is a Lely of his mother-in-law posing with a flower in her hand. This was Anne Hyde, Clarendon's daughter, who became pregnant by the Duke of York, the future James II, secretly married him and thus became mother to two of England's most self-effacing (though not uninteresting) monarchs, Mary II and Anne.

Wren now turns the corner of the palace into the queen's rooms through a series of closets. These formed, in effect, the royal family's **Private Apartments** with their own staircases to the Privy Garden below. Though they lack the intimacy of, for instance, the Restoration closets at Ham, they must have been a blessèd relief from the pomposity of the audience rooms. Today they contain a number of early Old Masters, including Holbein's dramatic 'Noli Me Tangere' in the King's Dressing Room, a curiously stylized piece when compared with the vividly naturalistic 'school of Holbein' works round it. There is also a Mabuse (Jan Gossaert) of 'Adam and Eve' and a delicate Cranach of 'The Judgment of Paris', its lascivious soldiers and naked girls full of medieval sensuality. Queen Mary's closet beyond contains more Cranachs (or 'Cranachs') and a famous Breughel the Elder, the 'Massacre of the Innocents' with the children painted out by a later censor. The simple peasant figures and pure white snow, deprived of the horror of the murdered infants, now seem rather tame, the mothers' anguish inappropriate. Is it not time to restore the original?

The queen's *enfilade* was not completed by Wren until after Queen Mary's death in 1694 and was therefore decorated with the emblems of Anne and the first two Georges. The **Queen's Gallery** is a splendid room, given a greater warmth than the other state rooms by a complete Grinling Gibbons' carved cornice and by its wall tapestries. These were made in 1662 from Gobelins designs based on Le Brun paintings depicting scences from the life of Alexander the Great. Over the fireplace Alexander has a friendly encounter with Diogenes in his tub. The **Queen's Bedroom** dates from 1715 and is upholstered in faded red damask, faintly suggestive of a house of ill-repute. Here Thornhill had an opportunity to outdo his rival Verrio: he chose to depict Aurora in a chariot rising from the sea with Night and Sleep lying beneath. On the wall is a delightful Lely of James II's daughter, Princess Anne, as a child with a bird.

Next door in the **Drawing Room** this delicate girl has become a queen and Lely has become Verrio. Queen Anne is portrayed as Justice, surrounded by Peace, Plenty, Fame and other assorted deities. The Glorious Revolution clearly did nothing to restrain the Stuart daughters from imitating their father's self-glorification as denizens of Heaven. Over the marble mantelpiece stands Anne's sottish husband, George of Denmark, as Lord High Admiral, pointing his baton at the British fleet. Opposite him Cupid in a seashell rides the waves with the fleet again in the background. Swags, shells, fronds and fruit droop in luscious *trompe l'oeil* from the coving of the ceiling. For all its absurdity it is a breathtaking composition. When we turn to the windows we see Charles II's vistas stretching out across the Home Park and down the Long Water to Kingston. The effect of room and view together could not be more dramatic.

149

If Wolsey's palace was cornets and sackbuts, here are all Marlborough's trumpets and drums. This is the room which might have inspired Pope to his ironic lines on Hampton Court: 'Here thou, great Anna! whom three realms obey,/Dost sometimes counsel take – and sometimes tea.'

The **Queen's Audience Chamber** follows, a dark room with the chair of state facing away from us – it would normally have been approached from the far end. Here is a portrait of Henrietta Maria's dwarf, Jeffery Hudson, by Mytens. Hudson was a mere eighteen inches high when he was 'served up' to the King and Queen in a pie when they visited his home county of Rutland. At the age of thirty he suddenly grew to just over three feet, and had an adventurous life, being twice enslaved after capture at sea and even killing a man in a duel. He died in 1682 and his clothes are preserved in the Ashmolean Museum, Oxford.

With the **Public Dining Room** Hampton Court becomes Georgian. William Kent worked here in the 1730s and lays his classicism on with a trowel. The massive fireplace embraces the coat of arms of George II and the walls are adorned with heavy mouldings and cornices. The paintings in this room are by the Venetians, Sebastiano and Marco Ricci – tough enough to trade blow for blow with Kent's decoration.

The *enfilade* continues with the Prince of Wales' suite designed by Vanbrugh in 1716 for the future George II. Among its paintings are a triptych by Duccio, simple and serene after Wren's pyrotechnics, and a Gentile da Fabriano of the 'Madonna and Child'. In the Prince of Wales' bedroom is a magnificent four-poster designed by Robert Adam for Queen Charlotte. Its floral embroidery recalls the intricate needlework of the Gheeraerdts painting in the Wolsey rooms.

From here we pass through the queen's private chambers: a series of small rooms overlooking the Fountain Court, with on their right the Presence and Guard Chambers equivalent to those leading to the King's rooms at the start of the tour. Included in this sequence are two washrooms, still with their marble basins, and a delightful small **Chapel** in which the Queen's chaplain would have said morning prayers while she dressed. The chapel now contains some fine paintings, including two 'school of Leonardos' with all the master's clarity and expressiveness of colour. There is also a George de La Tour of 'St Jerome reading with a glass'. The ceiling is worked in ornate plaster, with hidden monkeys looking down with smirking faces on the devout beneath.

The **Cartoon Gallery** was built by Wren to house the Raphael cartoons illustrating the lives of St Peter and St Paul, acquired by Charles I and now hanging in the Victoria and Albert Museum. In their place are seventeenth-century tapestries copied from the cartoons and presented to the palace in 1905. This is the best room of all the Wren additions – he seems to have found deeper inspiration in Raphael than he did in the boorish House of Orange. On the dark panelling below the tapestries hang a number of Tudor portraits, including a remarkable one of Henry VIII with his last wife Catherine Parr, in a renaissance setting. The Princesses Mary and Elizabeth are beside them and the court fool, Will Somers, stands in the background. Here also are two paintings recording Henry's meeting with Francis I on the Field of the Cloth of Gold in 1519. Henry's ship, the *Great Harry*, and the pavilions, tents and elaborate fountains of the field itself are meticulously represented – one of the first summit conferences of which we have a pictorial record. Henry's head was shrewdly cut out of one of them by a Royalist during the Commonwealth to make them unsaleable, and replaced on the Restoration. The artist is unknown.

We now pass round the west side of the Fountain Court along the **Communicating Gallery**, adorned with Lely's famous court beauties. The collection includes two of Charles II's more prominent mistresses, Barbara Villiers and Frances Stuart, as well as more reputable members of the aristocracy, who must have had their doubts at being included in such company. The similarity between all these doe-eyed ladies suggests Lely knew which side the bread of Stuart flattery was buttered. A small door on the left leads us into the **Wolsey Cabinet**, a tiny remnant of the previous palace. The ceiling is composed of overlapping octagons containing Tudor badges and motifs, a celestial quilt of golds and blues. The murals are scenes from the Passion of Christ, though with later overpainting. It is one of the most perfect early renaissance rooms in England, a jewelled casket which must have danced and shone in the evening candlelight.

Beyond the Cabinet is a set of chambers granted to the Duke of Cumberland by George II as reward for his bloodthirsty victory over the Scots at Culloden – others rewarded him with the nickname 'Butcher'. The rooms had been designed by Kent for the king in

1732 and are in a restrained Palladian style more in keeping with a Georgian townhouse than a palace. The state bedroom, for instance, is almost domestic compared with the grand opera sets of Wren's suites.

We now re-enter the Tudor palace along the **Haunted Gallery**. The relevant ghost was (or is) that of Catherine Howard, fifth and most ill-used of Henry's wives. Simple and pretty – 'a rose without a thorn' – she was accused by her enemies of having secretly married another before becoming queen. A suspicious Henry was never allowed to hear her side of the case and she was condemned to death. Legend has it that shortly before her execution she broke free from her guards at Hampton and ran screaming along this passage searching for Henry, who was at his prayers, to plead her innocence. She never found him – so still she runs. The royal pew of Henry's **Chapel**, where her screams would have been plainly audible, is reached through a door in the gallery. Thanks to its redecoration under Queen Anne, this is now one of the most elaborate rooms in the palace, a rich fusion of Tudor Perpendicular and Wren's Baroque. Earthy wooden pendants drop from the ceiling, capped with trumpeting angels peering down as if from the gondolas of celestial balloons. A fresco by Thornhill rises above Wren's reredos, carved by Gibbons and alive with scrolls, cherubs, fruit and ribbons. It is not so much a chapel as a cornucopia. Outside the downstairs doorway are panels in which Wolsey's arms have been replaced by those of Henry and a monogram in which H & A (for Henry and Anne) has been crudely altered to H & J (for Jane Seymour).

Continuing round the Haunted Gallery we shake the dust of Wren firmly from our feet and reach the two last survivors of Henry's palace, the Watching Chamber and the Great Hall. The ceiling of the **Watching Chamber** is composed of a complex hexagonal pattern of ribs with Tudor pendants and badges. Hunting trophies adorn the upper part of the wall, while below hang Flemish tapestries dating from Wolsey's time and of great rarity. They represent the triumphs of Fate, Fame and Time – appropriately abstract renaissance subjects. Age has melded their blues, silvers and reds together to give the room a warm sophistication.

The Horn Room now leads us into Henry's **Great Hall**, which wholly supplanted Wolsey's predecessor. After all the chilly pomp and ceremony through which we have passed, it is reassuring to

Osterley Park, with Jacobean façade converted by Robert Adam in 1763 and (*below*) the Etruscan Dressing Room, Adam's virtuoso exercise in stylistic innovation. His enthusiasm for Etruscan motifs was shared with the potter, Josiah Wedgwood.

Left Hampton Court Palace, showing Wolsey's gatehouse, Henry VIII's Great Hall and the William and Mary ranges designed by Sir Christopher Wren beyond. In the distance stretches Charles II's 'goose foot' of radiating avenues.

Left below Wren symmetry masking Tudor ostentation above the entrance colonnade in the Clock Court.

Hampton Court: View across the Clock Court under Anne Boleyn's Gate into the Base Court; *below* A set of Tijou gates in the Park. 'Tijou could make hard iron burst into leaf and flower.'

end the tour of Hampton Court back at the focal point of any medieval palace. Here would have lived no distant monarch, but a dancing, eating, fighting king, mixing at the end of the day (at least for a while) with his courtiers and retainers. The fire blazes in the centre of the room, its smoke rising to lose itself in the rafters. The dignity of the royal dining table is signified only by a perpendicular bay window rising the full height of the wall. The ceiling is like an upturned galleon, reminiscent of the great church roofs of East Anglia, but distinguished by renaissance ornaments on the pendants and spandrels. Flemish tapestries of the story of Abraham adorn the walls, works which have been showered with superlatives, for their scale and for the intricacy of their craftsmanship. The nineteenth-century antiquarian, W. H. Hutton, remarked that 'Nothing like them has been produced till in our own day' – praise indeed from a Victorian. The only sadness is that this wonderful room should be kept so empty of people and laughter, the minstrels gallery silent overhead. Someone should use it for a really good party.

From the Great Hall we make our way back to the Base Court through what was in effect a large hotel: the king's beer and wine cellars (intermittently open to the public), the serving rooms, the Great Kitchen and Wolsey's Kitchen, and corridors of stores, pantries, laundries and stables. These supported a standing army of servants, even when the royal family and court were not in residence.

While the Palladian Renaissance was bringing about its revolution in English architecture, the ideas of the French gardeners, André Mollet and André Le Nôtre, brough back by Charles II after the Restoration, had a similar impact on the English garden. The Tudor **grounds** of Hampton Court had been a series of neat patios and arbours with behind them the extensive hunting grounds of Hampton and Bushy. Charles, although he left the palace itself unchanged, had Mollet lay out a giant *patte d'oie* (goose foot) to the east of the old buildings, similar to those laid out at Greenwich and St James's. Three avenues radiate from a central semi-circle, the middle one converted into a canal (the Long Water) by channelling a conduit from the Thames. Along their course were planted lime trees, and game was left to roam the spaces in between. It was the same effect as that which Carlo Rainaldi was producing at that time at the Porta de Popolo in Rome, though with architecture rather than nature.

Harrow-on-the-Hill, 'lost in a world of bridleways, rookeries, tuck shops and boaters, its patrician nose in the air'.

William and Mary's enthusiasm for rebuilding Hampton Court was equalled, if not surpassed, by their zest for redesigning the gardens. The Dutch influence now replaced the French, with plants supplied from the horticultural emporium of George London and Henry Wise at Kensington. Daniel Marot relaid Mollet's semi-circle as well as the Privy Garden with *parterres* of clipped box and yew. These miniature hedges were patterned into intricate scrollwork and acanthus leaves, embracing emblems of monarchy. Gravel paths wove round them and thirteen fountains danced across the scene. To the north of the palace, Henry Wise laid out a wilderness, an asymmetrical conceit of evergreen hedges full of doodles and mazes impossible to comprehend except from the upstairs rooms of the palace itself (on this front, never to be built).

The best approach to Hampton Court grounds is through the Fountain Court and directly out on to the 'heel' of the *patte d'oie*. From here, the seventeenth-century's formalism has taken on a slightly dishevelled maturity. The *parterres* have long since been replaced and the lime avenues have developed a more wayward profile. The yews of the Great Fountain Garden directly ahead of us were once tidy obelisks, leading the eye outwards to the vistas. They now stand about the Broadwalk like giant courtiers waiting for royal preferment. Round to the left, the wilderness has become a calm English orchard and Henry's old Tiltyard (with one watch-tower still standing) is a rose garden. But one relic of Wise's ingenuity survives, the triangular **maze** in the northern corner laid out in 1714. It is not the most complex of mazes, having only four blind alleys, and the centre should be reached in five minutes. However, the experience of Harris in *Three Men in a Boat* stands as an awful warning to over-confident visitors.

By turning right out of the Fountain Court we reach the **Privy Garden** and other gardens to the south of the Palace. From this point we can capture the full scale of Wren's two main façades, with twenty-three bays to the east and twenty-five to the south. His classical orders and elegant stone dressings put the homely Tudor palace quite out of mind. This is a scene created for an exile, of brick walls, gravel walks and rare evergreen plants intended to give off the scents of Holland. Today the evergreen has grown into a mysterious forest, making the garden seem more privy than ever. But Queen Mary's bower of wych-elm still runs down one side to where her Water Gallery once stood. Here she lived while she watched the new palace under construction and from here she supervised the apparently continuous replanting. Of this gallery nothing remains.

The river end of the Privy Garden is raised to display one of the finest works of art at Hampton Court, the screens commissioned by William from the French artist, Jean Tijou. The twelve panels produced in wrought iron the same combination of rococo form and naturalist content as Grinling Gibbons achieved in wood and Wren's Italian craftsmen in plaster. Grapes ripen, harps play, roses bloom and cherubs dance as if all spun from glass. Tijou could make hard iron break into leaf and burst into flower. What a pleasure it would have been to see him at work.

We now pass through into the **Tudor Gardens**, an intricate patchwork of steps, beds and shrubs, including the famous knot garden. They seek to recreate the original sixteenth-century intimacy, but not by means of authentic Tudor flowers (to the fury of some purists). Overlooking them is Queen Anne's orangery, and beyond is the **Greenhouse** containing the giant Hampton Court vine. Planted in 1769, its huge umbrella still produces up to six hundred bunches of grapes a year (sold to visitors in autumn), while its roots are reputed to stretch deep into the bed of the Thames. The gnarled profile of its trunk is a magnificent symbol of Hampton Court's living antiquity. Opposite, the **Lower Orangery** has been converted for the display of the Mantegna cartoons of the Triumph of Caesar, much repainted by Laguerre. Great treasures though they are, I find it hard to adjust to them after the domesticity of the gardens which surround them.

Hampton Court is so massive a monument that few visitors have the energy to search out the pleasures which lie round about it. **Bushy Park** was intended by Wren as the triumphal way to his new north front. Today it is one of the most forgotten parks in London. Its twin avenues of chestnut and lime, dotted with deer and refreshingly free of people, could be the discarded set for a period film. Fanelli's 'Diana' Fountain, sitting proudly on its pedestal by Wren, waits serenely for the drama to reach its climax. Yet the only drama is provided by the crows in the treetops and the noise of children in a distant playground.

Upstream of the palace and facing the Green, are a jolly cluster of barracks and other outbuildings, gradually merging into riparian villas and a jumble of boats and boathouses. Not to be missed is Hucks' Chalet, an original Swiss house imported by a boatbuilding firm at the turn of the century and re-erected on the banks of the Thames so carefully as to look like a pastiche. Beyond, the river begins to reassert itself and occasional stretches of park briefly recreate scenes from eighteenth-century Middlesex. Towards the village of Hampton, for instance, we enter David Garrick territory. The actor purchased an estate here in 1754 and had Robert Adam complete a new front to his house overlooking the river. In the gardens below, Capability Brown designed an octagonal temple to contain the statue of Shakespeare by Roubiliac for which Garrick, with characteristic egoism, offered himself as model. The setting is still recognizable from two charming Zoffany pictures (privately owned but much reproduced) showing Garrick and his friends desporting themselves on this same grass. The house is now divided into flats and a constant torrent of traffic cuts it off from the gardens.

Hampton Village is all but crushed by this traffic and must soon shudder completely into dust. But beyond it is a curiosity. This is the point at which, in the nineteenth century, Parliament permitted the metropolitan water companies to take water direct from the Thames for piping into the capital. The result is a sudden outcrop of Victorian industrial architecture. Most remarkable is the creeper-clad pumping station of the Southwark and Vauxhall Water Works Company, looking like some austere house of correction. Beyond stretch the filter beds and pumping houses of the other private companies. Today the Metropolitan Water Board holds sway over what are acres of reservoirs south to Molesey and west to Staines. From the air this part of London looks like a vast untamed lakeland. It has become a bird sanctuary of European importance, mercifully inaccessible to wingless bipeds.

CHAPTER TWELVE

Harrow

HARROW has always seemed to me an out-of-sorts place. In appearance it should be part of the cluster of hill-villages round the northern heights of London. Yet here it is, stranded on its mound above the flatlands of Middlesex, besieged on all sides by the red roofs of suburbia. Sometimes, when the moisture rises round it from the valleys of the Colne and the Brent, the hills of Stanmore and Bushey seem to reach out a helping hand in its direction. But Harrow always drifts away, lost in a world of bridleways, rookeries, tuck shops and boaters, its patrician nose in the air.

The area on which Harrow turns its back is one of the most remarkable developments in London's history: the series of estates which grew up along the path of the Metropolitan Railway in the years between the wars, known collectively as Metroland. The development was the result of a profitable alliance between property and housing companies and transport pioneers on land served by the Metropolitan Railway in the years after 1918. The railway itself ran from Baker Street through Neasden and Wembley and out to Harrow, Pinner, Northwood and Rickmansworth, with subsequent spurs to Ruislip and Watford. The estates were privately built, largely for owner-occupation. They had no particular architectural unity, though the 'Tudor' style was a favourite for communities which self-consciously saw themselves as 'villages'. They still have little to startle the modern tourist. But their appeal is growing at a time when such affectionate revivalism is back in fashion. We shall return to them at the end of this chapter.

First 'the hill', and the institution with which, since Elizabethan times, it has been synonymous, Harrow School. Just as the manorial commons protected Hampstead Heath from early development, so this landlord has defied the encircling army of development with an outer bailey of woods and playing fields. The old village within is a curiously isolated community, increasingly dependent on its

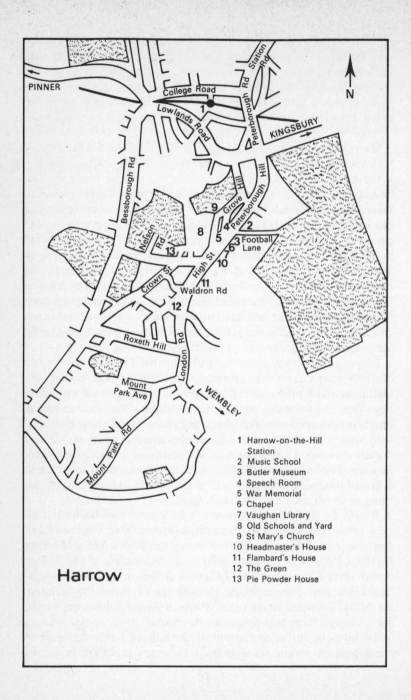

PINNER

College Road

Lowlands Road

KINGSBURY

Peterborough Rd

Station Rd

1

Bessborough Rd

Grove Hill

Peterborough Hill

9

8

4

2

5

3 Football Lane

Nelson Rd

13

6

High St

10

Crown St

11

Waldron Rd

12

Roxeth Hill

London Rd

WEMBLEY

Mount Park Ave

Mount Park Rd

N

1 Harrow-on-the-Hill
  Station
2 Music School
3 Butler Museum
4 Speech Room
5 War Memorial
6 Chapel
7 Vaughan Library
8 Old Schools and Yard
9 St Mary's Church
10 Headmaster's House
11 Flambard's House
12 The Green
13 Pie Powder House

Harrow

one industry, the school, and therefore empty of much of its life in the vacations. It is approached either uphill from the underground station or along the famous Harrow Road from London to the south-east. We shall take the former route, which means a bracing climb up rural Peterborough Road into the heart of the school 'campus'.

Harrow School was founded in 1571 by John Lyon for local boys – he specified, not girls. There were no fees but Lyon allowed that if the £30 a year salary was insufficient the master could take in 'foreigners' as borders to supplement his income. These foreigners inevitably came to take up more and more places, dominating the institution and eventually establishing its national reputation. Local people complained so bitterly at being deprived of their legacy that in 1874 the governors felt obliged to found the Lower School of John Lyon at the bottom of the hill to carry out their founder's intentions (this school is now run by the local authority). The original foundation saw its greatest expansion between 1845 and 1885, under two of those awesome headmasters who seem to bestride Victorian education, Dr Vaughan and Dr Butler. These men were responsible for most of the present school buildings.

As we climb Peterborough Road, Harrow's distinctive version of 1860s architecture is immediately apparent. On the left are the Garlands, the Knoll and Hillside, dormitory houses in which the boys sleep, while eating and studying communally. Their coloured brickwork, stepped gables and bargeboard dormers do little to relieve their somewhat forbidding façades. The architect of most of these dormitories was C. F. Hayward, a brother of one of the house-masters. They are hardly homes from home, and must have made a grim impression on homesick small boys clambering from the London coach on a dark autumn night.

Kinder by far is the architecture of E. S. Prior and Basil Champneys of two decades later, represented farther up in Football Lane by the former's Music Schools (1890) and the latter's Butler Museum (1886). Champneys' museum is an excellent example of the 'Queen Anne' revival at its best: bold Flemish gables, jolly oriel windows and a dramatic open staircase running the height of the building. As Mark Girouard remarks, it is 'like a Board School on which, for a change, there was money to be spent'.

Turning the corner at the top of the hill, we reach the heart of the school. A plaque set into the wall warns us: 'Take heed, the first recorded motor accident in Great Britain involving the death of the driver occurred on Grove Hill on February 25th 1899.' Harrovian sportscar enthusiasts roar past it unimpressed. Down Grove Hill to the right are more boarding houses, as well as the Art Schools, where the young Winston Churchill learned to paint. A plaque on the wall (Harrow has more wall plaques than anywhere in London) commemorates a visit from Charles I in 1646. Legend has it that he watered his horse on this spot, looked towards London and decided its Roundhead sympathies made it too risky a destination. He turned back towards Oxford and eventual defeat.

Next to the Art Schools is the **Speech Room** designed in 1872 by William Burges. It has one façade flush with the street and a semi-circular rear, recreating the effect of a Greek theatre. The school had asked for a light building and tall spires to harmonize with the chapel opposite. But Burges, architect of Cardiff Castle, was not the man for such stylistic deference. Like many of his structures this ponderous work has a curiously Moorish aspect. It is, however, the venue for one of the most emotive events in the English public school calendar, Harrow School Songs. It was to this that Sir Winston Churchill would return each year to bellow out his favourite lines:

> Forty years on, when afar and asunder, parted are those
> who are singing today,
> When you look back and forgetfully wonder, what you
> were like in your work and your play,
> Then it may be there will often come over you, glimpses
> of notes like the catch of a song,
> Visions of boyhood shall float them before you, echoes of
> dreamland shall bear them along.

The Prime Minister would weep copiously.

Next door is the **War Memorial**, built in 1926 to commemorate the Harrow dead of the First World War. It was designed by Sir Herbert Baker, architect of South Africa House in Trafalgar Square. He was not the most inspired of classical revivalists, but this is a friendly structure, stylistically a cross between a Flemish town hall and the Tudor of the Old Schools next door.

The architectural notes now become discordant. The **Chapel** opposite was built in 1854 by Sir Gilbert Scott, architect of the Foreign Office and St Pancras Station. If nothing else, Harrow chapel demonstrates his versatility. It is based on the Ste Chapelle in Paris, from which he borrowed the tall apse windows and the spindly *flèche* on the roof. Next door is the **Vaughan Library**, also designed by Scott but ten years later. Its foundation stone was laid by Lord Palmerston, another old boy, in 1861. Palmerston was Prime Minister at the time. Though aged 77, he rode down from London on a white horse in driving rain, performed the ceremony, refused all hospitality and promptly rode straight back again. The building's exterior is redbrick with patterned encaustic tiles and blind arcading along the ground-floor wall. The Gothic here is simpler, the window tracery more plain; a good illustration of the evolution of the style in mid-century from a pure revivalism to greater independence of spirit. But this collection of buildings does not make a happy essay in Victorian architecture. The materials clash, and despite the obvious effort by each architect to fit his work into the setting, the effect is of four egotists all talking at the same time. For relief, we may slip between chapel and library to where the gardens sweep down to the football fields and swimmimg pool (Duckers to Harrovians) in the distance. Ahead stretches a magnificent view across the Weald towards Hampstead and the towers of London.

Returning to the main street, we come to Harrow yard and the **Old Schools**. This is where boys assemble for rollcall (or Bill) in front of John Lyon's original schoolroom. The left wing contains the room itself, built in 1615, and the right wing of 1820 is a copy of it. Access to the building, as to all the school premises, is not easy. It is possible only during term on prior application to the Custos. But the old schoolroom is worth the effort. Now renamed the fourth form room, it is a remarkable relic of early English education: panelled, with a throne for the master, a large fireplace and continuous benches running lengthways for the boys. Books had to be balanced on knees. A cupboard stands ready to reveal the birch. Four Prime Ministers – Palmerston, Aberdeen, Peel and Churchill – are among the boys who have carved their names on the schoolroom panels. The right wing of the building contains a small art gallery containing works by a mixed bag of Romney, Tillemans, Turner, Girtin, Cotman and two old boys, Churchill and Victor Pasmore (open variably during the school term). It was from one of these windows, so another plaque tells us, that the young Lord Shaftesbury was horrified to see a pauper's funeral procession pass by on its way to church. The wretched and drunken pallbearers dropped their load right in front of the school. So moved was the boy by this sight that he dedicated his life to the relief of poverty. Shaftesbury's memorial now stands in the heart of the West End: the Eros statue and the avenue which bears his name.

The church to which the coffin was travelling was **St Mary's**, up Church Hill directly behind the Old Schools. The church stands on the site of an ancient pagan temple – for which the Saxon is *hearg*, reputedly the origin of the name Harrow. There are fragments of a Norman arch and chevron tracery at the base of the tower. The nave and chancel are thirteenth century, transepts and clerestory are Perpendicular. But the most famous feature is the spire, medieval and encased in lead. It can be seen from every vantage point in London and has a beacon on top to warn off low-flying pilots. St Mary's is a big church, extended by the ubiquitous Scott in the nineteenth century. He restored it heavily, covering it in his favourite flint, and as a result it seems more Victorian than medieval. Vandalism has led to its closure except for services, but it contains some excellent brasses, including one of John Lyon himself in sixteenth-century dress, flanked by his wife.

The **churchyard** is a peaceful sanctuary famous for the inspiration it gave another famous Harrovian, Lord Byron. It was his practice to sit on the 'Peachey tomb' and gaze out westward over the Thames valley:

> Again I behold where for hours I have pondered,
> As reclining at eve on yon tombstone I lay;
> Or round the steep brow of the churchyard I wandered,
> To catch the last gleam of the sun's setting ray.

So many latter-day Byrons have sought inspiration from the same tomb that it has been encased in an ugly iron cage. Below is a small terrace from which we can look down over the fields to the shoreline of suburbia lapping at our feet. The view is currently marred by a huge gasholder with the letters NO written on it – not a gesture of despair but a pilot's pointer to Northolt Aerodrome.

From here we walk back through the school to Harrow itself, imagining if we can the rows of medieval cottages which must once have linked village and church before the growth of the school. The first building on the right after Old Schools is Druries House, again 'Harrovian grim' in style, but with a curious recessed bay at the back whose architectural significance eludes me totally.

Opposite is the more sedate Headmaster's House. Then, quite suddenly, we are in a simple Georgian high street. After so much Victoriana, it is like coming across an old friend again. There is nothing special about Harrow **High Street**. There are simply no jarring notes, and in modern London this is sufficiently rare to catch our attention.

On the right as we enter the High Street is a branch of Gieves the tailors, a school shop of blazers, flannels and boaters. A discreet pair of jeans may be displayed in a side window. Beyond it is a shop called the Round House, a treasure trove of books, timetables and bric-a-brac for the railway enthusiast. Here you can buy early telegraph equipment, signal arms or porters' caps, and find out which engine pulled the night mail to Crewe in any year you care to mention. Opposite is Flambards House, a handsome Georgian residence on the site of the old manor house. It takes its name from a local family who first rose to prominence as financial advisers to William Rufus (there is a Flambard brass in the church). On the left stands The Park, built early in the last century for Lord Northwick, whose family were lords of the local manor throughout the eighteenth and nineteenth centuries. It has been part of the school for many years, and its garden has another fine view out over London. Nos. 25–33 High Street have well-preserved early-Victorian shopfronts, spoiled only by the use of plate glass in their windows. Nos. 29–31 is the Harrow School Tuck Shop.

We now reach the **Green** in front of the King's Head pub, from which the London coach used to depart. It is still a lively place, with wisteria and ivy outside and thick brown panelling in its bars. The king in question was Henry VIII, who reputedly used the building as a hunting box. The King's Head enjoyed an hour of dubious glory in the 1970s when feminists demonstrated against its 'men only' bar. A house on the far side of the Green with urns set into its façade is an essay in the history of suburban entertainment. It has been successively a dance hall, a music hall, and a series of cinemas with such names as the Elite, the Cosy and the Cosy-Carlton. Between the wars it found custom hard to come by and even tried running a free bus service for patrons from the suburbs down the hill. It finally closed in 1939. The building has now reopened as a Steak House – *O tempora, O mores.*

Harrow High Street now becomes the London Road, lined with trees, large houses and, increasingly, blocks of flats. A quarter of a mile along, just past the junction with Roxeth Hill, is the entrance to the **Mount Park Estate**, developed in the 1880s in the grounds of a house called the Mount, now a convent. It was one of the earliest developments of north-west London's pre-Metroland period and contains a number of houses in the 'Queen Anne' style. Here the gables, oriel windows and stone porches of Pont Street and Melbury Road are transported to what was then secluded woodland. There are no numbers here, just names such as The Oaks, St Margarets, Egerton and Duneaves – with a blue plaque on the last to commemorate the the residence of R. M. Ballantyne, author of the sort of schoolboy adventure stories which fit suitably into a Harrovian setting.

Returning to the centre of town, we turn left down Waldron Road just to the right of the King's Head, into Crown Street and **West Street**. This curious working-class neighbourhood was the site of the annual Harrow Fair, a lucrative and rowdy privilege first granted the town in 1262 and not discontinued until 1850, when the terraces of Nelson Road sprouted on the hillside in its place. West Street itself has some attractive half-timbered cottages. Here the Harrow Gazette was published, owned for a while by the local Member of Parliament, Sir Oswald Mosley.

Hidden away amid factory buildings behind an old terracotta schoolroom lies the Tudor **Pie Powder House**. In this building, medieval courts used to pass summary justice on those visiting the fair – the name is derived from *Pieds Poudres* or dusty feet. From here we can walk back up the hill over a field known as High Capers. Beneath us, on the other side of Bessborough Road, lies a small building, weather-boarded and with a red-tiled roof, in a row of suburban houses. This architectural chameleon is the ancient Roxeth Farm, guarding its memories of open meadows and country lanes.

The railway first arrived in the Harrow Weald as early as 1838: Robert Stephenson's famous London and Birmingham on its way down to Euston. But the residents of Harrow Village forced the company to divert the track well away from the hill and place its station at Harrow and Wealdstone, a mile to the north. Half a century later, Harrovians received the Metropolitan Line with greater hospitality, though it was not until electrification in 1905 that building began in earnest in the fields round the foot of the hill. Within two decades, Harrow was enveloped by the great tide of **Metroland** as it swept outwards from Neasden and Wembley to engulf fields, woods, villages and churches in concrete and brick. Or almost engulf, for the builders of Metroland sought meticulously to maintain '*rus in urbe*', to give their customers the illusion that this was not town at all, just as their Georgian predecessors had done in Bloomsbury or Regent's Park. Alan Jackson, in his study of early suburbia, has recalled some of their advertisements: 'A village green, a beautiful old church, a little moss-grown churchyard, long vistas of green fields ... you can have your home in the old rectory garden.' You could indeed – until everyone else came after you. Some of the earliest estates were truly bucolic (Pinner or Moor Park, for instance), their detached 'Tudorbethan' houses surrounded by large gardens shaded from each other by mature trees. Less satisfying was the subsequent development, where builders sold off subsidiary plots and mediocre estates were crammed into whatever land had proved less attractive initially.

Two routes out through north-west London can be recommended to enthusiasts. The road to Harrow is dominated by one of London's most famous inter-war monuments, **Wembley Stadium**. Built in 1923 by the firm of Simpson and Ayrton, its four domed towers and scruffy concrete detailing have become the nostalgic symbol of the great days of English soccer – of a world of Brylcreem, shin pads and goalies in flat caps. The stadium was joined by the British Empire Exhibition of 1924, laid out on land to its north and intended as a permanent memorial to imperial achievement. It never attained permanence, but a number of its pavilions remain as gaunt shells along the Empire Way, sprouting occasional Egyptian doorways, classical pediments and even imperial lions. On the hillside above it, the Metroland suburb of Wembley Park looks down in disdain.

From here the early Metropolitan Line ran out through Northwick Park and Harrow to **Pinner**. Here was the paragon of Metroland, a real Tudor high street, a medieval church and a scatter of farms and cottages. There was even – and still is – an original moated manor house and tithe barn situated a mile to the east at Headstone. The infilling of Pinner High Street with neo-Tudor shops and other buildings has been sensitively done. A medieval barn has been converted into a steak house and the two ancient pubs, the Victory and the Queen's Head, claim doubtful association with Nelson and Nell Gwynn respectively. At the top of the street stands St John's Church – heavily restored Tudor with quaint dormers in the nave

165

roof. In its churchyard is an extraordinary monument built by the garden architect, John Loudon, for his parents, who had wished to be buried above ground. The coffin is halfway up an obelisk.

From here, a pleasant walk of under a mile leads up Church Lane to the right of St John's, left into Moss Lane and back via Paines Lane. It takes us past Church Farm, the Vicarage, Pinner House and a series of Tudor cottages almost indistinguishable from their twentieth-century imitators. In Moss Lane is East End Farm, an immaculately preserved group of rural buildings dating from the sixteenth century. This is how Metroland was meant to be. No one should sneer at London's suburbs who has not walked the lanes of Pinner.

The second route runs north of Wembley, where Kingsbury and Queensbury stretch tediously towards the hills of Stanmore. At **Kingsbury**, however, are two remarkable churches, both dedicated to St Andrew and both sharing the same churchyard. The older one, situated at the rear of the site, is medieval with early-Norman walls. The larger Victorian building was transported here stone by stone in 1933 as its former congregation, in Wells Street Marylebone, was contracting – many of them doubtless fleeing to these same suburbs. Begun in 1847 by Dawkes and Hamilton, it was famous as a centre of Anglo-Catholic worship and thus became a treasure house of High Church art. As a result here in Kingsbury we have a pulpit and chancel screen by Street, a litany desk by Burges, a lectern by Butterfield, a font cover by Pearson and an east window by Pugin!

Farther north, we enter the former estates of the eighteenth-century Duke of Chandos. Nothing now survives of his magnificent home of Canons, apart from fragments scattered all over southern England (including the gate to Hampstead parish church). But its opulence lives on in **St Lawrence Whitchurch Lane**, near Canons Park tube station. This is one of the oddest churches in Middlesex, entirely due to Chandos. Apart from the Tudor tower, the church dates from 1715 and is in the sort of Baroque one would expect in Italy or Germany rather than England. It is decorated by Laguerre, but the effect is gloomy rather than elevating, not helped by bulky box pews vigorously asserting English social stratification. The Chandos mausoleum, with the duke in marble glory, is to one side.

Stanmore itself contains a romantically ruined church and two

buildings of historical importance. **Bentley Priory** is an eighteenth-
and nineteenth-century house which became the headquarters of
R.A.F. Fighter Command in the war. It was gutted by fire in 1979,
but is now being rebuilt. East of Bentley Priory, a series of country
lanes brings us to **Grims Dyke**. This began as the fortification for
probably a Saxon camp. More noticeable is the house of the same
name, built in 1872 by Richard Norman Shaw for W. S. Gilbert
(his operatic partner, Arthur Sullivan, lived in an equally extraordinary house in Harrington Gardens, Kensington). The house
is characteristic of Norman Shaw's early period – Tudor half-
timbering, tile-hanging, steep gables and tall chimneys. The luxuriant
gardens contain the lake in which the elderly Gilbert died of a heart
attack while trying to rescue a child. The house is now an excellent
restaurant.

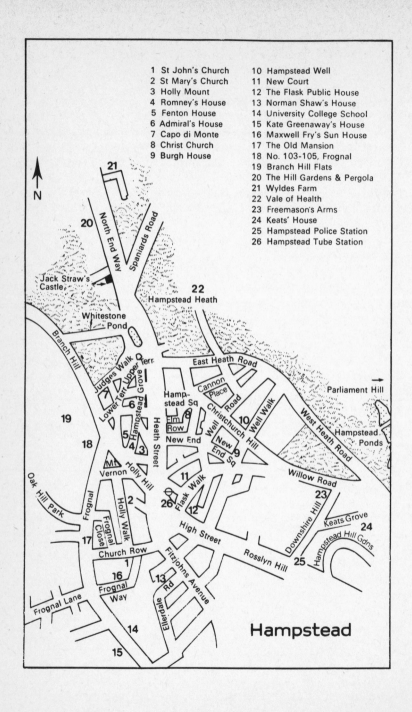

1 St John's Church
2 St Mary's Church
3 Holly Mount
4 Romney's House
5 Fenton House
6 Admiral's House
7 Capo di Monte
8 Christ Church
9 Burgh House
10 Hampstead Well
11 New Court
12 The Flask Public House
13 Norman Shaw's House
14 University College School
15 Kate Greenaway's House
16 Maxwell Fry's Sun House
17 The Old Mansion
18 No. 103-105, Frognal
19 Branch Hill Flats
20 The Hill Gardens & Pergola
21 Wyldes Farm
22 Vale of Health
23 Freemason's Arms
24 Keats' House
25 Hampstead Police Station
26 Hampstead Tube Station

N

Hampstead

CHAPTER THIRTEEN

Hampstead I

HAMPSTEAD is an easy place with which to fall in love. It offers the perfect fusion of urban bustle and rural privacy, as if all the elements of English townscape had been tossed in the air and fallen on this hillside with hardly a piece out of place. The people of Hampstead – pump-room rowdies, 'Bohemian' commuters, left-wing intellectuals – are merely its passing phantoms. The lasting Hampstead is a maze of steps, alleyways, turnings and sudden views. It is sprays of clematis, wisteria, ivy and holly scattering sunlight on to red brick and white stucco. It is grand mansions, terraced cottages, Victorian extravagance and workhouse simplicity contained within a surprisingly intact eighteenth- and nineteenth-century hill town, defended on three sides by a rambling heath and on the fourth by the stern ramparts of Italianate Belsize Park. The twentieth century has lobbed an occasional grenade over these ramparts. But Hampstead's defenders have become increasingly adept at lobbing them back. For once, it is probable that the town we see today is the town we shall bequeath to our descendants.

The pleasures of Hampstead are not those of a set piece. They are for a lifetime's strolling rather than a day's brisk walk, and choosing a suitable route for the latter is not easy. My first walk takes in the heart of Hampstead (two to three hours) and the second covers the outskirts and the Heath itself (three to four hours).

Hampstead has always been a suburb and no one fastidious about that term should pretend otherwise. It first developed round the springs which found their way down its swampy slopes to the Thames via the Tyburn brook and the Fleet river. They formed the basis of its earliest industry, laundering, and of its earliest fame as a spa for London day trippers. Its main spine was and still is the old road to Hendon from Charing Cross and its hub is the junction of Heath Street and the High Street where Hampstead tube station now stands. The station itself, for all its London Transport dowdiness, is a period piece. Opened in 1907, it is the deepest in London, with ancient lifts plunging passengers into the bowels of the hill, but providing a useful air-raid shelter during the War. Its 'self-cleaning' tiles, green inside and ox-blood red outside, are typical of the Northern Line in its heyday. The gusts of warm, dusty air which blow from its entrance are a reminder that, whatever fancies Hampstead may have in store for us, it is pinned firmly to the Metropolis.

The crossroads of Heath and High Street look deceptively urban. They were rebuilt and widened late in the 1880s, an early instance of metropolitan slum clearance, while at the same time Heath Street was pushed through a jumble of ancient courtyards to link with the newly-built Fitzjohn's Avenue (see p. 181 below). This redbrick, gabled redevelopment probably did more to protect Hampstead from twentieth-century spoliation (which tends to prey on Georgian high street properties) than any amount of preservationist activity. The best of these buildings is the old fire station at the foot of Holly Hill. Built by George Vulliamy (master architect of Victorian fire stations) in 1870, its famous clock must have traced the passing hours for a thousand assignations 'outside the tube station'.

Crossing the road, we proceed down Heath Street's southern extension past the Everyman cinema. **Church Row** on the right comprises (with restoration) an almost perfect early-Georgian ensemble. The Row dates from the 1720s when Hampstead was finding its feet as a health resort. Most of the houses are of the same period with brown bricks and red dressings, segment-headed windows and simple hooded doorcases on ornate brackets. Many of the iron railings are original, with stands for the linkmen's torches. Nos. 16 and 17, however, are a later development. The windows here are straight-headed and recessed into the wall – a reflection of the 1709 Building Act which outlawed exposed woodwork round windows as a fire risk. Yet if all the houses are of the same period, why this difference in conforming to the regulations? The house at No. 5 on the north side of the street, with weatherboarding and an oversailed first floor, looks earlier but is in fact later than the rest – presumably a resident eager for a bit of extra room.

Church Row culminates in **St John's Church**, like St Mary's Harrow a famous London spire with an equally secluded church-yard. It stands picturesque behind a pair of intricate iron gates brought from the Duke of Chandos' demolished mansion at Canons in Stanmore. It was begun in 1744 (later than Church Row) by a man named John Sanderson, on the site of a medieval structure. A better-known local architect, the Palladian Henry Flitcroft, offered to design a new church free of charge provided there was no competition involved. But the parish declined this offer. The tower is set at its east end, unusually for an Anglican church, rising not behind the main pediment in the style of St Martin-in-the-Fields but through it. Together with the battlemented tower, this gives the façade a toughness in which some have seen echoes of Hawksmoor. The interior, usually locked, is barrel-vaulted with Ionic columns rising through the gallery, a rather frigid composition.

The **churchyard** is a total contrast. It is packed with the tombs of Hampstead's citizens and thick with evergreen. Many graves are helpfully inscribed with the achievements of their occupants – a favourite of mine is that of John Harrison (d. 1776) near the south transept, who, though an untrained north countryman, became the leading clock inventor of his day, solving the problem of producing an accurate clock for estimating longitude at sea. So scornful of his background were the authorities that they withheld from him the promised reward for his achievement, until eventually both the king and parliament interceded on his behalf. The best-known grave is that of the painter, John Constable (d. 1837), and his wife and children. Constable's name crops up in the history of almost every part of Hampstead, renting one house after another from 1819 until his death. Like many Hampstead artists, Constable kept on his London house in Fitzroy Square as a studio but found the air on the hill so agreeable that he and his family spent more and more time there and it became their favourite home. 'Here let me take my everlasting rest,' he said of the place. Though Hampstead does not figure quite as prominently as Flatford or Salisbury in the Constable iconography, his pictures of the Heath at the Tate and the Victoria and Albert Museum are among the finest memorials of the town's past.

From the churchyard we now walk up Holly Walk to **Holly Place**. This enclave dates from the early 1800s and was the centre of a French community of some two hundred people who fled here from the Revolution (others settled in Marylebone and Somers Town). St Mary's Church was built in 1816 by the French Abbé Morel, who had arrived in Hampstead in 1796. It was one of the first Roman Catholic churches to be built in England since the Reformation, and forms the centrepiece of a cluster of brick and stucco terraces of West Country quaintness. Not for these *émigrés* the dinner tables of the Mayfair aristocracy, but instead the homely intimacy of Prospect Place, Benham's Place and Hollyberry Lane. Even the modern houses opposite seem to smile inoffensively on the scene. At the corner of Hollyberry Lane stands Hampstead's old watch-house. The decorated arch to the main door looks pleasantly amateur, perhaps the work of a local craftsman on his day off?

The path leads up to Mount Vernon, named after George III's *aide-de-camp*, who was Governor of the Tower of London and possessed of 'the worst temper of any man'. On the left is Mount Vernon House, sharing with most of Hampstead's better mansions the characteristic of hiding behind both a high wall and a thick coating of ivy. Ahead is Holly Hill, which was – and for some daring drivers still is – the main track over the hill from the High Street. Its steep incline must have been churned into a quagmire on wet days before the invention of tarmac. Clambering down its bank we reach **Holly Mount** on the far side, marked by a sign pointing to the Holly Bush pub. The latter is unspoilt inside and has a frosted glass window announcing it improbably as a coffee house. Beyond is a typical Hampstead backwater. Some of the houses date from the seventeenth century. No. 16 was the town's first Baptist chapel, now converted into an artist's studio. Next to it, Holly Bush Steps lead down to Heath Street, Montmartre style. Halfway down is Golden Yard, filled with colourful hydrangeas in summer.

Retracing our steps to Holly Hill, we reach Hampstead Grove, passing on the right the house built as a studio by the artist George Romney in 1797. Romney came to Hampstead partly to escape the pollution and expense of central London and partly to escape its distractions. After a career of portraiture, he now sought inspiration, in his biographer's words, for 'the vast historical conceptions for which all this travail has been undergone'. He found only illness and depression and eventually packed up his paints and went home to his family in Kendal. The house was subsequently converted into lecture rooms where speakers such as Constable and Faraday would address the early Hampstead intelligentsia. In 1929 the antiquarian architect Clough Williams Ellis redesigned it as his own residence, before disappearing to north Wales to create a less orthodox fantasy at Portmeirion. Opposite is one of those astonishments which only the Victorians would dare perpetrate. I suppose age and broadmindedness have rendered the National Institute for Medical Research nearly toᵢᵤrable, but not quite – have I seen its original somewhere on the Loire? Windmill Hill, overlooking the small green in front of it, is dominated by four large and much-altered Georgian townhouses of about 1730. The view from their upper rooms is superb.

Now for Hampstead Grove proper. According to Christopher Wade (whose *Streets of Hampstead* is a masterpiece of local history), the cottages on the right, Nos. 4 to 14, could well have medieval foundations dating from the time when the monks of Westminster would have visited their property here on the hill. Their attraction is of the chocolate box variety.

Fenton House, behind the long wall opposite, was built in 1695 and is 'William and Mary' at its best – before the Palladians crushed much of the gaiety out of London architecture. Its steep-pitched roof, strangely nautical balconies on the street façade, undersized pediment and oversized cornice all seem utterly cheerful. Even the classical colonnade tacked on to the side when the entrance was moved there after 1800 manages to add to the welcome. (The house is open Wednesday to Saturday 11.00 to 5.00, Sundays 2.00 to 5.00, weekends only in winter). Little is known of the house's early owners, but it takes its name from the Fenton family, City merchants who acquired it in 1793. It was James Fenton who convened the first meeting of Hampstead residents at the Hollybush Tavern in 1829 to fight for the preservation of the Heath. The house has remained virtually unaltered since. It retains much of its old panelling and a fine staircase with twisted balusters and fluted handrail.

When Fenton House was left to the National Trust by Lady Binning in 1952, it acquired both her collection of furniture and porcelain and the Benton Fletcher Collection of **Musical Instruments**. The instruments were first assembled by an army officer, Major George Benton Fletcher, who held strongly to the view that classical music should be played on contemporary instruments. Each room in the house now contains one or more of his harpsichords, spinets or virginals, frequently with students practising on them. The main dining room downstairs is used for concerts, with the largest eighteenth-century harpsichord ever made in England, a Burkat Shudi of 1770. The Porcelain Room has collections of Chelsea and Meissen, including a fine Harlequin set of the latter. But my favourite room is the Fentons' **Drawing Room** on the first floor. London

173

is surprisingly poor in domestic interiors open to the public, but here is a modest survival of the taste of a wealthy merchant of the Regency period. The room is filled with satinwood furniture, embroidered fireguards, Worcester porcelain and needlework pictures. It requires only a Jane Austen heroine to pose in one of its chairs, waiting for a suitor to call. Up above, the attic rooms are cluttered with instruments in various states of repair. From their windows, there are marvellous views over London. To look out from here, when the house is silent but for the soft playing of a harpsichord below, is to enjoy one of those moments of private romance which all cities should be able to offer, but so few can.

The **grounds** of Fenton House are still intact inside their original walls. The front garden runs down to the ornamental gates on Windmill Hill designed by Jean Tijou, and at the back is an extensive terrace walk round what would have been a seventeenth-century *parterre*. It is a good place for children to play while parents visit the house.

Continuing up Hampstead Grove we pass Old Grove House, a Georgian mansion with a colossal Tuscan doorway and secluded garden and New Grove House attached to it. The latter is also eighteenth century but was given a Tudor veneer in the 1840s. It was the last of the four houses in the district occupied by George du Maurier, whose novel *Peter Ibbetson* contains a number of Hampstead scenes. Du Maurier is best remembered for his *Punch* cartoons – the most famous of which was 'The Curate's Egg'. His son, the actor Sir Gerald du Maurier, created Captain Hook in the first Peter Pan in 1904. To our right, the narrow lanes of **The Mount** run down towards Heath Street. This was the area whose 'little square of slum houses' so detracted from the charms of New Grove House for du Maurier's novelist granddaughter, Daphne. They are slums no more, and today are admired and photographed while the old house itself is increasingly decrepit.

Opposite the entrance to The Mount stands **Admiral's House**, named after Admiral Matthew Barton, who died in 1795. He had the distinction of being shipwrecked naked on the Barbary coast, enslaved by the Moors, ransomed by the British government, court-martialled for losing his ship, acquitted and eventually promoted admiral. Since by then his health had understandably collapsed, he took his command to Hampstead and constructed a bridge-like balcony on the top of his house. Here he installed two cannons, firing them at moments of naval celebration to the consternation of his neighbours. The house was subsequently lived in by the Victorian architect Sir Gilbert Scott, begetter of the Foreign Office, St Pancras Station and the Albert Memorial. Next door, at **Grove Lodge**, a blue plaque records the residence of the novelist John Galsworthy from 1918 until his death in 1933. Here he completed *The Forsyte Saga*. I like to think of Scott and Galsworthy, artists whose creations span and symbolize what we think of as the Victorian age, working peacefully in this backwater of Georgian taste.

Opposite these two houses a short rustic path leads past an old brewhouse to Windmill Hill. There are, I am told, the tombstones of an old dogs' cemetery buried in the undergrowth here, but I have not found them. Two modern houses at the junction of Admiral's Walk and Windmill Hill have suitably nautical names, Fleet House and Broadside, the latter in a style which is best described as Pasadena Vernacular.

The area was, as its name suggests, once covered with windmills, none of which survives. Instead, a typically Hampstead grouping of cottages, terraces and secluded mansions leads us up to Judges Walk and our first taste of the Heath. The Walk takes its name from a tradition that High Court judges, fleeing the plague, held their sessions here in the 1660s – a tradition, says James Thorne (writing in 1876), which is 'seemingly a very modern one'. The tiny heathside cottage on our left is famous both for its name, Capo di Monte, and the S over its door, recalling a stay by the actress Sarah Siddons in 1804. From here is a panorama of Harrow and the hills above Stanmore, the setting for many of Constable's best-known Hampstead canvases. In summer there are donkey rides for children along to Whitestone Pond.

We leave the Heath to our next walk and return via Upper Terrace and the old reservoir to the top of Heath Street. Here on summer weekends, local artists display their wares; the style is patently chosen to appeal to tourists, though it is better than the sort of work found along Bayswater Road. Down the hill, Turpins Restaurant commemorates one of the more famous villains to frequent the Heath. Next to it and gentler by far is the Quaker Meeting House. Hampstead has always had a substantial Quaker community. Joshua Gee, an early resident of Fenton House, had Quaker connections, as did the banker Samuel Hoare, who lived at Heath House by Jack Straw's Castle. The Meeting House was designed by a member of another prominent Quaker family, Fred Rowntree, in 1907.

Beside it, a narrow lane leads down to Hampstead Square – all brick walls hung with greenery – and Christ Church, constructed in 1852 to relieve the pressure on St John's in Church Row. In those days the district immediately beneath the church was composed largely of slums, and a marked social divide must have separated the two churches. It is a solid Victorian Gothic structure, its spire a notable landmark on this side of the town. Before descending into New End, we persevere through the Square to find **Elm Row**, a line of houses of the same period and scale as Church Row. Anywhere but Hampstead, Elm Row would be an architectural celebrity. Here it merely winks at the passer-by and retreats into itself.

Now comes an abrupt change of character. A flight of steps opposite Elm Row leads down to the entrance of the New End Hospital. This building began life in the 1830s as a workhouse but was later converted into a hospital with a neo-baroque façade and novel circular wards. It is still in use as a hospital today. Farther down **New End**, a wall plaque commemorates a dispensary and soup kitchen established here in 1853 and gives thanks to God for sparing New End from a cholera epidemic at the time. Towering over the southern dogleg of the street is the Edwardian elementary school, a large structure built in 1906 in what was Brewhouse Lane – renamed Streatley Place in an effort to raise local morale. The school's four corner towers rise up on the hillside, stone dressings above the windows imitating the rays of the sun.

New End leads round into New End Square where **Burgh House** stands almost entombed in council flats. The house was built in 1703 for a prosperous local physician, but it takes its name from a later occupant, the Reverend Allatson Burgh, a Regency musicologist. A recent threat to convert it into offices has been averted and it is now available as a centre for receptions and concerts.

We are now in the Wells district, developed in the early 1700s following the discovery of medicinal properties in the chalybeate springs in what is now **Well Walk**. The only surviving trace of these springs is a Victorian fountain halfway down Well Walk sternly labelled 'Not Drinking Water'. The original pump house stood directly opposite, marked by a plaque on Wellside next to the entrance to Gainsborough Gardens. The Long Room, without which no eighteenth-century spa was complete, extended as far as

Harrow School: the Vaughan Library (1861) by Sir Gilbert Scott, from the Yard steps.

Left Hampstead: the entrance to Fenton House (1695).

the Wells Tavern with a bowling green beyond. Unlike Bath or Tunbridge, Hampstead Wells were not fashionable for long. Their proximity to London attracted a less desirable clientele and local profiteers were quick to capitalize on this early mass market. Admission to concerts in the Long Room was cheap, and carriages were available to take customers to and from London at all times. Apart from drinking houses and gambling dens, the Wells were also able to supply 'Fleet marriages'. One hostelry advertised in 1716 that it had a minister constantly in attendance at its 'chapel' and that 'All persons on bringing a licence and who shall have their wedding dinner in the gardens may be married in that said chapel without giving any fee or reward whatsoever.' There was no shortage of other establishments able to supply a wife if necessary.

Not surprisingly, the Wells suffered a swift eclipse as a health resort. The springs fell into disuse and the original Long Room achieved a sort of nemesis by being converted into a proprietary chapel in 1732. A forlorn attempt was made to revive their popularity with a new and respectable Long Room next to Burgh House – visited by Alexander Pope and Fanny Burney – but this in turn became a private house, eventually the home of the poet laureate, John Masefield. It vanished beneath council flats in 1948.

Well Walk is nonetheless worth a detour, especially for those who find fascination in tracing some link between the *genius loci* of a street and the famous people who have inhabited it. Well Walk can boast Marie Stopes at No. 14; John Constable, for a brief period, at No. 40; the socialist Henry Hyndman at No. 13; D. H. Lawrence at No. 32; and J. B. Priestley at No. 27. At the end of the street on the left is Foley House, a mansion of 1698 built for John Duffield, the first proprietor of the spa. He must have come to regret the riotous assemblies his venture unleashed just over his garden wall. Immediately uphill from Foley House is **The Logs**, a Victorian house of 1868 and defying stylistic description. Its pinnacles, gargoyles, gloomy tower and sombre grey brickwork made it the natural setting for one of Sherlock Holmes' most sinister characters, Charles Augustus Milverton. Even Hammer Films might regard it as over-done.

We return to the town centre via **Flask Walk**. This street takes its name from the flasks of well water which were bottled here to be sold in London 'at the Eagle and Child in Fleet Street every morning at 3 pence per flask; and conveyed to persons at their

Hampstead: St John's chapel with Georgian galleries and pews intact inside.

own homes for one penny per flask more. The flask to be returned daily.' Its history was a chequered one: here 'second rate persons are to be found occasionally in a swinish condition' wrote the novelist Samuel Richardson. Not now, however. Flask Walk is an excellent amalgam of houses from all periods of Hampstead's history, each one an individualist – and including some lively modern new-comers. Yet how many visitors – or residents even – have strayed off it into **New Court**, halfway up on the right? Here survives a remarkable cameo of London philanthropy from the Victorian era: two gaunt blocks of five-storey tenement flats, and climbing up the hill behind them the black chimney and circular ward tower of New End Hospital, the cliff of the Elementary School and the pinnacles of Heath Street Baptist Church. This is a very different Hampstead – it might be the backdrop to a Lowry townscape.

At the summit of Flask Walk, the Flask Tavern is Hampstead's best-known pub – not to be confused with the equally distinguished Flask at Highgate. It has today grown so rowdy that the authorities have banned drinkers from spilling out on to the pavement of a summer evening. The fastidious residents of Flask Walk would not have lasted long in the eighteenth century.

Back Lane brings us finally up into Heath Street behind the new **Kingswell** shopping precinct. This structure, designed by Ted Levy, Benjamin and Partners, typifies the split personality of modern Hampstead. As its swirl of white split levels, mansard roofs and bubble-gum lamps went up in the early 1970s, it evoked the rage of local conservationists. 'Costa Brava' architecture, they called it. Yet it well sums up the spirit of this part of **Heath Street**. Two hundred yards farther up, where we last met it at the Meeting House, this thoroughfare still had the gentility of a retiring spa town.

But as it sweeps down, pouring cars into the gluepot of the High Street, Heath Street begins to look more and more like Chelsea's King's Road. Restaurants acquire French names or dabble in the lastest fast-food fad. Boutiques come and go with nods in the direction of Carey Street. And by the time we are back at the tube station and turning left into the High Street the old town appears to have succumbed altogether to what in Earl's Court is referred to as the 'three t's': traffic, tourism and trash.

After a hundred yards, however, Hampstead begins to find itself again. Here the studious and the chic scurry about sticking up notices of protest meetings in friendly shop windows, children slung like piccaninnies over their backs. Here are health-food restaurants, delicatessens with French cheeses and homemade pâté, and that parish pump of intellectual Hampstead, the High Hill Bookshop. With tree-shaded pavement and an atmosphere of colourful bustle, the High Street and Rosslyn Hill present that rare phenomenon – a London community on public parade.

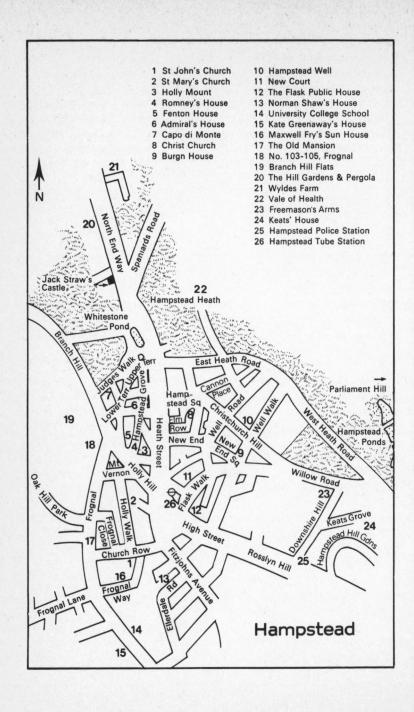

1 St John's Church
2 St Mary's Church
3 Holly Mount
4 Romney's House
5 Fenton House
6 Admiral's House
7 Capo di Monte
8 Christ Church
9 Burgn House
10 Hampstead Well
11 New Court
12 The Flask Public House
13 Norman Shaw's House
14 University College School
15 Kate Greenaway's House
16 Maxwell Fry's Sun House
17 The Old Mansion
18 No. 103-105, Frognal
19 Branch Hill Flats
20 The Hill Gardens & Pergola
21 Wyldes Farm
22 Vale of Health
23 Freemason's Arms
24 Keats' House
25 Hampstead Police Station
26 Hampstead Tube Station

Hampstead

CHAPTER FOURTEEN

Hampstead II

୬

THE Hampstead through which we have been walking so far was for the most part built over in the eighteenth century when the town was still detached from London by fields and lanes. In the middle of the nineteenth century a new Hampstead began to develop. The march of bricks and mortar made its way north from Regent's Park, invading first the Eyre Estate in St John's Wood, then the Eton College Estate in Primrose Hill and the Church lands round Belsize Park. Farms and country mansions were surrounded and swallowed up and fields plunged into a frenzy of brickmaking and roadbuilding. The white stucco of early-Victorian Italianate contorted itself into Gothic and Tudor disguises before finally giving way before the redbrick of 'Queen Anne Revival'. The sounds of the country gave way to the clatter of horses and carriages and the whistle of the steam engine.

We now circle the old town clockwise, reaching the Heath by the richest product of this development, the street known as Frognal. From the tube station, we head towards **Fitzjohn's Avenue**. The land down to Swiss Cottage was sold for development in the 1870s by the Maryon-Wilson family, Lords of the Manor of Hampstead, against bitter protest from local residents. 'The long hill, which used to be so rural and pretty, now is all red brick and cockney prose,' complained Henry James to George du Maurier (employing quite the wrong metaphor for the avenue). The Victorian housing reformer, Octavia Hill, lamented to the local paper: 'How freshly the air blew over these fields and what fine views their hilly slopes commanded.' But all to no avail. From the start the avenue was intended to be magnificent. Pink chestnuts were planted along its line and the developers to whom plots were sold were enjoined to employ the best architects of the day: J. J. Stevenson, Basil Champneys, T. K. Green and Richard Norman Shaw. The American magazine *Harpers* referred to it in 1883 as 'one of the noblest streets

181

in the world'. And Thomas Barratt in his *Annals of Hampstead* (1912) said: 'The houses were considered very wonderful by a generation accustomed to the frowning dinginess of Georgian bricks and mortar.'

The sweeping gables and asymmetrical façades which now appeared in Hampstead remained popular not just in the 1870s and 1880s but through to the First World War. Norman Shaw and his school designed explicitly as an 'English' reaction against the classical and Italianate styles of their predecessors, well illustrated in the terraces recently constructed immediately to the south. Here amid the creeper-clad walls of the new Hampstead it is easy to see traces of the farms and early manors which the young Norman Shaw and his friends spend so much of their youth sketching. The style, which spread across many of the wealthier suburbs, was sadly easy to debase. Green's heavy bargeboard eaves, for instance, became a common Hampstead cliché.

On no building did Norman Shaw expend so much care as on his own home at No. 6 Ellerdale Road, near the crest of Fitzjohn's Avenue. Here he planned the works of his later years: New Scotland Yard, Cragside and Bryanston. It is classic Shaw, essentially a simple Queen Anne box with steep pitched roof, two gables on the front and two massive chimneys. On to this he applied his variations, to the left a three-storey projecting bay and to the right a three-storey oriel window with leaded glass and 'Ipswich' pargetting. Other windows were distributed asymmetrically as the interior plan demanded, yet always in balance. The addition of a porch and extension has drastically altered this balance, but it is still unmistakably the house of the master.

From Ellerdale Road we can walk via Arkwright Road into **Frognal** itself. This, nestling by its lane beneath St John's Church, was once as ancient a hamlet as Hampstead. Today it has no shops or pubs and is simply a residential through-road to the south of the Heath. Yet no other London street better conveys the richness of English domestic architecture from the seventeenth to the twentieth centuries – contriving to do so in less than half a mile.

Turning right out of Arkwright Road, we come to **University College School**. It was designed by Arnold Mitchell in 1907 in a scholarly baroque revival much in vogue in the Edwardian period. The king of that name has his statue in a niche above the main entrance. The centre block has recently been restored after its destruction by fire in 1978. Opposite at No. 39 is the house Norman Shaw designed for the artist, Kate Greenaway. Here she created a fantasy world of children, trees and blossom for her huge following among Victorian parents and their offspring. The house, in which she lived alone with her parents, manages to appear both handsome and cosy – its tall chimneys suggestive of warm comfortable fireplaces inside. The attic studio twists to catch the north-eastern light and outside it is a small terrace where, as Andrew Saint says in his biography of Shaw, 'the little visitors might be sketched before they were entertained in the tea room next door; or from which Kate could watch the toy-like children bowling their hoops down the quiet lane from Hampstead village'. Shaw and Greenaway were both so abused by imitators that it is hard today to recapture the magic of their original invention. But both in their different fields were artists of happiness and good humour.

The architectural idiom now becomes more academic. Frognal Close is vintage 1930s, by E. L. Freud, and opposite in Frognal Way is a remarkable congeries of inter-war styles, including a seminal work of twentieth-century architecture, Maxwell Fry's **Sun House**. Nowhere is the revolutionary nature of the International Style (later known as the Modern Movement) better illustrated than here, surrounded by timid neo-Georgian contemporaries. The house is three-storey, of reinforced concrete with a terrace running the length of the first floor. It is an immaculate composition – the façade might be a painting by Mondrain – with none of the frigidity and squalor which so often accompanies concrete surfaces. We might be gazing at some exotic yacht beached for a while on the sandy slopes of Hampstead. Across the road, is a completely different thirties flirtation: Spanish colonial, with arches, white stucco and green pantiles. And No. 20 at the end of the cul-de-sac is also colonial, but this time unmistakably South African, built in 1934 for Gracie Fields and her husband, Archie Pitt.

Back at the corner of Frognal, modernism rears its head again at No. 66, by Connell, Ward and Lucas, but not so successfully. The horizontal emphasis is oppressive and the concrete ugly – dangerously close to a cheap Mediterranean hotel. We now move back in time to No. 88, a straightforward early-nineteenth-century lodge looking out over a private garden. No. 92 announces itself 'The Turrett', with much early-Victorian castellation. And then suddenly we find ourselves in the heady days of Fenton and Burgh

Houses. The Old Mansion dates from the end of the seventeenth century and is as sleek as the façade of a millionaire's stud farm.

A sedate villa opposite guards Oak Hill Park, not as we might expect, an Italianate mansion but almost a suburb of Washington D.C.: luxury flats dotted among the mature trees with young executives stepping in and out of Mercedes cars. Undeterred by this intrusion, Frognal shakes its head again and gives us No. 100, neo-Queen Anne with an extraordinary pinnacle on its corner turret. No. 79 on the other side is Georgian but with an odd gazebo perched on the roof. No. 95 is all pretty turrets. And then comes Frognal Mansions, a large block of Edwardian flats booming self-confidence. The singer Kathleen Ferrier lived here until her tragic death from cancer at the peak of her career in 1953. Walking past the block late on a summer evening I once heard her rich voice drifting out of a window across the trees. Was it a gramophone or her ghost?

Still Frognal has not finished with us. Nos. 104–6 are early-Georgian terraced houses, Frognal's modest answer to Church Row, while No. 110 is late-seventeenth century with a projecting entrance bay towards the front garden. On a bluff overlooking the road opposite sits **Frognal House**, a substantial mansion of about 1740, which was occupied by General de Gaulle during the war. Then comes a final flourish almost hidden from view: Nos. 103–7 are a group of townhouses by the Palladian architect Henry Flitcroft, designer of St Giles-in-the-Fields, one for his own occupation (but much altered). Another, No. 103, was the home of Ramsay Macdonald, the first Labour Prime Minister, from 1925 to 1937.

Frognal now becomes Branch Hill. But before climbing up on to the Heath, we can turn left past a Victorian gatehouse to Branch Hill Lodge, a survivor of the many private mansions which once dotted this side of the hill. It is a gaunt neo-Jacobean building designed by Samuel Teulon in 1875 on the site of an eighteenth-century house appropriately known as Bleak Hall – an adjective Teulon might have had in mind in producing this work. The house has since been altered and unsympathetically extended by Camden Council to make an old people's home. But the real object of this detour lies in the grounds beneath the house.

Branch Hill Flats were completed in 1978 as the last word in high-density modern living. They cling, gleaming white, to the hillside like monks' cells on Mount Athos. Each unit is split level, with a spiral staircase and its own front door giving on to a grid of stepped alleys running across and down the incline. The flats are less than practical; all goods have to be manhandled from the nearest parking bay and the ubiquitous steps are treacherous for young children. But their chief claim to fame is their cost. At approximately £80,000 per unit, they were probably the most expensive public housing ever built in Britain, if not the world. Designed by Camden Council architects, they were enveloped in controversy from their inception and represented the last extravagant gesture of the public housing boom of the 1960s and 1970s. They could also be the last gesture of the Modern Movement itself. As such they would make a fitting climax to the era begun four decades, and half a mile, earlier at Maxwell Fry's Sun House in Frognal Way.

We now strike out across the Heath to **Whitestone Pond** and Jack Straw's Castle. The pond is four hundred and forty feet above sea level and is named after a white milestone near the top of Heath Street, $4\frac{1}{2}$ miles and 29 yards from Holborn Bars. On summer days the pond is much used by animals and model boat enthusiasts, usually in conflict. But its chief fame is as the focal point of what has for the past century been London's most treasured open space.

The saving of **Hampstead Heath** was the first and noblest of all London's preservationist battles. It lasted for half a century from 1830 and was not fully successful until the 1890s. The absentee Lord of the Manor, Sir Thomas Maryon-Wilson, who lived across town in Charlton House, was eager to realize the Heath's development value as suburban London pressed northwards. Local people enjoyed putative grazing rights on the 'commons' of the Heath, but all Maryon-Wilson required was a private Act of Parliament enabling him to enclose and build. Most manorial lords obtained such acts almost for the asking. But the wealth and influence of the early Heath Protection Committee (led by the Quaker banker, John Gurney Hoare, and including four Members of Parliament) ensured that every one of Maryon-Wilson's applications was refused. The result was what the historian Sir Walter Besant called 'Hampstead's guerilla war'. Maryon-Wilson began selling thousands of tons of Heath sand, creating what now seem attractive dells in the hillside, and his men tore up the undergrowth and planted ornamental trees where he hoped to run streets of houses.

A protest meeting at Hampstead Vestry Hall on 21 April 1856, was one of the fiercest preservationist rallies in London. The curses heaped on Maryon-Wilson's head were bloodcurdling. The protest-

185

ors and their Parliamentary allies held out until Sir Thomas's death in 1870. His son then admitted defeat and sold the first two hundred and forty acres of the Heath to the Metropolitan Board of Works for a modest £45,000. Parliament Hill Fields came within the fold in 1890 and other sections were gradually added whenever money and opportunity permitted. So parsimonious were the Board, however, that no effort was made to rectify Maryon-Wilson's damage and the groundsmen were merely ordered to walk about scattering gorse seed. The Heath's wild appearance is thus not the product of a romantic design, but of private greed, public protest and official meanness – so often the foundations of London's charm.

Immediately beyond the pond stands **Jack Straw's Castle**, a pub dating back to medieval times and named after Wat Tyler's accomplice in the 1381 rebellion. Straw ended his days with his head on a stake and his connection with this pub is unclear. The castellation and weatherboarding are the work not of some medieval insurgent but of the architect, Raymond Erith, who restored the building in 1964. Across the road is Heath House, an eighteenth-century mansion which was once the home of Samuel Hoare. Its open aspect suggests the Hoare family's concern for the future of the Heath was tinged with self-interest.

From this point we continue down North End Way past The Hill, renamed Inverforth House when it became a hospital in the 1950s. The house had been rebuilt by a previous owner Lord Levehulme, in 1914, and includes an extensive sequence of pergolas which run from the formal gardens (now called The Hill and open to the public), over a public footpath and out along a magnificently dilapidated terrace. With the Heath rolling away beneath, it is one of the most mysterious spots in all London. The road now descends through a narrow defile to **North End**, another of Hampstead's outlying hamlets and the only one still recognizable as such. On these trees in the seventeenth century, the body of a convicted highwayman was left dangling as a warning to future miscreants. The deterrent was clearly not effective – numerous convictions are recorded – but it must have terrified many a late-night traveller. At the foot of the hill is the Old Bull and Bush tavern, which began life as a farmhouse before becoming a popular haunt of Hampstead artists in the eighteenth century. The well-known song to which the pub gives its name is helpfully inscribed, words and music, on the front wall.

Behind lies a curious small enclave, still very much Hampstead despite its proximity to Golders Green just down the road. Turning right up North End and then left along a short lane, we come to a remarkable relic of pre-suburban London, **Wyldes Farm** (once known as Collins Farm). The buildings have been occupied since Tudor times; the tenants, when they have not been farmers, have included the Hampstead artist John Linnell and the architect, Sir Raymond Unwin, creator of Hampstead Garden Suburb. Charles Dickens also stayed here in 1837. To all of them it must have seemed an idyllic relief from the crowded city over the hill. It is now carefully preserved and was used recently as a photographic set. If it is to retain its agricultural pretensions, it could do with a pig or two about the place.

North End Avenue leads us back past **Byron Cottage**, home of the redoubtable Lady Houston. She started life as a warehouseman's daughter and chorus girl, progressing through three aristocratic husbands to inherit £7 million from the last of them in 1926. Her use of this fortune showed considerable imagination: beneficiaries included women's suffrage, poverty-stricken coalminers, Hull tramwaymen, the *Saturday Review*, Liverpool Cathedral and the development of the Spitfire and Hurricane, for which the government had refused funds. She even offered money for London's anti-aircraft defences before the last war – an offer politely refused. So devout was her patriotism that she painted the rooms of Byron Cottage red, white and blue.

Across the road, **Pitt House** marks the site of a house of the same name which saw one of the more bizarre incidents of British history. There the first Earl of Chatham incarcerated himself in 1767 when still Prime Minister. He refused to see anyone; his servants had to push his food to him through a double-sided hatch. Only after eighteen months of this was his resignation formally accepted by the king. Chatham later recovered from what must have been a mental collapse and returned to public life. The house was demolished in 1952, but the gardens remain, in effect an extension of the Heath.

A path leads from North End Avenue up to the left of Heath House and across **Spaniards Road**. This road takes its name from the Spanish community which used to live near the former tollgate of the Bishop of London's Highgate estates. Persistent attempts to demolish the gatehouse to improve the traffic flow have been successfully resisted, not the least by those eager to reduce that flow.

The Spaniards Inn, like the Bull and Bush, was a favourite resort for Victorian day trippers. Its moment of glory was during the Gordon Riots, when the proprietor gave free beer to a mob on its way to burn down Kenwood House – thus delaying them long enough for the militia to be summoned and Kenwood saved.

Immediately beneath Spaniards Road a fold in the hill contains one of the oddest of Hampstead's many outposts, the **Vale of Health**. The Vale was developed from the late-eighteenth century on the site of a malarial swamp named Hatches Bottom, where the town had uncharitably located the parish poor house. After draining the swamp, builders were clearly eager to improve the district's image – hence one possible origin for its strange name. The Vale was never laid out as an estate, houses and terraces going up whenever the site of a shack or smallholding fell vacant. The result is a warren of narrow lanes and alleyways giving directly on to the Heath. The Vale's most distinguished resident was James Leigh Hunt who came to live in South Villa in 1816, bringing with him a circle of radical friends including Shelley, Byron, Coleridge and Lamb. Here they planned their ruthless satire on the Prince Regent, an offence for which Hunt had already spent two years in prison. Keats would often walk over from Wentworth Place to visit him and even lived here briefly, until a servant inadvertently opened one of his love letters and so upset him that he left. D. H. Lawrence, Edgar Wallace and Compton Mackenzie were later residents.

Immediately south of the Vale is a curious relic of its proletarian past, a permanent fairground, occasionally with roundabout, side-shows and donkeys. Twice a year, at the Spring and August bank holidays, this expands into one of the largest fairs in London, part of it located below Spaniards Road and part down at South End. At such times all London appears to descend on the neighbourhood. Much fun is had and many purses vanish.

The path down from the Vale leads towards Hampstead Ponds over rough wooded terrain mercifully free of landscaping. Veering to the right, we cross East Heath Road at Willow Road, named after the grove of trees planted by Maryon-Wilson as part of his abortive attempt to develop this section of the Heath. The entrance to **Downshire Hill** is indicated by the Freemason's Arms, a pub sitting on the old course of the Fleet stream. This road is remarkable in retaining almost completely its original early nineteenth-century appearance, each house reflecting the confusion of styles of the late

Regency, early-Victorian period. Some are Italianate, some Gothic, some neo-Tudor, one is even Greek classical. The centrepiece of the composition is the proprietary **Chapel of St John** at the corner of Keats Grove. Built by a local developer, William Woods of Kennington, it has a simple façade in a style reminiscent of a New England church; its Georgian galleries and box pews are still intact inside.

Turning down Keats Grove we reach Wentworth Place, renamed **Keats House**, on the right, where the poet lived for part of his adult life. It is now the Keats Museum (open 10.00 to 6.00. Sundays 2.00 to 5.00) and wonderfully preserves both the atmosphere of a small Regency house and the sense of tragedy which surrounded its famous resident. It was built in 1816 by Keats' friend, Charles Brown, and was one of the first houses in the district. Shortly after Keats came to share one half of it with Brown, a Mrs Brawne and her three daughters came to live in the other half – it must have been a crowded place. One of the Browne girls, Fanny, immediately captured Keats' heart. Visitors can now see the room in which Keats composed his love letters to Fanny. In the garden outside was the tree (now replanted) under which he wrote the 'Ode to a Nightingale'. And in the curious tent bed upstairs he coughed the famous drop of dark blood which told him he was dying of consumption. Shortly afterwards the antiquary, William Hone, saw Keats in Well Walk 'sitting and sobbing his dying breath into a handkerchief, gleaning parting looks towards the quiet landscape he had delighted in'. His doctor ordered him to spend the winter in Italy, and Fanny, now at last wearing his engagement ring, prepared his clothes and stitched a silk lining into his travelling cap. Soon after his arrival in Italy his condition worsened and he died in Rome at the age of twenty-five.

It is hard to remain unmoved by Keats' story as presented in this house: by the gentle proportions of the rooms, the friendly portraits and the simple memorabilia of the poet and his friends. Even the sentimental painting of 'Keats listening to a nightingale' by Joseph Severn seems quite in place. Upstairs, by his bed, is written an appropriate epitaph: 'I am certain of nothing but of the holiness of the heart's affection and the truth of imagination.'

Returning to Downshire Hill, we pass No. 47, one of the artistic shrines of Hampstead. Here the mid-Victorian painter, Gaetano Meo received Rosetti, Burne-Jones and the Pre-Raphaelites. Then Hilda Carline and her husband Stanley Spencer took the house and entertained Nevinson, Bevan, Gertler and other artists of the inter-war years. During the war, the building became headquarters of the Artists Refugee Committee. Either the place must have a muse for a ghost or the food must have been plentiful – Richard Carline has mildly suggested the latter. Farther up the hill on the right, literature takes over at No. 7, where the poet and critic Edwin Muir lived for three years in the 1930s and at No. 21 Pablo Picasso would visit his friend, Sir Roland Penrose.

We reach Rosslyn Hill at one of Hampstead's most distinguished public buildings, the **police station**. It was built in 1903 by the official police architect, J. Dixon Butler, who had worked with Norman Shaw on New Scotland Yard. Here he uses a much freer version of Queen Anne: a huge gable, stone window surrounds and long, graceful corbels to the door canopy. London's public architecture was unsurpassed at this time. Here is a building which speaks of the days when all police stations were shrouded in fog, all crimes were murky and an 'officer of the force' invariably arrived just *after* Sherlock Holmes had found the villain.

We can now return to the tube station up Rosslyn Hill – though enthusiasts for late-Victorian architecture should not miss **Hampstead Hill Gardens** immediately down the hill to the left, by the excellent 1870s firm of Batterby and Huxley. The estate is overlooked by two of Hampstead's best church buildings, Samuel Teulon's St Stephen's and Alfred Waterhouse's Congregational Church. Both masterpieces are now disused and in danger. Hampstead has overcome such challenges before.

CHAPTER FIFTEEN

Highgate

SINCE the Middle Ages Highgate has stood guard over the northern approaches to London. Had England's history been more precarious, it would have been the site of some great fortress. Instead it was merely the first stop on the main road out of town, its tollbooth, inns and coaching yards beckoning travellers up the steep gradient of Highgate Hill for refreshment and a change of horses. As early as the fourteenth century a hermit named William Philippe was granted the right to levy a toll to pay for the upkeep of the road past his hermitage on top of the hill. Pond Square is a relic of the pit from which the necessary gravel was dug. The tollgate (or 'Highgate') marked the entrance to the Bishop of London's land to the north.

By 1809 the pressure to avoid this bottleneck and its steep hill was so great that a private company was formed to drive a tunnel through the hill a mile to the east of the village. The venture was not a success and the tunnel collapsed before completion. A deep cutting was dug instead, with an arched bridge designed by John Nash (now replaced) to carry the lane to Hornsey over it. As a result, the village of Highgate was left stranded on its hilltop, deprived of the prosperity channelled down Archway Road to the east. It has remained stranded ever since. Even its metamorphosis from coaching village to residential suburb has been discreet. In contrast to the razmatazz of Hampstead along the hill, Highgate is an English gentlewoman showing the rest of London how to grow old with dignity.

The village can be approached from either Highgate or Archway stations or along the road from Hampstead. We shall approach from Archway up Highgate Hill: the historic point from which young fortune-seekers would catch their first sight of the towers and spires of a city 'paved with gold'. Near the foot of the hill is the spot where one fortune-seeker, Dick Whittington, is alleged to have heard the chimes of Bow Bells in Cheapside calling him back to be Lord Mayor of London. This strange legend, enshrined in annual pantomime, takes many forms. One version has Whittington working in a kitchen ruled over by a tyrannical cook with only his cat for company. The cat leaves on a trade voyage with the master of the house, and Dick decides to leave also and seek his fortune in the north. He is recalled at Highgate by the sound of Bow Bells and discovers that his cat has returned and earned him a fortune already, by clearing the palace of an African ruler of a plague of mice. This windfall enables him to become, as the bells predicted, 'thrice Lord Mayor of London'.

The extraordinary feature of this story is not so much its implausibility – it would make an excellent advertisement for a Highgate hearing aid – as why it should have attached itself to Sir Richard Whittington, who was indeed Lord Mayor three times between 1397 and 1419. The real Whittington was the son of a wealthy merchant and his prosperous business as a mercer ensured his status as a leading City figure with considerable prominence in contemporary politics. He was also a prodigious benefactor of City charities, one of which gave rise to the hospital which bears his name at the foot of Highgate Hill. There is no record of his having worked in a kitchen, let alone of his owing his fortune to a globetrotting cat. Nor, even in legend, did 'Dick Whittington' take the cat with him up Highgate Hill, despite an inn sign on the hill portraying them there together. Similar cat legends exist in many medieval cultures and we must suppose that Whittington – one of the last of the great City merchant princes – was the sort of popular figure to whom later generations might attach such a legend.

Highgate proper begins at the crossroads known locally as 'Holy Joe's'. **St Joseph's Church**, with its adjacent monastery of the Passionist Fathers, was built in 1888 by an architect appropriately named Vicars. The style is Romanesque but with an oriental flavour lent it by the onion domes which form its most prominent feature. Together with its gaunt monastery, it could be anywhere between the Tuscan hills and Moscow, but certainly *not* in Highgate. Like Sacré Coeur in Paris, Holy Joe's is a curious stylistic import, yet over the years it has worked its way into the spirit of the place.

Immediately opposite, Hornsey Lane runs east over the **Archway Road Bridge**. The bridge is a replacement of John Nash's noble original. But the view from it is still the one Nash intended: of the

Highgate: Robert Adam's library at Kenwood House (1769), 'one of Adam's richest and most extravagant interiors'.

Stylistic contrast on the Northern Heights: Northern Line *art nouveau* at Hampstead tube station;
below Regency ironwork decorating a porch in Holly Terrace, Highgate.

towers of the City shimmering in the distance dominated by the dome of St Paul's. Returning to Highgate Hill, we reach on the left a white stucco building named **Lauderdale House**. This was the Highgate already fashionable in the seventeenth century, early 'ribbon' development in the clean air out of town but well placed for the City. Lauderdale was Scottish Secretary to Charles II (with his later residence at Ham) and legend has this as yet another of Nell Gwynn's residences. Legend also has it that as the king passed by the house one day, Nell dangled an as yet untitled royal bastard from the window, shouting that she would drop him if ennoblement were not forthcoming. 'Then save the Earl of Burford,' cried the king with a promptness required of such stories. (It should be added that the same tale is told of 'Nell Gwynn' houses elsewhere.) The present building dates from the seventeenth and eighteenth centuries, with a pretty colonnade and *parterre* at the back. It has been in municipal care since 1889 and this, together with a serious fire, has left little of interest inside. Beyond is Waterlow Park, given to Highgate by Sir Sidney Waterlow in 1889 to be 'a garden for those who are gardenless'.

On the other side of the road is a different proposition. **Cromwell House**, built in the 1630s by a merchant named Richard Sprignell, is one of the few mansions in London surviving from the pre-Restoration period (compare Lindsey House in Lincolns Inn Fields). The house is seven bays wide, the three centre ones projecting slightly, and crowned by a cupola. The façade is in a rich red brick with carved surrounds to the main windows and scrolls on either side of the centre one – Mannerist to Lindsey House's Palladian. To the right is an extension over the entrance to the stable yard. An unusual brick balustrade fronts the garden. The house is now in the hands of a missionary society and can be visited by appointment. Inside is the original staircase with warriors on the newel posts and boldly carved panels instead of balusters.

Highgate Hill clearly finds it hard to sort out its legends. There is no evidence for any link between Cromwell House and the Lord Protector himself. And the same applies to the supposition that his son-in-law and close associate, General Ireton, inhabited Ireton House next door. The terrace comprising Ireton House, Lyndale House and No. 110 is plainly eighteenth century. The closest connection with the Commonwealth is probably with Ireton's brother, Sir John Ireton. He was Lord Mayor of London in 1658, occupied

Highgate

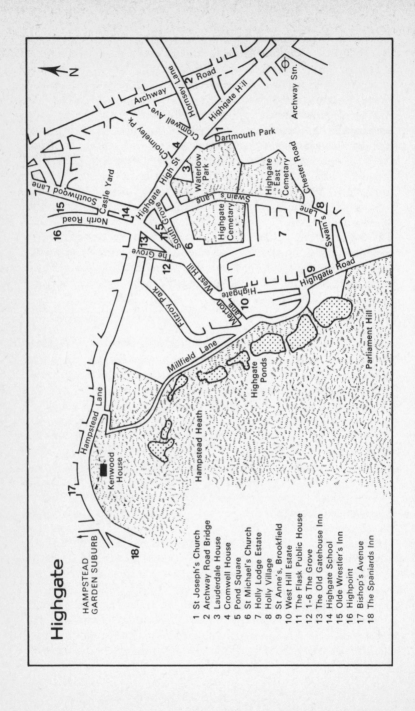

HAMPSTEAD
GARDEN SUBURB

N

Archway Road

Hornsey Lane
Highgate Hill
Archway Stn.

Archway
Cromwell Ave.

Dartmouth Park

Cholmeley Pk.

Highgate High St

Waterlow Park

Highgate East Cemetery

Chester Road

Castle Yard

Highgate Cemetery

Swain's Lane

Southwood Lane

North Road

South Grove

The Grove

Highgate West Hill

Highgate Road

Swain's Lane

Fitzroy Park

Millfield Lane

Hampstead Heath

Highgate Ponds

Parliament Hill

Hampstead Lane

Kenwood House

1 St Joseph's Church
2 Archway Road Bridge
3 Lauderdale House
4 Cromwell House
5 Pond Square
6 St Michael's Church
7 Holly Lodge Estate
8 Holly Village
9 St Anne's, Brookfield
10 West Hill Estate
11 The Flask Public House
12 1–6 The Grove
13 The Old Gatehouse Inn
14 Highgate School
15 Olde Wrestler's Inn
16 Highpoint
17 Bishop's Avenue
18 The Spaniards Inn

Lauderdale House and was known to have owned other land in Highgate.

There is yet more unauthenticated history on the roadside opposite: a plaque recording the site of a cottage once lived in by the seventeenth-century poet Andrew Marvell. Sadly there is no documentary evidence for his ever having resided in Highgate. Doubt also surrounds yet another famous Hill story, that it was here the Jacobean statesman and scientist, Sir Francis Bacon, conducted his early experiment in refrigeration, stepping down from a coach to stuff a newly killed chicken with snow to study its rate of decay. The chicken bore up remarkably well but Sir Francis contracted a chill, was unable to return to his London house and died shortly afterwards. Such tales naturally attached to Highgate, given its status as gateway to London. Famous men and women were continually to be seen travelling through and stopping at its inns and houses, while local people were eager to 'remember them well'.

Highgate **High Street** runs along the summit of the hill like the windy thoroughfare of some clifftop village. It is an amalgam of Georgian townhouses, shops and inns, the proliferation of places of refreshment reflecting the days when the street would have been thick with thirsty ostlers, coachmen and their passengers. None of the coachyards survives in anything like their original form, but some of the atmosphere of snorting horses and clanking harness can be found behind the Duke's Head, where a few outhouses remain. Since the pubs have been steadily reconditioned, it is now the houses and shops which make the High Street so attractive an ensemble. It has none of the urbanity of Hampstead or Greenwich, rather the atmosphere of a small country town. Two shops still have painted wooden arcades, once a common feature of a London high street, but now sufficiently rare to look like a Western filmset. Most remarkable of all, the street still boasts a butcher, baker, greengrocer and iron-monger – with only the incursion of the Dragon Seed Chinese restaurant a portent of things to come.

While the High Street curves round to the site of the old gatehouse, we turn left into South Grove and Pond Square. This was the centre of the village, protected from the main road and with a group of eighteenth-century buildings set round what would once have been the village pond. Unfortunately this has been filled in and the resulting garden appallingly municipalized, with little walls and parking spaces. To restore Pond Square to its former state would turn this spot into a major tourist attraction (which is perhaps why the residents will not let it happen). We must therefore simply admire the calm dignity of South Grove along to St Michael's Church, a fine sequence of individual Georgian townhouses, with views to the rear which have long been the envy of passers-by.

Cutting down between them runs Swain's Lane, steep, dark and narrow and an appropriate entrance to the austere necropolis of **Highgate Cemetery**. Vandalism has now closed the main (west) cemetery to the public, but open days are occasionally held and are not to be missed. Since its post-war dereliction, Highgate Cemetery has become one of the most astonishing places in London: a vivid demonstration of the Victorian concept of death wrestling with the eternal vitality of nature. It is architecture's answer to Hieronymus Bosch or Berlioz' Grande Messe des Morts.

The cemetery was begun in 1838 and was, like Brompton and Kensal Green, part of the early-Victorians' attempt to decentralize the crowded graveyards of central London into new landscaped parks on the outskirts. These were mostly privately-run and seldom offered paupers' graves. Tombs could be extremely ornate, surrounded by well-tended groves of evergreen trees. The companies would be careful to provide a chapel, a catacomb and an avenue for family mausolea. The whole undertaking was highly profitable.

All this can be forgotten at Highgate today, for the outside world is invisible and irrelevant. Here is now a vast, clammy forest tearing apart memorials, spilling open graves and imprisoning everything in dank greenery. Not for nothing did Bram Stoker locate one of the more gruesome scenes in his Gothic masterpiece, *Dracula*, in this place. Paths seem to twist back on themselves as if destination were no longer important. Creepers droop down from treetops to entwine stone angels and marble cherubs. Everywhere memorials are split and tombstones askew, ivy oozing from every crevice. The air is heavy with moisture and any movement leads to a flapping and screeching of birds grown accustomed to their privacy. By struggling through the undergrowth, the intrepid may discover a ring of catacombs guarded by an entrance in the style of an Egyptian tomb, with an old cedar tree draping its branches over its walls. Here family vaults stand ruinous, their doors horrifically ajar as if the spirits themselves had tired of the place and made their escape. Over it all towers the mausoleum of the diamond magnate, Julius

Beer, crowned by a stepped pyramid. Its carved marble interior and sarcophagus are now a wretched sight, thick with bird droppings and the carcases of dead pigeons. *Sic transit gloria* indeed. From the mausoleum it is possible, though not easy, to climb up on to a stone terrace immediately beneath St Michael's Church and look down into the purgatory beneath. It is a vision of the city handed back to the earth from which it sprang, and perhaps the very preciousness of this vision justifies our leaving it quite alone. But nature is now gently destroying whatever vandals left unwrecked. Highgate Cemetery is worth a little help from man or it will disappear altogether.

The east Cemetery lies over the road from the main entrance. It is open all day, is maintained and is correspondingly less interesting – more like Père Lachaise in Paris. Its best-known grave is that of Karl Marx in the north-east corner, dominated by his larger-than-life but rather genial bust. Beneath is carved in bold lettering the famous exhortation, 'Workers of the world unite', and also the more prosaic, 'Philosophers have only interpreted the world in various ways. The point, however, is to change it.' Crowds of Japanese tourists can usually be seen photographing it furiously. When I was last there, two unsmiling gentlemen, tieless but in square-cut suits, solemnly added to the pile of red flowers regularly by the tomb. Embassy staff on carnation duty?

We can now either retrace our steps uphill to South Grove or continue down Swain's Lane past the **Holly Lodge Estate**. The Lodge, now demolished, was the suburban home of one of the nineteenth century's wealthiest women, Angela Burdett-Coutts. Heiress at twenty-three to the Coutts banking fortune, she was a model of careful Victorian philanthropy. She was closely associated with contemporaries as diverse in their interests as Charles Dickens, the Duke of Wellington, Brooke of Sarawak and General Gordon. Her money built Columbia Market in the East End, St Stephen's Westminster and numerous ragged schools, hostels and learned institutes. She supported Stanley's search for Livingstone, the extension of the Church of England in the colonies and the relief of Gordon at Khartoum. Rich and poor alike trooped out to enjoy her summer hospitality on this Highgate hillside and she came to hold a place in the esteem of Londoners second only to that of Queen Victoria herself. She was the first woman to be raised to the peerage on her own merits. When she died in 1906 she lay in state at her Stratton

Street house, while thirty thousand Londoners came to pay their last respects. As William Howitt wrote after her death, had she only performed her good works in the Roman Catholic faith, 'she would have been canonized as St Angela'.

The house which might have become her monument was promptly sold and the Holly Lodge Estate turned over to development – a neo-Tudor spread of flats and houses protected from intrusion by gates across the roads leading into it. But the baroness did leave one local memorial. At the foot of Swain's Lane lies H. A. Darbishire's unmistakably mid-Victorian **Holly Village**, in a picturesque Gothic of 1865 with gatehouse and semi-detached villas set round a landscaped garden. The place was intended for the estate's servants and is a curiously lighthearted fantasy for a lady so serious in her ambitions. Its pinnacles, gables and carved bargeboards round a village green comprised an improbable Victorian ideal of rustic living.

Those who have persevered this far down the hill should continue into Highgate West Hill and turn right past **St Anne's Brookfield**, built in 1855 and important as Sir John Betjeman's early introduction to Victorian architecture (he lived as a child at No. 31 farther up the hill). Betjeman has well captured the atmosphere of turn-of-the-century Highgate:

> I see black oaktwigs outlined on the sky,
> I ask my nurse the question, 'Will I die?'
> As bells from sad St Anne's ring out so late,
> 'And if I do die, will I go to Heaven?'
> Highgate at eventide. Nineteen eleven.

The twentieth century has filled in the acres which at that time separated Highgate from its surrounding villages, and motor cars have eroded the individual character of each of them. It was Betjeman's good fortune to have experienced that individualism while it lasted and his genius to have captured it in verse.

Left off Highgate West Hill, **Millfield Lane** runs up to the Heath, overlooking Highgate Ponds and extending as far as Kenwood on the lane to Hampstead. It was a favourite rendezvous for the Romantic poets of Hampstead and Highgate and saw the famous first meeting between Coleridge and John Keats, whom the former described afterwards as 'a loose, sleek and not too well-dressed youth'. We turn off at Merton Lane, past the West Hill estate designed by Ted Levy, Benjamin and Partners. It is in the 'Hampstead Mediterranean' style so popular with English domestic architects of the late 1970s. They fought back against the concrete and glass of post-war modernism with an abundance of pitched roofs, pantiles and yellow stock bricks. The architecture of these cottages is so retiring, almost apologetic, that within a few years they will have vanished completely beneath their coating of assorted creepers.

Back on West Hill, a gate marked 'Private' leads into **Holly Terrace**. A discreet stroll along this terrace reveals some of the best Regency ironwork in London adorning the garden façades of houses backing on to West Hill itself. Especially good is the porch of No. 5 and the 'Gothic' verandah of No. 6: time was when most terraces in London could boast ironwork such as this, though much of it was removed for armaments manufacture during the war.

Farther up the hill we reach the site, marked by a plaque, of the old Fox and Crown Inn. A former proprietor achieved immortality by saving the life of the young Queen Victoria and a friend by seizing the reins of their carriage horses as they bolted down the hill outside. For this bravery he was rewarded with a royal coat of arms, but the glory did him little good. James Thorne recorded laconically in 1876 that 'he died in poverty some years back'. Beyond is the entrance to Witanhurst, built in 1913 in a neo-Queen Anne style and one of the largest private mansions in London. Successive attempts to demolish it and develop its extensive grounds since the war have all failed and it was purchased in 1977 by a member of the Saudi Arabian royal family. It has since been resold and its future remains in doubt.

The summit of Highgate West Hill is marked by a soaring pinnacle of English Gothic. Where would the hill villages of London be without these splendid obelisks? Harrow, Richmond, Hampstead, Blackheath are all blessed with them. The **Church of St Michael** was designed in 1830 by Lewis Vulliamy to replace the previous chapel in the High Street. It is a tall, graceful structure with ogival windows pushing upwards towards the tower and spire. The church is usually locked and has little of interest inside apart from the memorial to Samuel Taylor Coleridge, moved here from the old chapel. Opposite stands the Flask, dating from the seventeenth century and one of London's most characteristic pubs (not to be confused with the other Flask in Hampstead). Despite the traffic teeming past, its courtyard it is a seething mass of humanity in summer. Its bars are traditional bars, offering darts and billiards, and its food is a robust revival of traditional pub food. It is a place which will disappoint neither the tourist nor the enthusiast – though the beer, I fear, is not the best.

Opposite the Flask lies the serene **Grove**, for long the home of Highgate's *haute bourgeoisie*. Nos. 1 to 6 date from the turn of the eighteenth century and are fine examples of their period. Out here where land was presumably cheaper, builders could afford to be more spacious. No. 3 was the residence of Coleridge for eighteen years until his death in 1834. He arrived here with his family in 1816 to stay as permanent guest of a Doctor Gillman and his wife. Here Coleridge at last found a sort of stability; his opium addiction abated and he had hosts whose devotion to him became total. 'The gentlest and kindest teacher; the most engaging home companion,' was the Gillmans' epitaph on his memorial. He could wander free through the lanes of Highgate and Hampstead, visited by friends such as Wordsworth, Lamb and Hazlitt, taking them to his upstairs room and showing them his beloved views over London. Carlyle saw him 'sitting on the brow of Highgate looking down on London and its smoke tumult, like a sage escaped from the inanity of life's battle . . . a kind of *magus* girt in mystery and enigma'. Leigh Hunt recalled him more intimately, 'taking his daily stroll up and down, with his black coat and white locks and a book in his hand: a great acquaintance of the little children'.

Today the houses of the Grove still have their extensive gardens running down the hillside towards Fitzroy Park, most of them on two levels. Nos. 5 and 6 still have their fire plaques from the days when insurance companies operated the fire engines and needed to know whether a house was paid up and thus worth saving. To the north, the Grove becomes late-Georgian, and at No. 12 is a modern brick house built by and for the Russian Embassy. It is not out of keeping with its surroundings, but closer inspection reveals a deep 'moat' round it and ground-floor windows which seem uncommonly narrow. In the middle of the Grove is an old reservoir which, like the patio in Pond Square, spoils what would otherwise be a marvellous spread of grass.

At Hampstead Lane, we turn right to the Old Gatehouse Inn and Highgate School. The inn is on the site of the original gatehouse and tollbooth which used to straddle the road at this point. It is a neo-Tudor pub of the best sort – timbered gables and oriel windows smartly turning the axis of the High Street to face the road to the north. The mid-Victorian buildings of **Highgate School** opposite are dull by comparison. The school was founded by Sir Roger Cholmeley in 1565 (predating Harrow) adjacent to what was then St Michael's Chapel. Highgate was still under the parish of St Mary Hornsey and parishioners would have had a long walk to service each Sunday without this local place of worship. The chapel was itself established on the site of the medieval hermitage, which was in turn the historical precursor of the tollgate. So inn, gate, school and church are all closely linked Highgate institutions.

After the building of the new St Michael's in South Grove, the school demolished the chapel (though not its graveyard) and rebuilt both it and the schoolhouse for what was then a rapidly increasing number of boys. The new buildings, opened in 1866, were designed by F. P. Cockerell in the type of Public School Gothic which goes with cloisters, games masters, memorial windows and fervent hymns. Big School is balanced by the chapel on one side and the cloister on the other. The monogram of the founder can be made out on the lead parapet of the main block together with three reliefs showing boys playing rugby, hearing a lesson and saying their prayers before bed.

North Road is the sort of highway we might expect leading out of a county town such as York or Norwich, lined with Georgian houses and jolly inns, and hinting at open fields just a mile away. On the left is Byron Cottage (not to be confused with Byron Cottage in Hampstead's North End Avenue), where the poet A. E. Housman lived while working as a civil servant and writing 'The Shropshire Lad'. Here his mother demanded to 'inspect the landlady' and a new cook refused to work for any 'poet', having had nothing but trouble from that Mr Swinburne down in Chelsea. Farther down on the right is Ye Old Wrestlers Inn, Tudor in origin but frequently rebuilt and the only pub to maintain the ceremony of the Swearing on the Horns. This medieval rite, once practised in many Highgate pubs, involves paying a shilling 'for the good of the house' and swearing a nonsense oath that 'by the rules of sound judgement you will not eat brown bread when you can have white, except that you like brown the best ... that you must not kiss the maid while you can kiss the mistress, except that you like the maid the best or have the chance to kiss them both ...' and so on. This is done with considerable shouting and drinking and ends up with the initiate being given the 'Freedom of Highgate'. The rite was sufficiently well-known to gain mention in Byron's *Childe Harold*:

And many to the steep of Highgate hie.
Ask ye, Boeotian shades, the reason why?
Tis to the worship of the solemn Horn,
Grasped in the old hand of Mystery
In whose dread name both men and maids are sworn.

The probable origin of the rite is that the horns were symbols of the gatekeepers' authority and the ritual was a satire on the payment of the toll.

Directly opposite this quaint survival rise the twin blocks of **Highpoint**, designed by the Tecton partnership in the 1930s. They were the first 'point blocks' built in London in the Modern Move-ment style. No. 1 on the right, designed in 1935, is cement-rendered, the only visible decoration being curved parapets to the balconies. As if finding this too bleak, No. 2, designed two years later makes greater use of brick and tiles on its façade and has two caryatids supporting its *porte cochère*. These caryatids are the best-known feature of the buildings: according to Pevsner, 'a case of surrealism in architecture ... the figures are deprived of their original meaning. Instead of all turning one way, one of them seems to have decided on an independent right turn.' Highpoint became world-famous among architects in the thirties and forties, and served as prototype for many of the point block developments of postwar housing. As such it has a lot to answer for. Though No. 1 has a handsome simplicity, I find both of them lacking either charm or beauty. Le Corbusier acclaimed them as a 'vertical garden city'. Enough said.

From Highpoint, we return to the High Street down Castle Yard, whose neat cottages have had to be protected from through traffic by huge fenders against which cars are continually crashing. South-wood Lane runs east to Jackson's Lane – an old track over the hill to Hornsey – and west to the High Street. On its right are twelve almshouses founded in 1644 by Sir John Wollaston, another High-gate Lord Mayor. They were rebuilt in 1722. Georgian houses line the lane to the left and down behind them were the 'drifts' along which early drovers would direct their sheep and cattle to avoid the tollgate. Today the drifts provide dramatic views over Muswell Hill to Alexandra Palace and the East London basin beyond.

Half a mile along Hampstead Lane from Highgate lie the house and grounds of **Kenwood**. The house is situated on a wooded slope, above a fold in the hillside, which has always given it a remarkable privacy. It was one of the many seats of the Dukes of Argyll in the early eighteenth century, then passing to the Earl of Bute and finally to the Earl of Mansfield in 1754. Mansfield, then Lord Chief Justice of England (and scourge of the Gordon Rioters), employed the architect Robert Adam to redesign and extend the building, a commission carried out when Adam was at the height of his reputation in 1767–9, with Syon and Osterley already under his belt.

The **exterior** of Kenwood well demonstrates the revolution Adam brought about in British eighteenth-century architecture. He starts on the entrance façade with a restrained composition of Ionic portico, only mildly enriched with swags and ribbons in its entablature and a single medallion in the pediment. On the garden front, however, he produces a complex arrangement of ten pilasters above a rusticated ground floor. The full enrichment of this façade has only recently been completed by the owners, the Greater London Council, using designs from Adam's original pattern books. The effect is not totally successful. The absence of a strong central feature is uncomfortable when the house is viewed from a distance. Adam's rival, Sir William Chambers, would have shaken his head and advised another portico.

The **grounds** of Kenwood were laid out in the 1790s by Humphrey Repton, with a lake and Chinese bridge designed by Adam. An open-air orchestra pit has been built on the far side of the lake, and Dr Johnson's thatched summer house has been brought from the Thrales' old garden in Streatham and set down by North Wood. (Is Streatham so careless of its own history?) The grounds are now virtually part of Hampstead Heath and, at least in summer, no other building is visible from them, an incomparable asset. Municipal refreshments are available in the old coachhouse.

The great treasures of Kenwood, however, are inside (open 10.00 to 7.00, 10.00 to 4.00 in winter). The house was bought by Lord Iveagh in 1925 and when he bequeathed it to the public in 1927 he left with it his collection of old master **paintings**. The result is one of the best small galleries in London, not at all overwhelming and a particularly good way of introducing children to paintings. The only problem is to know where to begin: whether to start in England with Gainsborough and Reynolds and build up to a climax with Rembrandt and Vermeer, or to begin chronologically with the Dutch masters and end with the eighteenth-century English pictures. I have tried both ways many times, and find the former more intellectually satisfying, the latter more exciting. So let us choose the latter.

This means commencing with Kenwood's best-known pictures hung in the former dining room. Here is Hals' kindly 'Man with the Cane', a dramatic Cuyp of Dortrecht and, next to it, 'Yarmouth' by John Crome, this last showing that East Anglia could provide the artist with the same effects of light on clouds and water as could the scenery of Holland. Then facing each other across the room are the gallery's two most outstanding paintings. Rembrandt's 'Self-portrait' in old age gazes back at us, full of sadness but with the calm assurance of a lifetime's work well done. Opposite hangs its contrast, 'The Guitar Player' by Vermeer, painted in Holland at about the same time. Here is none of Rembrandt's directness. Vermeer's young girl tilts her head enigmatically away from us, her eyes all allusion, her mouth opening for a song. The play of light makes her plain face seem radiant; her guitar is almost audible.

The marble hall leads us through into the vestibule and thus to the **library**, one of Adam's richest and most extravagant interiors. Themes and motifs gleaned by Adam from his studies of the Diocletian ruins at Split in Yugoslavia were here applied with gusto to a classical English room. The apses at either end (where the few books for which Adam left room were confined) are divided from the main room by screens of giant columns. Walls and ceilings are covered in delicate plasterwork by Joseph Rose with panels painted by the Italian artist Antonio Zucchi. It was while employed at Kenwood that Zucchi fell in love with Angelica Kauffman, who was also working here, and eventually carried her off to Rome.

The sequence of rooms along the garden front contains a variety of eighteenth- and nineteenth-century works. These include J. M. W. Turner's 'Fishermen on a Lee Shore in Squally Weather'; a popular picture by Joseph Wright of Derby entitled 'Dressing the Kitten'; and a seventeenth-century painting by Claude de Jongh of old London Bridge, looking placid and sunny as if crossing the Arno at Florence. Finally we reach the English eighteenth-century pictures. In the Orangery is a vast Stubbs of 'Whitejacket' rearing up on the end wall as if about to gallop off down the hill outside, and Gainsborough's 'Lady Brisco', a sombre study in grey painted at the time of her marriage – and surely not to her satisfaction.

The lobby and music room contain paintings by the great Georgian masters, Reynolds, Romney, Raeburn, Lawrence and Gainsborough, including a number of portraits of children in varying stages of improbable innocence. Gainsborough's Miss Brummell (sister of 'Beau') looks about to burst into tears, while Raeburn's Sir George Sinclair, the 'Harrow Prodigy', is made unnaturally angelic. Lawrence's Miss Murray, dancing with flowers, has adorned the lid of many a chocolate box. The collection also includes a famous Romney of Lady Hamilton at the spinning wheel, her delicate hands looking quite unused to such toil. But my favourite is Gainsborough's 'Mary Countess Howe' in the music room. Here is the calm assurance of an English aristocrat, set against one of Gainsborough's most stormy backgrounds, the twin emotions fused in a whirlwind of pink satin and white lace. To add to the sense of drama, she appears to be walking out of the picture towards us. It is a painting full of movement and even menace – the best memory with which to leave Kenwood on a stormy day, its vast trees bending in the wind outside and clouds racing overhead.

The routes north from Highgate, either up the old Great North Road (A1000) or up the A1, pass through what can at times appear a seamless weave of suburbia. To the west lie Golders Green and Hendon, where development was initiated in the 1900s by an American syndicate headed by one of Charles Tyson Yearkes. He and his friends saw the property potential of this area if only a railway line could be pushed through Hampstead Heath from Charing Cross. This line, now the western branch of the Northern Line, reached the rural crossroads of **Golders Green** in 1907. As Alan Jackson points out in his study of this development, 'The Americans knew from home experience that given favourable conditions, a frequent service of electric cars to places just beyond the edge of towns or cities soon caused the fields to disappear beneath bricks and mortar.' As throughout the home counties, railway engineer and property developer moved hand in hand – though why it needed Americans to exploit this opportunity is a mystery. Today Golders Green is chiefly notable for its massive Hippodrome cinema (now under conversion) and for its reception of tens of thousands of the more well-to-do European *émigrés*, particularly Jews, before and after the last world war.

One vigorous social reformer, however, was eager to avoid the perils of over-rapid suburban development – Dame Henrietta Barnett. Fearful that Golders Green might spread up on to Hampstead Heath, she planned perhaps the best-known of London's Edwardian enclaves, **Hampstead Garden Suburb**, on a stretch of high ground above the Finchley Road. Inspired by the garden city movement of Ebenezer Howard and by its first manifestation at Letchworth, she recruited Letchworth's architects, Raymond Unwin and Barry Parker, to design the initial layout. It was firmly intended as a socially integrated neighbourhood where, as Alfred Lyttleton put it in a patronizing Hampstead phrase (quoted by Jackson): 'the poor shall teach the rich, and in which the rich, let us hope, shall help the poor to help themselves'. Needless to say, it did not take long for the Suburb to become as select as any private estate – if not more so.

Unwin's spacious layouts can be best appreciated from Falloden Way (A1) up Northway, or from Temple Fortune in Golders Green. Some still have traces of the late-Victorian 'Queen Anne' school but demonstrate the most neo-Georgian lines of the twentieth-century housing estate, here on a grand scale. Much of their appeal lies in the lavish planting which was so dominant a feature of the garden cities, abetted by the Suburb's avid gardeners. But the oddest relic of Dame Henrietta's enthusiasm is **Central Square**, with its Anglican church (St Jude's), its Free Church, its institute and school (but no pubs or shops). All these buildings were designed in 1908–10 by Sir Edwin Lutyens, and **St Jude's** is his ecclesiastical masterpiece. It is a confident application of Queen Anne Revival to the traditional church form – making Norman Shaw's church in the earlier model suburb of Bedford Park seem confused in comparison. With its bold spire rising out of the tapering tower it is one of the best twentieth-century church exteriors in England. Inside, Lutyens' humour gets the better of him. The combination of rustic woodwork, architectural eclecticism and murals-with-a-message, symbolize the cultural ambivalence of the Suburb's progenitors. But the murals, by Walter P. Starmer, are great fun and include a feminist ensemble in the Lady Chapel, its subjects ranging from Elizabeth Fry and Queen Victoria to a modern Girl Guide.

Due east of Hampstead Garden Suburb runs **Bishops Avenue**, its large, predominantly twentieth-century mansions encrusted with anti-burglar devices, while their gardens are a patchwork of swimming pools, tennis courts and barbecue patios. In line of descent from Park Lane, Kensington Palace Gardens and Avenue Road, Bishops Avenue has acquired the appellation of 'Millionaires Row'. It is the nearest London comes to Beverley Hills – banknotes are hanging from every tree. But it is all rather restrained, lacking the architectural panache of its Los Angeles sister.

North up the old Great North Road the suburban grain becomes coarser and undeniably tedious. But at Totteridge a delightful walk can still be had between the hill villages of **Totteridge** and **Mill Hill**. The former has the eighteenth-century Church of St Andrew with yew trees and pound; the latter has a village pond, cottages, alms-houses and Mill Hill School set in the ornamental grounds planted by the eighteenth-century botanist, Peter Collinson. As a schoolboy here in the 1950s I well remember travelling up from our 'commuter village' in rural Surrey, wandering off the Ridgeway towards Folley Brook and thinking that here at last I had found true countryside. This is one place where that quaint post-war planning concept, the 'London Green Belt', has proved to be as good as its name.

Barnet was the first coach stage north of London and, unlike Highgate, did not avoid the architectural battering such a commercial opportunity involved. But it has a good, largely Victorian church (St John's), with a canopied seventeenth-century tomb to Thomas Ravenscroft in his own chapel. Immediately north of the town lies **Monken Hadley**, regarded as the prettiest Georgian 'village-scape' in outer London. Its angular spaces flow out of one another – as at Ham and Blackheath – punctuated by tall trees, old houses and sweeps of rough grass. It is an enchanted place.

CHAPTER SIXTEEN

Islington

𝔇

ISLINGTON is the London suburban archetype. Ever since it first bruised the fields north of the City in the eighteenth century, it has been the hill towards which the City clerk has lifted up his eyes in search of a place to call his own. In the early nineteenth century William Hone could commend it ecstatically (and a little satirically) to: 'You who are anxious for a country seat/Pure air, green meadows and suburban views/Rooms snug and light, not overlarge but neat/ And gardens water'd by refreshing dews.' To the heights of Islington came such social aspirants as the Smiths of Leigh Hunt's *Sunday in the Suburbs* and Mr Guppy of Dickens' *Bleak House*. Immediately to its north, to Holloway, came the Grossmiths' Mr and Mrs Pooter. Here was order and moderation, cleanliness and respectability.

Apart from the green meadows, Hone's advantages still remain. For its modern residents Islington can offer acre upon acre of three and four-storey terraced houses within a mile of Holborn and the City. A small army of architects and builders stand ready to adapt the time-honoured formula to each new arrival's needs. The young couple share a house if they cannot at first afford their own. As the family grows, a bathroom extension is put up here, a wall erected or knocked through there. Paint is removed and reapplied, tiny gardens planted and replanted. Decorators, antique dealers and second-hand stores are more patronized than any food shop. And the frenzied activity continues right up to the moment when the third child is on the way, a larger garden is called for and the outer suburbs beckon. The cycle starts again.

Yet Islington also has deeper virtues as a city community. Despite its image of new respectability, it is still predominantly a working-class district. Its architecture may impose a homogeneity of status: each Islington terraced house has a similar quiet dignity. But the homogeneity is not social. As the original nineteenth-century leases came to an end in the early twentieth century, the growth of sub-

Highgate cemetery, begun in 1838 and now derelict, 'a vast, clammy forest, tearing apart memorials, spilling open graves and imprisoning everything in dank greenery'.

The two Islingtons open up for business: a fruit stall in Chapel Street market and (*below*) an antique dealer unwraps her wares in Camden Passage.

letting admitted a poorer group of lodgers and transient workers. Many of these were from the Irish immigrant community which spread across north London's inner suburbs between the wars, supplanting families fleeing up the commuter lines to the north. In Islington in particular, the Irish infected local life, especially local politics, with a rip-roaring personality more typical of New York (or Boston) than of London.

The extension of public housing in the borough in the 1960s and 1970s has meant that much of this personality is likely to survive even the present spread of 'gentrification' through the older terraces and squares. Modern Islington is thus a suburb still with its feet firmly on the ground. The young wives of Barnsbury scurry home of an evening shocked by the drunks of Liverpool Road. The costermongers of Chapel Street market mouth jovial obscenities not a hundred yards from the refined sensibilities of antique dealers in Camden Passage. And the local town hall is the only one in London where the police must occasionally be called on to restore a modicum of order.

We start with the central monument to this 'other' Islington, the **Angel** pub. This once was one of the most famous London inns, situated on a prime site at the junction of the road north from Smithfield and the New Road from Marylebone round to the City. Periodically rebuilt, it stands today in the late-Victorian dress of the pub architects, Eedle and Meyers, in baroque terracotta with turrets and a dome. For over ten years it has remained derelict in the 'care' of the Greater London Council. The same goes for almost all Islington's short High Street, once resplendent with music halls and tall 'Dutch' gabled shop buildings. Opposite the Angel, the old Philharmonic Hall (later the 'Grand' and then the 'Empire') still peers over the top of its council hoardings, Greek statues clinging tenuously to the classical pediment. Few places are a sadder monument to municipal inertia than this. However, rehabilitation at least of the Angel is at last in hand.

From the junction with Liverpool Road, the High Street becomes Upper Street, lined with the chain stores found in any suburban shopping street. But **Chapel Street**, to the left, is one of the best-known and liveliest of London's open markets. There is little nonsense about antiques here. Chapel Street gets down to basics: food, clothes and household goods sold with traditional Cockney backchat. To the right of Upper Street is a characteristic Islington con-

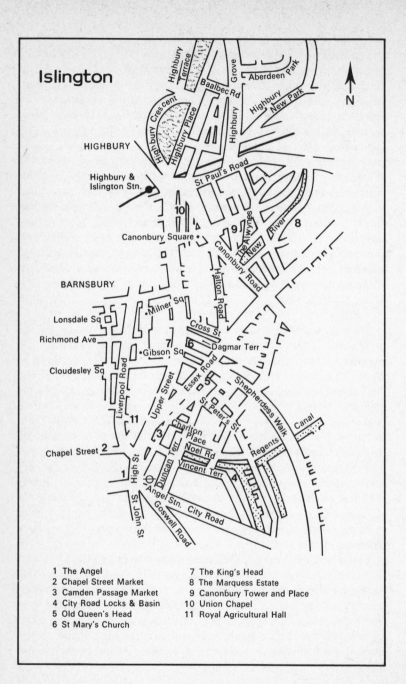

Islington

HIGHBURY

Highbury & Islington Stn.

BARNSBURY

Lonsdale Sq

Richmond Ave

Cloudesley Sq

Chapel Street

Highbury Terrace

Baalbec Rd

Grove

Aberdeen

Highbury New Park

Highbury Crescent

Highbury Place

St Paul's Road

Canonbury Square

Milner Sq

Cross St

Gibson Sq

Dagmar Terr

Essex Road

Shepherdess Walk

Halton Road

Canonbury Road

The New River

Liverpool Road

Upper Street

St Peter's St

Charlton Place

Noel Rd

Vincent Terr

Duncan Terr

Regents

Canal

High St

Angel Stn. City Road

St John St

Goswell Road

N

1 The Angel
2 Chapel Street Market
3 Camden Passage Market
4 City Road Locks & Basin
5 Old Queen's Head
6 St Mary's Church
7 The King's Head
8 The Marquess Estate
9 Canonbury Tower and Place
10 Union Chapel
11 Royal Agricultural Hall

trast. The row of antique shops comprising **Camden Passage** rose to prosperity in the late sixties, aided by the arrival of a gourmet restaurant run by Mr Robert Carrier. As happens with such enclaves, its character is changing fast, with specialist shops being ousted by restaurants and enclosed markets. But it remains a bustling place with splendid engraved glass in the Camden Head pub and some typically scruffy Islington council flats in the middle. The smartness only degenerates in parody at the far end with a 'Georgian village'. A smoked-glass *porte cochère* quite unnecessarily fronts a warehouse which has been converted into an antique hypermarket.

We do better to dive down the delightful curved row of Charlton Place to **Duncan Terrace**, which once stood on the banks of the New River. The river itself was a colossal undertaking begun in 1613 by the Jacobean entrepreneur Sir Hugh Myddleton, to provide the City of London with an alternative water supply to the heavily-polluted Thames. The water came from thirty-eight miles away in Hertfordshire, crossing Highbury in wooden pipes and ending at the New River Head in Clerkenwell. Its route through Islington was covered over in 1861 and the conduit ceased altogether in 1946.

The Terrace's most distinguished resident was the City clerk and essayist, Charles Lamb, at what is now No. 64 (much altered). Here in 1823 Lamb wrote an enthusiastic account of his new home: 'The new river (rather elderly by this time) runs (if a moderate walking pace may be so termed) close to the foot of the house; and behind is a spacious garden with vines (I assure you), pears, strawberries, parsnips, leeks, carrots, cabbages to delight the heart of an old Alcinus. You enter without passage into a cheerful drawing room, three windows full of choice prints. I feel like a great lord, never having had a house before.' His friends were more cynical. The poet Thomas Hood replied that it seemed 'a cottage of ungentility for it has neither double coach-house nor wings'. Smarting perhaps from such rejoinders, Lamb moved to Edmonton after only five years in Islington.

In the centre of Duncan Terrace rises the monumental and incongruous Roman Catholic **Church of St John the Evangelist**, neo-romanesque with twin towers crowning the façade. It was begun as early as 1843, when High Gothic was still the fashion for such suburban places of worship – perhaps the Catholics preferred a less obviously Anglican design. The Gothic propagandist, A. W. Pugin, singled it out for special contempt: 'The most original combination

211

of modern deformity that has been erected for some time past.'

Between Noel Road and Vincent Terrace, steps lead down to the **Regent's Canal** and the locks of City Road basin at the point where the canal passes through the half-mile Islington tunnel. The canal, built in the 1820s by John Nash (as part of his Regent's Park development), links the docks at Limehouse Reach with the Grand Union Canal at Paddington – a boat from here could, and can still, pass from the Thames to the waterways of the north of England. In its early days this basin would have been a hive of commercial activity: coal barges, lighters and long-boats packed like gipsy caravans with canal people and their attendant animals. At the tunnel, the towing horses had to be led up and along Chapel Street to the Caledonian Road exit while the bargees 'walked' their loads through the tunnel, lying on their backs and pushing at the roof with their feet (they were later assisted by a steam tug). Passing through it today is still an eerie experience, the water oily black and the pinprick of daylight an impossible distance away at each end. Only motorized craft are permitted to enter, and a strong light is essential: accidents have happened!

The waterway is now the preserve of canal enthusiasts, whose numbers are increasing so rapidly as to give this historic London artery a new lease of life. Narrow-boats are being reconditioned as summer cruisers or permanent homes, and the colourful paintwork on hatchways, doors and crockery has become a new cottage industry. The Regent's Canal locks have been restored in their original manual form, but here at City Road a lock-keeper will pop out from his cottage to help when a boat hoves into view.

The basin below the lock was once a substantial inland wharf. It is now a wasteland of smashed windows and rotting garbage, with only the sails and canoes of a local boys club to enliven the scene. But the canal towpath can be walked, with a few gaps, right through to Victoria Park eastwards and (from Caledonian Road) to Maida Vale westwards. The latter three-mile walk is one of the pleasantest in inner London, a continuous museum of industrial archaeology, passing the 'St Pancras Yacht Club' and a series of locks up to Camden, from where pleasure boats run through to the zoo and Little Venice.

The canal is overlooked at this point by the back of **Noel Road**, its ground floors curiously crenellated and rusticated – a stern Georgian terrace revealing its romantic nature to the world of commerce behind. Some of the windows have their original Gothic tracery. The artist, Walter Sickert, lived for a time at No. 56. He portrayed the backs of these houses in a well-known engraving, 'The Hanging Gardens of Islington', admirably capturing the flickering light of the sun on ash trees and old brick. No. 8 is clearly an oddity: it was hit by a bomb in the war and one of Islington's extensive colony of publishers secured permission to rebuild it in a 'freer-than-Georgian' style. The tubular railings on the roof terrace are a splash of sixties unconventionality.

From Noel Road we can make our way to St Peter's Street through terraces restored by enthusiasts in the 1960s and 1970s. Beyond lies the Packington Estate, a famous battleground between advocates of rehabilitation and redevelopment – a controversy settled by Richard Crossman, the local government minister at the time, in favour of a compromise. The restored terraces now face a Wates-built modern development over the way. The terraces are quintessential Islington; the Wates houses could be anywhere.

On Essex Road stands the modern replacement of what a Victorian antiquary called 'one of the most perfect specimens of ancient domestic architecture in the vicinity of London', the **Old Queen's Head** inn. In 1829, so the local newspaper reported, 'the exertions of a number of labourers have at last accomplished that which had withstood the encroachments of Old Father Time for three centuries'. The labourers, however, kept part of the Tudor bar and this has been incorporated in the modern building. It was reputedly one of the haunts in which Sir Walter Raleigh indulged in the new-found habit of smoking tobacco.

St Mary's Church, up Dagmar Terrace opposite, is Islington's Parish Church. It was bombed in the war and Mottistone and Paget's rebuilt nave is a poor replacement, looking like some institutional memorial hall. But the tower of the original Georgian church survives, as does the handsome front porch with its unusual segmental pediment. The tower was begun in 1751 by Launcelot Dowbiggin, a little-known architect who claimed his design was an amalgam of the towers of St Bride's, Bow and Shoreditch churches. It is a vigorous composition, with heavy corbels framing the clock faces and billowing convex buttresses to the spire – 'Baroque blood flowing through Palladian veins,' says Ian Nairn.

Next door in **Upper Street** is the friendly Congregational Church, looking more like a stockbroker's 'Norman Shaw' mansion than a place of worship. And opposite stands the 'Northern District Post Office', a late-Victorian exercise in Mannerist Revival with four strenuous caryatids holding up its entablature. The Post Office does not breed architects such as this today – and more's the pity. To its left is the King's Head pub, taken over in the 1960s by an American named Dan Crawford and converted into London's first true 'pub theatre'. It has been a remarkable success, customers happily sitting in a scruffy back room with drinks and a plate of food while watching the show. Over the years, pub and theatre have merged their personalities to create a noisy, virile place of entertainment with the added eccentricity of quoting all its prices in pre-decimal currency. *Kennedy's Children* had its première here.

Retracing our steps through St Mary's Churchyard and Dagmar Terrace, we reach **Cross Street**, rising gently from Essex Road. The street is a survival from the 1760s, before the growth of the surrounding squares and terraces and its doorcases are an essay in eighteenth-century design. No. 22 dates from the 1780s in an Ionic style reminiscent of much earlier patterns. But No. 33, although also built in the 1780s, is borrowed directly from Robert Adam's Adelphi buildings off the Strand. The architectural historian, Dan Cruickshank's description of its Adam Street parent fits this door exactly: 'The pilaster capitals are copied from the Temple of the Winds in Athens while in the centre of the frieze two sphinxes gaze at each other across a vase.' No. 24, the Pattern House, is a fine example of a Regency warehouse, with its crane and pulley still intact. And No. 32 is a later version of the same, this time with glazed tiles covering its façade.

Farther up **Essex Road**, prepare for a shock. The ABC cinema's neo-Egyptian façade (1930) of red and yellow *faïence* tiles was intended to create an architectural sensation, enticing Islingtonians away from the Depression into a world of escapism and romance, what C. Day Lewis called 'this loving darkness, a fur you can afford'. Now a bingo hall, the building is badly in need of restoration – London has lost too many relics of this period already. Behind the ABC cinema in Halton Road we are deep in working-class Islington. Students of English public housing can feast their eyes (or bruise them) on a museum of styles dating back to the nineteenth century. Dutch gables jostle with neo-Georgian windows, 'fifties' balconies look up to 'twenties' mansard roofs. And housewives who 'Remember the war' complain to the milkman at newcomers driving up prices in the local shops. The architects have all missed that essential Islington characteristic, the dignity of one's own front door on to the street. Here wall plaques record housing committee chairmen, not residents.

At Canonbury Road we rejoin the 'other' Islington among the genteel groves of the Alwynes estate. Here the New River survives as a series of ponds, landscaped with rocks, mounds and roses. It is best appreciated by walking along it to Willow Bridge, where the Marquess Tavern stands guard over the old stream. The pub has gold-painted pilasters covering its façade and proudly announces itself as a Free House – able to sell any beer it wishes (including good ones). Up Douglas Road is the back of the **Marquess Estate**, one answer to the grimmer works of Halton Road. Designed by the architects Darbourne and Darke in 1966, its brown brick and grey slates merge into their surroundings rather than clash with them. Two-thirds of the houses were designed specifically to have front doors at street level as well as their own gardens. It is one of the few places in London where I have found myself walking through a council estate without instantly realizing it.

We now progress uphill through the semi-detached villas of the Alwynes to **Canonbury House**. This is Islington's only pre-eighteenth-century historic building. The house, and indeed most of Canonbury, has been in the same family ownership since Tudor times. The house and manor were bought by the Lord Mayor of London, Sir John Spencer, for £2000 in 1570. Spencer was a characteristic City figure of the Tudor period, immensely rich from manipulating Spanish and Mediterranean trading monopolies, avaricious and mean to boot. Like Shylock his most prized possession was his only child Elizabeth who, to his rage, fell in love with an impecunious provincial nobleman, William Compton (of Compton Wynyates). Compton was so angered at Spencer's opposition to his suit that he used his influence at court to have Spencer imprisoned for maltreating Elizabeth, an action which did nothing to improve Spencer's opinion of him. Compton eventually eloped with Elizabeth, reputedly smuggling her out of Canonbury Tower in a baker's basket. As in all the best fairy stories, the queen herself intervened to bring peace to all parties. Compton won not only Spencer's blessing but, more to the point, a fortune estimated at £500,000 on his death. His descendants, the Marquesses of Northampton, have retained their hold on the estate ever since.

The Comptons seldom lived in the house. As early as 1616 it was rented to Francis Bacon and in the following century Oliver Goldsmith took rooms in the tower. But in 1770 a Mr John Dawes leased the whole property, demolished the south range and built what is now Canonbury House and Place on the site. Only the old tower remained. In the nineteenth century, the American author, Washington Irving, rented Goldsmith's room in an effort to recapture his muse, but was infuriated to discover it was infested by 'a perpetual streaming of citizens and their families to look about the country from the top of the tower and to take a peep at the City through a telescope to try if they could discern their own chimneys'. The creator of Rip Van Winkle had to endure the landlady telling some visitors that his room was 'occupied by an author who was always in a tantrum if interrupted, and I immediately perceived by a slight noise at the door that they were peeping at me through the keyhole. By the head of Apollo but this was quite too much.'

Today the **tower** belongs to the Tavistock Theatre Club, a repertory company using a hall in what would have been the former courtyard. Two seventeenth-century panelled rooms are intact and can be seen by appointment (with a modern version of Irving's landlady who struggles to keep the stairs spotless and checks every ledge for dust). On the first floor is the Spencer Room, its walls entirely oak-panelled with fluted pilasters and a large fireplace with a stone lintel. On the second floor is the Compton Room, where the panels over the fireplace contain deep relief carvings of two women. This is a gem of a room, peaceful and unnoticed (though available, as always, for hire). It has looked out over Islington for three and a half turbulent centuries and, apart from some gunshot holes in part of the panelling, has survived them unharmed. The climb up the remainder of the tower is a steep one, but justified by the magnificent view out over the City and the Thames basin beyond.

Of the rest of the house, some plaster ceilings of the sixteenth century survive inside the houses flanking Alwyne Place, and the two hexagonal pavilions which marked the southern wall of the garden have been incorporated into later villas – the best is attached to No. 4. Alwyne Villas. **Canonbury Place** is a curiously urban enclave. No. 5 was the home of the Grossmith brothers, creators of the Pooter family in *Diary of a Nobody*. Modern Grossmiths still look down from lofty Islington and satirize the later suburbanites of Pinner and Neasden, though without the affectionate sympathy the Grossmiths showed towards the Pooters.

Canonbury Square is a distinguished late-Georgian ensemble begun in the early years of the nineteenth century by a speculative builder named Jacob Leroux. It is marred only by the traffic engineer who ensures that huge lorries hurl themselves at it from every point of the compass. Evelyn Waugh lived at No. 17A while writing *Decline and Fall*: Harold Acton came across him in what was then 'this shabby-genteel square such as Sickert loved to depict, no longer a fashionable quarter but agreeably symmetrical and soothing to the eye'. And George Orwell lived at No. 27B. Islington was then passing through a depressed phase, its houses unconverted and many of its residents transient. Was it from this that both writers drew their common pessimism?

Round the corner in Upper Street, stands Leroux's Compton Terrace, dominated by **Union Chapel**, a famous Islington eyesore which is acquiring some admirers in its old age. The style is a bold red-brick Gothic (by James Cubitt in 1876), its huge tower crushing the adjacent terrace, but visible from all over north London. A classical church had been built on the site and its replacement shows the Victorians' desire for relief from the Georgian façades which surrounded them. These churches were of great social importance to these early suburbs. Even before its rebuilding, Union Chapel had eight hundred and fifty communicants and contributed two hundred volunteer teachers to Sunday and ragged schools in the neighbourhood. South along Upper Street is a much later municipal institution, Islington Town Hall. It is inter-war neo-Classicism at its most insipid.

To the north, Upper Street meets Highbury Corner, still bearing the scars of its devastation by a flying bomb in the last war. Beyond is Islington's only park, **Highbury Fields**. Begun as early as 1774, this is the smart end of Highbury. The 'Place' and 'Terrace' shoot off curiously at odd angles from each other, as if they had gone sleep-walking from Canonbury and lost their way. Walter Sickert held court from 1927–34 at No. 1 Highbury Place, where he had a school and studio. And at No. 38 lived Abraham Newland, the apotheosis of the Victorian bank clerk. Newland was born in Southwark whence, according to the Islington historian, Thomas Coull, 'being educated for the counting house and showing great aptitude in the application of the rules of arithmetic, at the age of eighteen his father contrived to get him an appointment as junior clerk in the Bank of England. Here his businesslike habits, punctuality and sagacity soon gained for him the notice of the directors.' Newland rose swiftly to reach the pinnacle of Chief Cashier (and signer of bank notes) in 1782, a post he held for a quarter of a century. He never married and slept in his office at the Bank every night of his cashiership, declaring that he derived 'more happiness from a single hour's attendance on the duties of office than a whole day spent in the most convivial and entertaining company'. Not averse to status, he bought himself one of the new houses being built in Highbury, suburban yet convenient for the Bank. But he merely visited it each evening after dinner to take tea with his housekeeper before returning to his office.

Aberdeen Park and Highbury New Park, east off Highbury Grove, were once exclusive private estates of large Victorian mansions, with laurels in the shrubbery and crunching gravel underfoot. Most of these houses have been demolished, though a few survive amid the modern flats to give a hint of glories past. Victorian enthusiasts should visit instead the streets round **Baalbec Road**, also off the Grove. Here is a raucous Cockney answer to the Georgian good manners of the Fields: an 1880s essay in what a firm chisel could do with red bricks, terracotta and a builder's pattern book. The small houses are covered in carved leaves, swags, dentils, every conceivable stylistic gimmick. This is the London which tourists will want to see in a hundred years' time – and there is miles of it north into Holloway.

Now back through Highbury Corner to **Barnsbury**. Anyone following this route by car should beware. In 1970 Barnsbury became London's first major experiment in 'traffic management'. To prevent its geometric grid of streets from being saturated by commuter traffic, most of the entrances to the neighbourhood were closed off, such that there was no through route in any direction. To the infuriated drivers and those living on the periphery roads, the scheme was not a success. But to the delight of those living inside the charmed circle, the scheme is now permanent. Visitors should walk – or regret it.

Barnsbury is almost all of a piece. The stock brick or white stucco houses, neat shops and pubs spread themselves confidently over a hillside nearly half a mile square, only occasionally punctuated by a church or school in clashing stone or red brick. The colonization

– or recolonization – of Barnsbury by middle-class residents in the 1960s (when the proportion of its professional and managerial residents increased fourfold) has restored houses which elsewhere in London would have been condemned as obsolete. The local Labour Council's reaction to this colonization was a series of pre-emptive strikes, buying up what streets it could, clearing them of residents and demolishing them – all too often without sufficient resources to build new estates in their place. The heart-breaking consequence of this policy can be seen on the lower slopes round Richmond Avenue and Matilda Street, barricaded open spaces where once stood decent houses. Nonetheless the same council has rehabilitated a considerable amount of the Cloudesley Street and Liverpool Road area for working-class housing.

Two pairs of squares on either side of Liverpool Road form Barnsbury's nucleus: Milner and Gibson, Lonsdale and Cloudesley. Leaving Upper Street at Barnsbury Street, we run into the top end of the first sequence. **Milner Square**, a recent council restoration, has become a test question for architectural historians: what did the eccentric mid-Victorian architects, Roumieu and Gough, think they were doing? Though contemporary with the area round it Milner Square (of 1841) is evidence of an attempt to break out of the straight-jacket of Georgian Classicism. The ground floors are conventional enough, but about them rise closely-spaced brick pilasters leading to a restless attic of unevenly arched windows. As a design, it must be judged a failure, an experiment which should never have left the drawing board. (Why a modern architect should have tried to parody it on a site in the north-west corner defeats me.) But it remains a London curio, and I must admit to spending longer in Milner Square than in the ordered terraces of Gibson Square to the south. In the centre of the latter is a modern classical folly by Raymond Erith: a ventilation shaft for the Victoria Line tube.

We pass back through Milner Square and turn left into **Liverpool Road**, a long thoroughfare running from the Angel to Holloway flanked by a series of eighteenth-century terraces. Immediately to our north is Lofting Road, where a local housing association has tried to recreate the spirit of Barnsbury in a modern idiom. Designed by Pring, White and Partners, the estate has the correct scale and sense of privacy. But why turn so bleak a façade to the passer-by – something a Georgian would never have done?

From this point we can work our way down the hillside to the broad sweep of Thornhill Square or cut south to Lonsdale Square, where the Georgian eccentricities of the contemporary Milner Square are disregarded and straightforward neo-Tudor used instead. Richmond Avenue, however, does still show traces of Milneritis: bizarre Egyptian window surrounds, with stone sphinxes guarding each entrance. The effect is extraordinary – as if Mr Pooter were making his entrance to the triumphal march from *Aïda*. Cloudesley Square and Street are earlier (1820s) and more urban in atmosphere. In the middle of Cloudesley Square is Charles Barry's perpendicular Gothic Holy Trinity Church, a breezy version of King's College Chapel by the architect of the Houses of Parliament.

Back in Liverpool Road stands the biggest, if not the most beautiful, building in Islington. The **Royal Agricultural Hall** was built in 1862 as a livestock exhibition hall for the Smithfield Club. Until the last war it housed agricultural shows, revivalist meetings, military tattoos and athletic displays. Blondin walked the tight-rope here; in 1870 a full-scale Spanish bullfight was staged under its roof; and in 1916 it saw London's first 'Used Motor Show'. The R.A.H. was also the venue for the annual Cruft's Dog Show from its foundation by Charles Cruft in 1891 until his death in 1938. 'Aggie', as it is affectionately known, now stands derelict in the ownership of the local council. As with so much of Islington, the hall is currently being fought over by various interest groups – its twin towers and battered façade waiting patiently for the local community to make up its mind.

The course of Myddleton's **New River** once ran across open fields to reach his reservoirs above Sadler's Wells. Although today it is little more than a necklace of ponds, its fourteen-mile path out to Hertfordshire can still be traced (with a car and a good map) in a fascinating game of hide and seek. Eight streets named after Myddleton provide occasional clues. The route passes through two of north London's most attractive local parks, those of Clissold and Finsbury, and then runs north to Alexandra Palace and Muswell Hill. **Alexandra Palace**, built in 1875 as north London's answer to Crystal Palace, is now almost as friendless as the Royal Agricultural Hall. In 1936 it was London's first television centre and was later the first transmission base for the Open University. Part of it occasionally used for special displays and events, such as jazz concerts and the holding of supervised public examinations. Concerts were also held to give the huge Willis organ a chance to show its paces. No sooner was a proper restoration under way in 1980, however, than a fire, horribly reminiscent of that at Crystal Palace in 1936, completely gutted its interior.

Out near the Hertfordshire border, **Forty Hall** in Enfield is one of London's least-known 'stately homes'. It has a rich, stone-dressed William and Mary façade and fine early-seventeenth-century rooms inside. Much of the original period furniture is still in place (open daily except Mondays, 10.00 to park closing time). The New River finally reaches open country in the grounds of James I's former palace of Theobalds. Here, overlooking one piece of London history, stands another, Christopher Wren's **Temple Bar**. There have been countless plans to return this treasure of English architecture to some appropriate site in the City. For the present it remains in its field, a naughty pupil sent out of class for getting in the way of Fleet Street's traffic.

CHAPTER SEVENTEEN

Points East

ઢ

LONDON east of Tower Hamlets is an acquired taste. Its greatest potential asset, the disused wastes of **Docklands**, have at the time of writing been under siege from planners for ten years. Their population has already been decimated by economic collapse and the young are escaping by every route they can find. The old Docklanders stand on their doorsteps, where they have been permitted to keep them, muttering against the authorities and the world in general. My mother drove an ambulance in Shadwell during the Blitz and can recall their vitality and courage when this corner of London became a raging inferno. But since then, neither they nor their leaders have found the elixir of renewal. A journey through their city takes us past a series of dejected walls, warehouses, and vandalized housing estates. In between are raw patches where the city's skin has been ripped away, first by bombs and then by senseless demolition.

But enough of such gloomy thoughts. If the promised rebirth of Docklands occurs this area may yet live again. Cynics may scoff at such prosperous colonies as those which have sprung up at Wapping and Narrow Street, Limehouse. But they are one means of revival. Another must be found for an almost complete set of Georgian wharves at West India Docks in Poplar (closed to the public). Hawksmoor's masterpieces, **St Anne's Limehouse** and **St George's-in-the-East**, still stand guardian angels over their respective communities: they are among the most dramatic and powerful structures ever built in London, though St Anne's in particular is sorely in need of friends. Then there are the pubs, precious oases surviving from the East End's past, not just the famous ones – the Grapes, the Prospect of Whitby and the Gun, Coldharbour – but the dozens of vigorous hostelries in which locals are still left in peace to remember the past and curse the present.

There are also the surprises: Regent's Canal Docks, its old quays waiting silently for a new era of pleasure boats to press them into service; the Gallions Inn off Manor Way, now derelict but in its day a beacon to weary dockers and seamen who would have seen its lights from miles around; the medieval church of St Mary Magdalene East Ham, in whose five-hundred-year history the rise and fall of the adjacent Royal Docks will seem a mere passing incident; and Eastbury Manor, Barking's own Tudor historic home (open Tuesdays), 'ready made for hauntings and screams out on the mud flats' (Nairn). All are places made the more precious by the grimness of their surroundings. But they need a map and a determined driver to seek them out.

North of Docklands on the banks of the River Lea (or Lee) is perhaps the most evocative of all east London set pieces. The Lea in the nineteenth century became what the Thames itself once was: a commercial sewer alongside which only the poorest would live, enduring the noise and stench as best they could. It is now a succession of gasworks, power stations, wharves and warehouses. Only an incurable optimist could call them beautiful. But such optimists exist, and they should travel to Bromley-by-Bow Tube station or park in Three Mills Lane off St Leonards Street.

The **Three Mills** are basically two. On the left is a block dated 1776 but looking earlier, with fake windows and sluice gates still intact to the rear. On the right is Clock Mill of 1817, with two oasts looked after by the wine firm of Hedges and Butler. These mills date back to the Middle Ages, when the land was occupied by Stratford Abbey, but the point of visiting them today is their setting. Gasholders, cooling towers and pylons dominate the view in every direction. Sluggish oily water moves silently between hump bridges, ramps and cobbled alleyways. I keep meaning to come here in a fog. It is London's answer to a tropical mangrove swamp.

By taking the towpath up what would have been the millrace, we reach Bisson Road and Abbey Lane. Here stands a truly magnificent example of Victorian industrial archtecture, **Abbey Mills** pumping station. Special permission is required to see inside, but even outside it looks like the creation of some nineteenth-century Shah Jehan. Sir Joseph Bazalgette was such a man. His sewerage system, constructed in the 1860s, is still one of the wonders of London, though thankfully a subterranean one. Its chief monuments were the Embankments along the Thames, built to contain his massive 'outfall' sewers (as well as the District Line railway), and two pumping stations were built near the sewers' downstream outlets to maintain the flow.

The Station at Crossness on Erith marshes is a near ruin (see p. 42), but Abbey Mills has been excellently restored by the Greater London Council. The council describe it as 'Venetian Gothic' but it is more a sort of Moorish Renaissance, with pinnacled cupolas and mansard roofs. Two tall minaret chimneys were demolished in the war, but the whole composition must once have shimmered over the Lea Valley like the Taj Mahal. The richness of the interior ironwork knows no bounds, created as much for the delight of the workpeople as for the glory of the directors. Immediately beyond the station we can clamber up on to the grassy embankment of the sewer itself. From here a curiously rural bridleway curves away south towards Canning Town, a dramatic forest of industrial architecture looming up on every side.

Half a mile north of Abbey Mills at **Stratford Broadway** is the most vigorous town centre in the East End. In the middle is St John's Church (by Blore in 1834), with dainty lancet windows more suited to a college chapel than a Cockney parish church. Round swirls a torrent of traffic. The new shopping centre is ugly but alive. A jolly *ziggurat* of offices has just been completed to the east of the church by Newham Council. And tucked in behind the shops is the Theatre Royal, Stratford, made famous in the 1960s when it was run with a mixture of political conviction and music-hall flair by the director, Joan Littlewood. *Oh, What a Lovely War!* was first staged here.

Round the corner in Romford Road stand two strong works of late-Victorian architecture, the **West Ham Municipal College** (now the North-East London Polytechnic) and next to it the **Passmore Edwards Museum**. John Passmore Edwards was a highly individual Victorian philanthropist. Born in the West country in 1823, he came to London to make his name as a publisher and social reformer. He became proprietor of a number of worthy journals and even went bankrupt before achieving financial security with *Building News*. His former creditors gave him a banquet to celebrate. His causes were diverse, including pacifism, drug abuse, Transvaal independence, the abolition of capital and corporal punishment, the suppression of gambling and electoral reform. His publications rejoiced in such titles as *The Public Good*, *Peace Advocate*, and the *Mechanics' Magazine*.

224

North London recreations: The Grand Union Canal at Noel Road, Islington;
below the former ABC *art deco* cinema in Essex Road.

God and Mammon in the East End: Hawksmoor's St Anne's, Limehouse from the embankment of the former London and Blackwall Railway and (*below*) Three Mills, Bromley-by-Bow, on the River Lea, 'perhaps the most evocative of all east London set pieces'.

Edwards founded no fewer than seventy charitable and educational institutions, and the college at West Ham was among the most splendid. Flemish, baroque, Queen Anne – anything taking the fancy of architects Gibson and Russell seems to have been tossed into the design. Yet in this most confident of eras (the 1890s) the result is never discordant. The museum to the right is an equally inspired essay in baroque revivalism.

Yet even here suburbia is not far away. North of Romford Road stretch the private estates surrounding **Wanstead Flats**. Although Colen Campbell's Wanstead House has disappeared, Hardwick's plutocratic classical church guards the entrance to the old park, which still has about it a flavour of the days of Capability Brown. (The Flats themselves manage to support a respectable herd of cows.) From Wanstead to Woodford, the East End turns prosperous in a sequence of leafy parks and avenues. Off Hermon Hill is the extraordinary Victorian pile of Wanstead Hospital, with one of the most delicately executed entrance porches I know (in florid Venetian Gothic). **Woodford** itself is the geographical and social high point of east London, strung out along the ridge overlooking the valleys of the Lea and the Roding. It consists of a series of pleasant houses and greens, though it never quite achieves the coherent identity of a Highgate or a Dulwich – despite having had Sir Winston Churchill as its M.P.

Woodford does, however, have one crowning asset, **Epping Forest**. The Forest was acquired by the City of London in 1878 to preserve it as an open space for City and East End inhabitants (as Hampstead was preserved for those in the north and west). It has served that purpose ever since. The railway line from Liverpool Street to Chingford was the traditional approach route. Tens of thousands of East Enders would pour out of soot-laden trains to breathe in air cleansed by oak, hornbeam and beech. Others would hitch up their costermongers' drays and go camping under the stars. At a time when Stepney and Whitechapel were the most crowded parishes in England, Epping was the one place where their populations could enjoy trees and grass, where they could play, run and make love without trampling each other underfoot.

Today the East Enders still come, now mostly by car and motor bike, tearing up Woodford High Road with their tents and transistors. But the Forest manages to absorb them as it always has. Its trees seem denser than those of Richmond or Hampstead, its dells certainly more sinister. (Once upon a time, no Bank Holiday was complete without a body discovered somewhere in the undergrowth.) Just near Chingford station is a curiosity, **Queen Elizabeth's Hunting Lodge**. This sixteenth-century structure was built to enable visitors to watch the hunt as it raced across the fields. Its top floor was thus an open terrace and Queen Elizabeth is reputed to have ridden upstairs to it on horseback in a moment of high spirits. The old oak beams were built to last 'till the crack of doom'. Like Epping Forest, they are still going strong.

Appendix of opening times
mentioned in the text

୨৯

Chapter 1: GREENWICH: I

Cutty Sark and *Gipsy Moth IV* (11.00 to 6.00, Sundays 2.30 to 6.00, closed at 5.00 in winter)
Royal Naval College (2.30 to 5.30, closed Thursdays)
National Maritime Museum including the Queen's House and Royal Observatory (10.00 to 6.00, Sundays 2.30 to 6.00, closed at 5.00 in winter)

Chapter 2: GREENWICH: II AND BLACKHEATH

Ranger's House (10.00 to 5.00, closed at 4.00 in winter)
Royal Artillery Museum (10.00 to 12.30, 2.00 to 4.00, closed Sundays)
Eltham Palace (11.00 to 7.00, closed at 4.00 in winter)
Hall Place (10.00 to 5.00, Sundays 2.00 to 6.00 except in winter)

Chapter 3: DULWICH

Picture Gallery and Mausoleum (10.00 to 5.00 except Mondays, Sundays 2.00 to 5.00, closed at 4.00 in winter)
Horniman Museum (10.30 to 6.00, Sundays 2.00 to 6.00)

Chapter 4: KEW

Kew Gardens (10.00 to dusk)
Kew Palace (summer only, 11.00 to 5.30)

Chapter 5: RICHMOND

The Park (closed at dusk)
White Lodge (2.00 to 6.00 in August)

Chapter 6: PETERSHAM AND HAM

Ham House (2.00 to 6.00, 12.00 to 4.00 in winter, closed Mondays)

Chapter 7: CHISWICK

Chiswick House (9.30 to 7.00, except Mondays and Tuesdays in winter, closed at 4.00 in winter)
Hogarth's House (11.00 to 6.00, 11.00 to 4.00 in winter but closed Tuesdays; Sundays 2.00 to 6.00, 2.00 to 4.00 in winter)

Chapter 8: SYON

Syon House (12.00 to 5.00 from Good Friday to end September, closed Fridays and Saturdays). Gardens open all year

Chapter 9: OSTERLEY

Osterley House (2.00 to 6.00, 12.00 to 4.00 in winter, closed Mondays)

Chapter 10: TWICKENHAM

The Octagon (2.00 to 5.30, closed at 4.30 in winter)
Marble Hill (10.00 to 5.00 except Fridays, closed at 4.00 in winter)
Strawberry Hill (by appointment on Wednesdays and Saturdays)

Chapter 11: HAMPTON COURT

The Palace (9.30 to 6.00, closed at 4.00 in winter, Sundays 11.00 to 6.00, 2.00 to 4.00 in winter)

Chapter 13: HAMPSTEAD: I

Fenton House (Wednesdays to Saturdays 11.00 to 5.00, Sundays 2.00 to 5.00, weekends only in winter)

Chapter 14: HAMPSTEAD: II

Keats House (10.00 to 6.00, Sundays 2.00 to 5.00)

Chapter 15: HIGHGATE

Kenwood (10.00 to 7.00, 10.00 to 4.00 in winter)

Chapter 16: ISLINGTON

Canonbury Tower, by appointment
Forty Hall, Enfield (10.00 to 6.00 except Mondays, closed at 5.00 in winter)

Index